A Father's Letters
To His College Daughters

WILLIAM COURTER M.D.

Copyright © 2016 William Courter M.D.
All rights reserved.

ISBN: 1518752152
ISBN 13: 9781518752155
Library of Congress Control Number: 2015917833
CreateSpace Independent Publishing Platform
North Charleston, South Carolina

To Skyler

*To her spirit and energy,
passion for life,
love of people,
ability to create joy,
and willingness to take a risk.
She has brightened our family
more than she knows.
It has been a privilege
to be her father,
to be part of her life.*

To Austen

*To her sensitive soul,
remarkable kindness,
God-given talent,
intelligence, and
ability to make us laugh.
She has enriched our family
more than she knows.
It has been a privilege
to be her father,
to be part of her life.*

CONTENTS

Preface	ix
Part One—Letters to My Elder Daughter, Skyler	1
Freshman Year	3
Sophomore Year	54
Junior Year	86
Senior Year	124
Part Two—Letters to My Younger Daughter, Austen	155
Freshman Year	157
Sophomore Year	205
Junior Year	236
Senior Year	267
Acknowledgments	303
About the Author	305

PREFACE

For any parent, there are phases of parenthood: the excitement of each pregnancy; the incredible explosion of initial joy; those first months of preparation, designing the baby's room; the nervous anticipation of delivery; at birth, the amazing realization at the depth of love for your baby; the early months of interrupted sleep punctuated by the wonder of the baby's development; the delight in experiencing the emergence of a child's early speech, personality, and intelligence; those early years of preschool education with so much personal growth; the realization, long since forgotten from your own childhood, of the importance of those grade-school teachers and how much they help shape your child's personal progress; the transitions through grade school, middle school, and high school with the increasing loads of homework and the rising competitiveness for acceptance into a good college; the shared relief of the first college acceptance letter and the realization of your adolescent's rapid rush toward adulthood; and finally, the bittersweet awareness of how the center of your world will be soon transitioning to an independent life.

For the final phase, the transition through college years toward adulthood, what do you want for your child? With the economic pressures, are you secretly—or not so secretly—hoping your child selects one of the most-in-demand majors, obtains high grades, and grabs one of the better-paying jobs? Are your child's future income, level of prestige, and social status your most important goals? What about freedom, exploration, and adventure? What about your child's development of new talents, new passions, and perhaps a sense of purpose? Are those goals on your list? What is your best approach over these next four years for your child's lifelong happiness? And are you helping or hindering your child? What if you were derailing your child's best chances for a great life? What if I could offer an example, as shown in this book, of a different, more open approach for supporting your son or daughter through college, helping your child reach his or her—not your—goals? Giving your child sufficient freedom and space, with your support, to discover his or her own path toward a better life?

When my two daughters attended college, I wrote endless heartfelt letters (usually e-mails), often composed late at night, offering a different approach for the college years. I secretly kept all of those letters. I collated them into two separate books, and I gave the books as surprise gifts to each of my daughters on Christmas, once they had graduated. They loved them. Their friends loved them. A boyfriend of one of my daughters was even spotted shedding a tear. When I shared the books with fellow parents, I often received a common response: "I wish I had taken that approach." In the spirit of sharing, and with the hope that my approach will offer a different philosophy for other parents to consider, I decided to share my letters and e-mails in this single book. I collected my favorite correspondence, selected the ones with the deepest emotions, the most honesty, and the best stories, and arranged them for this book.

Parents will have their own styles of maintaining communication with their children during these crucial years. Some parents will utilize the cell phone for texts with periodic calls. Other parents will use Skype to maintain contact. Parents, if they live close enough to the college, will visit, taking their share of photos. Facebook. Instagram. Other parents, like me, may resort to the dying art of letter writing. The different approaches do not matter. What counts is how we try to help our children through this crucial transition. What counts is how we frame our philosophy for finding the best, most satisfying path through life, and how we allow them the chance to accept—or reject—our own perspective. Within our individual philosophies, what also counts is how we attempt to become better parents and how we attempt to expand our initial parent-child relationships into eventual adult-adult friendships. Our children can become our closest, dearest friends. When this transition proves successful, it is a wonderful journey. I encourage parents to follow my approach. Reevaluate your thinking of life and what's important. Make that extra effort to share more of yourself, the best parts and the worst parts. Change your relationship to an equal, open partnership, primed to last a lifetime.

Through this process, I encourage each parent to record the college years in any fashion of your choosing. You have a chance to create more than a lifelong friendship. You have a chance to create a legacy of insights to leave to your children. That legacy can reveal your love and respect; it can also reveal your fears and concerns, and it can reveal more about you. With honest communication, it can be an avenue for sharing the *real* you. What can be more important for any parent? Nothing trumps the satisfaction of watching your child make that successful transition into adulthood. At the same time, wouldn't you want your child to get to know you a little better? How you struggled as he or she struggled?

With my letters, you will see my own efforts, where I often needed to grow as much as—if not more than—they needed to grow. Personal growth, for everyone, is the cornerstone of a great life. That truth applies to more than the child; it also applies to the parent. Here's hoping you can learn from the triumphs and setbacks of my endeavors through these college years. Here's hoping any new insights and any new behaviors can lead to a greater happiness for your children, coupled to even closer and stronger relationships for the entire family, with more shared love, respect, and time for one another.

PART ONE

Letters to My Elder Daughter, Skyler

FRESHMAN YEAR

8/28/06 Thanks for the Start of College

Dear Skyler,

It is 10:50 p.m. PST, and I have been up since 6:00 a.m. EST, so my bones are tired, my head is throbbing, and my cognition is more than disjointed, but I would be remiss if I did not make the effort to write you to express my sincere thanks. Thanks for just being you. Thanks for allowing me to accompany you to your freshman day move-in at New York University. It has always been a privilege to be your father (after all, your birth was one of the best days of my life!), and it was a special privilege to be part of this historic transition. I have always loved the little girl who you were: the little girl who loved the Snoopy dance; the little girl who entertained me with her conversations on the drive home after diving practice in grade school; the little girl who jumped at opportunities such as the transition from fifty-plus classmates in middle school at St. John's Episcopal School to four-hundred-plus classmates at Santa Margarita Catholic High School. But I equally love the woman you are becoming: the woman who so easily engages others; the woman who embraces new opportunities ("Shall we try something new each day, Dad?"); the woman who has the strength to leave the safety of home to face the unknown, always with a smile on her face and a positive outlook fixed in her expression. In my eyes, you have been terrific, and you are growing better and better with time.

After spending the weekend with you, I also want to thank you for having the courage to choose New York University. What's the line we love from Garth Nix? "Does the walker choose the path, or the path choose the walker?" I can't answer the question, but New York is a great fit for you. In a strange way, we are indebted to, of all people, your junior-year physics teacher. Are you nauseated at the mention of him? Think about it for a moment. For the first three years of high school, you were on my path, not yours. You were a straight-A student, were number one in your class, and you were being pushed, by me, toward the rigors of Harvard or Princeton. With that first B+ in honors physics at the end of your junior year, your path changed. It gave you the freedom to look at different options. It gave you a step toward autonomy, which is always good. Your college choice became yours, not mine. If that first B+ was one cornerstone for that changed path, the other cornerstone was our college exploration trip back east. While I was still busy making plans for you to apply to the Ivy League colleges, you discovered your own different vision of Manhattan and New York University. At first, I was resistant to your vision. Academically, you could have competed at any school. But watching how you fell in love with Manhattan and NYU, my resistance faded. You morphed from a girl, still dependent on her parents, to a woman, ready to face the world of her choosing, and you jumped from my forced path to your own path, with a growing sense of self. For the courage to make that leap, and the courage to forge your own identity, you have earned my respect.

Better yet, your ability to see your future has far exceeded my own. It's a lesson for all parents who struggle with dependence versus independence. Now, on your own, you will be taking the courses you like, participating in those activities that enrich your spirit, and having fun with tons of friends, not isolated in some library. It's what you envision for yourself—not what others see for you—that is so important. But, as I sip my green tea and munch on my gluten-free chocolate chip cookie, can I still offer advice? Or share some of my hopes? Over these next four years, I hope you find a career that fuels your passion, I hope you head into a world that gives you a group of wonderful friends, a chosen family for life, and I hope you find one special person, at some time far in the future, who makes your life complete. In Yann Martel's *Life of Pi*, a character retorts, "That's a tall order!" And the other character, with whom I agree, replies, "Not so tall that you can't reach." So, with this first letter, that is my message: don't underestimate yourself, and your own vision, in any endeavor. To accent that point, I am going to include my fatherly perspective on you, which I wrote for your high-school counselor at the start of your senior year. It was one of those required parental assignments, but I believed every word I wrote in my description of you, and I think every observation still applies to you today. *Dream*, Skyler, *dream* as if you were still that little girl, ready to face any challenge.

A Father's Perspective of Skyler Courter

From the beginning, when Skyler was conceived in June as a test-tube baby, frozen in CryoFreeze for four months, and then born in July of the following year, I sensed I would be dealing with someone special, someone different. When the much-awaited pregnancy test came back positive—one of the happiest days of my life—I remember having this mental image of an embryo grabbing the uterine wall, hanging on for dear life, and beating the odds, fueled by an inner power of spirit, an inner willpower. With no rational explanation of why she survived and was born while our other embryos failed, I have maintained that image over the years. In fact, over time, that belief has strengthened. Why? Because Skyler has always had an internal spirit, an internal level of energy, with which I am not familiar in myself. It's one thing to face a challenge and emerge victorious; it's another to approach that challenge with an optimistic view, a core level of confidence, and a rock-solid equilibrium, unruffled by minor, and even major, setbacks. Skyler, for her entire life, has always been that special type of person.

When she was two years old, sitting in her crib, and being threatened by a tired mother who was loudly proclaiming she was going to get Dad who was going to deliver some real punishment, what did Skyler do? Retreat to the corner? Start following Mom's directives? No! Instead, she rose to her feet, clutched the side rails, and screamed, "Dad!

Dad!" That attitude, that willingness to face life's challenges, even when they are cast as something horrific, is one of Skyler's trademarks. Better yet, that attitude comes with a sense that nothing can stop her. In grade school, when a teacher would assign a massive assignment and the kids would scatter with worries and complaints, Skyler would emerge from class with a smile. The bigger the project, the better she liked it, and the bigger the project, surprisingly, the better she did. Why? How? Even from a father's perspective, I am not quite sure. I do not know whether to call it confidence, or optimism, or simply an inner spirit. But whatever it is, she has it, and to this father, it is something she was born with and something she will always have.

There is the saying that people are derailed not from the walls they face or the disasters in life, but from the pebbles, the minor irritants, in life. That is another area where Skyler seems so different, so special. Through the years, from preschool to grade school to high school, each of us has witnessed kids who have become unraveled by some unkind remark, some offensive statement, or some unfair treatment. Skyler's path has not been easier than the paths of other kids. I remember her being teased for her curly hair, criticized for something by one of her peers, or excluded from some desired group. Yet, she has never seemed overly fazed. Better yet, I have never seen her react with anger, bitterness, or unkindness. There has never been moping, depression, or anger. Again, I am not quite sure how to explain her equilibrium. But I find myself coming back to her inner spirit, her inner confidence, and her inner outlook on life. She always manages to stay positive, constantly believing that she can make it. In some way, it's that same spirit that brought her into this world, and it's that same spirit that seems to be carrying her through life. In my eyes, it's as good as gold. In fact, in my eyes, she is as good as gold.

With those same sentiments, as strong tonight as when I first wrote those words, I hereby promise to support you, regardless of your path and regardless of how much that path may be different from my expectations for you. I also promise to support you, regardless of your success on that path. I promise to move away from my deficiencies as a father. Or were they mistakes, not just deficiencies? You do not need to send me any grades. I have pushed you too hard, with too many external rewards, for those grades in high school. Forget grades. I will love you for just being you. In *Sabriel*, the father says, "I have not been an ideal parent, I know…but behind this, there was always my love." That's how I feel tonight. I have made my mistakes. In that same *Sabriel* conversation, the father bemoans the distractions that have come his way, blocking parts of their relationship. I feel a certain kinship with that line. I wish I could have worked one job, not two jobs. I wish I could have had more free time at night and on the weekends, not constantly working 24-7. As a long-term planner, I have to accept some of the blame. I did not foresee my father's dementia and its impact on my weekend time. I did not anticipate the subsequent conflicts with my mother. I did not see her, with her gaining control of my dad's financial plan for us, holding on to every family dime. I did not see her as opposing any contribution to your education. My own misconceptions, or missed assumptions of my mother, cost me a shot at a reduced workload, but much more importantly, they cost me valuable time with you during your final years of high school. For that I am sorry. More time with you would have been far more valuable than any of the additional income.

Someday, I hope I can make up for my mistakes. I hope, as I head into my older years, we can have more, not less, time together. I hope we can enjoy many more trips, establishing them as golden moments. I hope we can keep our "tide" in, never going far out. Unlike some of the individuals in our lives (like my mother), I intend to keep my promises. For me, my first goal is to become a better father. My second goal is to try to create an even stronger family, one that will last for the rest of our lives. With these goals, there are underlying steps for each one of us, especially me: to break free of old ways of thinking; to focus on greater acceptance and appreciation of new opportunities; to become independent of society's opinions and expectations, even if they were once my own; and to embrace change and risk. Better yet, to embrace the challenge of developing a new sense of self with improved self-love and self-respect. On that note, I am going to end this initial e-mail, welcoming you to New York University. Do what you choose, not what anyone else chooses for you—not even me. Just don't lose the little girl in the emerging new woman. And follow my only dictum that ever made sense.

Be safe. Be good. Be you.
Babbo

8/30/06 Miss You Terribly

Dear Skyler,

It's Wednesday night. I just finished working on hospital cases for three hours, and I just headed upstairs to climb into bed. Once again, I am feeling much too tired for my own good, and once again, I am working far harder and longer than I should for my own mental and physical health. As I dragged myself upstairs, I swung by Austen's bedroom to see if her door was open. She might be only seventeen months younger than you, and just a junior in a performing arts high school, but you have trained her well. Your habits are now her habits. Privacy is sacrosanct. Her bedroom door was closed, so I found myself edging toward your doorway and your bedroom. I am certain you can visualize every detail of your bedroom without much difficulty. Picture this image: everything was neat, the bed was made, the childhood toys were carefully arranged across the bedspread and along the decorative wall shelf, and the desk and stack of last year's high-school books were clean and dusted. Even your favorite, well-padded, green reading chair was clean, not cluttered with books. But the reality? The room felt empty. Much too empty for my taste.

When I am busy with my evening work, I can push aside our geographic distance. With your high-school novel, *Knightfall,* on one side of my computer and *Life of Pi* on the other side, I can pretend you are home, working upstairs. After all, how many high-school nights did you work for hours, only for me to swing in for a quick good-night after Mom and Austen had already retired? But tonight that image faded as I paused at your bedroom door. For several minutes, I stood in the darkness, overwhelmed with sadness. I did not cry, as I only cry while watching movies, but I sure could have shed a tear. You are dearly missed. Really missed. Even your smells were missed. Standing between your bedroom and the bathroom, there was no smell of body gel, or nail polish, or perfume. In every "sense," you have been a vital part of this family. You have been the motor of this family—the one who gives all of us a lift in spirit and a lift in energy.

Now, why I am sharing this moment of sadness? Not to make you sad. I hope you pass through any initial homesickness and slip into your usual upbeat and positive mode. I am sharing my feelings because I want to emphasize how special you are, and how much you are going to offer to your new friends. You are as good as gold, and don't let anyone tell you anything different. If others do not see your special qualities and special spirit, that is their mistake, not yours. As they say, you cannot force anyone to love you; you can only allow yourself to be loved. If you ever are inclined to ask yourself, "Am I loved?" there is an easy answer: if you are loving, you are loved. You are going to make a great woman, a great wife, and a great mother who will bring energy, excitement, and happiness to her future family. Keep all of these positive attributes close to your heart as you march toward your new college career. And don't rush to your future. It is there and waiting.

As for us, do not worry. Geographic distance is easier than emotional distance. Right now, the tide feels "in"! I am sure we can keep it that way. Your calls, e-mails, and text messages really help. If we can feel a part of your experience, it will make us feel closer, regardless of the distance. Please share the good and the bad of all of your daily activities. I noticed how Mom moaned when told of how you missed one of your first classes by not finding the right building. That reminded me of your precollege orientation trip. When they had that three-hour lecture on how to get around Manhattan, you skipped the lecture and spent three hours exploring Manhattan, taking as many subways as possible. So you missed the part of the lecture on NYU's buildings. Regardless, New York University may prove to be an excellent training ground for life, as it will force you to find your own way to the next destination. There is the belief that the more mistakes you make, the more you learn. Be accepting of mistakes. No judgment from me. I am just glad to hear any news, good or bad. When you want to connect with us, call or write. We will do the same.

In closing, there is one other thing to keep in mind. This is only a transitional stage. You will be home for four months a year, although I can't promise it will be the highlight of your year. For this coming summer, I hope to take all of us to Maui. At least we can spend time together with another vacation of shared experiences. To repeat, shared experiences do not mean you have to be living with us. By writing, texting, and calling, we can keep those shared experiences ongoing through the entire year, not just during the summer months. For my part, I will keep writing my e-mails on a regular basis, possibly too frequently for your taste. For this e-mail, I just want to repeat that you are loved and missed. All three of us (Mom, Austen, and I) realize how lucky we are to have you in our family. No wonder I was so happy when you were born; it was a sign of things to come. I just never thought this far ahead, nor do most parents. I never imagined this transition to college, and the intensity of our feelings of loss.

We love and miss you.

Babbo

9/03/06 Labor Day Confessional

Dear Skyler,

    I have to confess, since your departure to NYU, I have developed a few more idiosyncrasies. Mom thought I had reached my limit. Wrong. Last night, as we were heading up to bed, Mom noticed how I have started turning on the front hall lamp each night, usually sometime after dinner. She observed that it seemed as if I were recreating those nights when I would turn on the lamp, scribble you a "welcome home" note to leave beside it, saying I was glad you had arrived home safely, hoped you had a fun night out, and wondered if there was a specific time when you might want to be awakened in the morning. Mom asked if I would be writing imaginary letters to place next to the lamp. She was, as are most of Mom's points, right on target. I was turning on the lamp in the front hall because it was giving me a reassuring feeling, as if you were coming home later that night. It was a new idiosyncrasy, helping me through the quiet evening. I intend to keep doing it, but don't tell Mom. What she doesn't know is that I have been sneaking into your bedroom, leaving the light off and plopping myself down on your overstuffed reading chair to soak in the Skyler ambience. That, too, seems to be helping. I won't share that idiosyncrasy. It will be our secret.

    When I look back on my life and think of my most difficult challenges, I might be tempted to list getting accepted into Stanford University and Williams College, or getting accepted into medical school, or writing the first draft of my five-hundred-page novel while living in Marbella, Spain. Now those challenges seem intellectual, not nearly as emotionally trying as what I'm experiencing now. They required discipline for daily nonstop work. So what? People do that every day. My bigger challenge? It is occurring right now. It's purely emotional. It's adjusting to your absence from home and the sizeable vacuum that now exists in our home and in our lives. I knew I was going to miss you. I just did not realize I was going to feel such an overwhelming sense of loss. Maybe other parents do not wince when their kids leave for college. Maybe some parents are relieved as they now have some peace and quiet. Not me. Austen was right in her e-mail to you. I, too, miss all your little things: your clothes scattered across your bedroom; the green-tea-body-cream smell wafting from your bathroom; your music blaring from the Honda as you pulled into the garage; the constant phone calls—all asking for you, not for any of us; the "Grand Central Station" feel of our house, as your friends gathered in ever-changing masses, sometimes to study, sometimes to party. I miss all of that chaos much more than I ever thought possible.

Again, I do not mention our collective sense of loss or our collective sadness to make you depressed. Just to show how much you are loved. I'm not like Austen, curled into the family-room couch, proclaiming she is going to need a strong antidepressant to survive your departure. Honestly, I don't think any drug, even an illegal one, would do the trick. How am I going to make it through these days? For me, there are two solutions. First, there are these e-mails, where I can express my feelings, cleansing my soul. Tolerate them to the best of your ability. Second, there are the interactions with you through phone calls and texts, where I can keep up with the activities of your college life. After your call the other day, I felt much better. As Mom and I walked the neighborhood loop, talking for about an hour, we chatted nonstop about you. I felt great. Then reality set in, and I was back to my work in an isolated computer room with a silent household except for my Enya music. Depression. Sadness. But there is a crucial point. Our adjustment to your departure is our parental challenge, not yours. It is our responsibility, not yours. Focus on your own transition, carving your independent path.

Although, I will admit how much it helps when you call in such a good mood with such upbeat spirits. The fact that you like NYU and your new group of friends is reassuring. At the same time, I want to be available for any rough periods. I would also feel better if I were helping in some way. Please call with any and all setbacks. Maybe that is why I loved working with you for that one month in the summer following your junior year of high school when you wrote your novel. Even when I awoke at 4:30 a.m., reviewed your chapter from the previous day for sixty minutes, and e-mailed you some suggestions before heading out the front door to work, it always felt good. It made me feel part of the Skyler team, and that is a great team of which to be a part. In college, I do not expect you will be requesting any assistance for any writing projects. That was just *me* pushing you for one of my goals—not one of your goals—when I should have stayed in the background, giving you more space and freedom, not more intrusion and confinement. However, if you ever want to share an essay you have submitted for one of your classes, I would love to read it. On that note, there is another request. Mom says she is not 100 percent certain of your class schedule. We would like to request a list of your class times, so that we can create our own *Skyler Class Schedule* and scotch tape it to the pantry wall. I wonder if that's a pattern for most parents of college students. Looking at it, while imagining where you are, will be a great way to start our day, especially since you will be in class while we are eating our breakfast.

There's still another way you can help me. I know. I lied. I claimed my adaptation to this separation was my responsibility, not yours. Oh well, all parents lie as it suits their needs. Picture me as the typical father. Here comes another request. It helps me when I know you are doing well, with comfort and health. This morning when I woke up, I was thinking about your dorm bedroom and its temperature. Is it warm enough? I remember the dorm at Williams College getting pretty cold at night. If you want to shop at the bed and bath store to obtain a comforter or something for your bed, please purchase what you need, and charge it to my credit card. It will lift my mood when I know that you are warm, safe, and cozy at night. Add some weight to your sheets and put a relieved smile on my face. Same goes for any coat, scarf, gloves, or boots that are needed to keep you warm. If you are physically warm, then I will be emotionally warmer. See? Isn't helping your dad far better than watching him pop some antidepressant medication?

In closing, you are probably wondering "What is happening to dear ol' Dad? Going crazy?" Don't worry. I have listened to the CD that you made for me, packed with your favorite songs, enough times to absorb some of the lyrics. *The times are a-changing.* I realize if I don't start swimming, I am going to sink like a stone. I also realize I have lost my little girl, but she is coming back each summer for the next four years. I realize it will get easier as I grow more accustomed to the separation. This process will make me a stronger person, right? Maybe even a better father. Let's hope so. On that note, I hereby repeat my apology for anything I have done wrong as a father. It could not have been that bad, yes? After all, you turned out great. Unlike Mom, who will claim you deserve all the credit, I will pretend some of your success is because of me. Enough said. I am talking mostly about myself, not you. Thanks. I am feeling better already.

Confessionals: they are good for the soul.

Babbo

9/05/06 Thanks for Sharing the Pain

Dear Skyler,

It's just after 9:00 p.m. on a weekday night. Austen went to sleep around 8:30 p.m., as she's been feeling run down by the stress of high school and the idiots in her classes. Mom went to sleep a little before 9:00 p.m., as she's sick with headache, fever, chills, and a stomachache. What do I always say? When the mood drops, the immune system drops? No wonder you are so healthy, and no wonder we are dragging and sick. It has been a challenge to adjust to your absence, more than you will ever know. My green tea and collection of vitamins can only do so much. I am sure your best friends miss you, but I will bet, with all my money, we miss you even more. My proof? Are any of them going to sleep at 8:30 p.m., tired and depressed? Are any of them sick when they never get sick? Really, when was the last time Mom was sick? And are any of them writing you nonstop e-mails at midnight as a way to handle their emotional instability? We each have our ways of dealing with the loss we feel after your departure. Don't despair. From pain and suffering comes strength. So think of it as helping us, your family, become better people. That's what college is all about, right?

Speaking of pain and suffering, thanks for sharing your frustration about your first English class. I was worried about the required freshman English class, especially since you were so well prepared in your high-school English classes. I did not expect you to receive a teacher who would be covering the same old high-school material. I wish I had some suggestions, and, you know me, I always do. No, I do not recommend you hand in your high-school essays on the same books. Instead, I recommend you visit the head of the English department. You don't have to complain. If you ask about the department and how much it offers, I think the head of the department would be a good resource for finding better courses with more interesting material. In a large university, you have to find some type of mentoring to have a shot at the best education. NYU will have many great courses. You may be stuck with this English course for a semester, but wouldn't it be worthwhile to avoid any other repetitive courses in future semesters? The solutions only come with action, like researching some other classes.

Which reminds me…my cell phone is fixed, and I would love to hear from you after Barbie's visit from George Washington University. Are you going to take her to the Met? Or one of the Broadway plays? If you want an expensive dinner, I have a four-year college offer for you. You are welcome to have one expensive dinner each month, with a friend, charging it to me. With all of New York's restaurants, you might as well enjoy what the city has to offer. In return, I have just one request: please share some of those good times. They will keep me away from the medicine cabinet or the liquor cabinet. They will give me a rationale for my constant load of work. At least it is paying for your college education, and I need something to remind me that my effort is worth it. My dad used to say his best financial investment was the money he spent on my education. Of course, for him, my entire education cost less than a year of today's private college. Still, I want to share that same feeling. I want the cost of your college education to be my best financial investment. I have reached that age where my happiness comes from you and Austen, not from my work. If my efforts, geared toward your college expenses, improve any part of your life, it will be well worth those efforts. Spoken like a true parent.

Any pick-me-up news is appreciated.

Babbo

9/07/06 Are We All Going Crazy?

Dear Skyler,

    Earlier this evening, my mom called and said that my dad, with his dementia, was forcing her to leave the house, claiming he did not want to sleep with an unmarried woman, especially when his own dad might be coming home in the morning. Of course, his dad has been dead for fifty years. He insisted this woman could not possibly be his wife, and he did not want his dad to become upset at him for any immoral behavior. I talked to my dad on the phone, trying to drive some common sense into him, but he kept going back to sex, an unmarried woman, and his dad's likely anger. He made little sense. You already know the secret of my dad having to marry my mother, at the start of his senior year of college, because of her unexpected pregnancy during their summer fling. Do you think his mistake is still haunting him? Sixty years later and his anger still burns? Mistakes in college can last a lifetime, and they can erupt no matter how dormant the volcano. After a drive to their house and a long confrontation, I talked my dad into letting this strange woman, his wife of sixty years, stay the night as long as she did not demand any sexual favors. Trust me, I did not ask him about the details about the potential sexual requests.

    However, I have a question for you. Do you think I was more shocked by my dad's behavior, or by the news that you are joining the diving team? Are you as crazy as my dad? Let me be clear. I encourage you to explore new areas and follow your passions. You should pay no attention to a parent's panic attack or to a parent's opinion. But how much of a commitment is it? How many days per week? How many hours per day? I love the idea of your exercising, staying in shape, and doing something athletic. You have always been a good athlete. But I am anxious about diving safety. If you remember, you hit the board on multiple occasions when you were diving in your pre-high-school years. I hope your coach starts you slowly, so you can rebuild your diving skills. In any case, whenever you call, I would love to know why you decided to join the team. No restraints from us—just the usual parental concern. No diving in high school, but diving in college? It would have helped, and made me feel less anxious, if your high school had finished building their on-campus pool during your four years, not after you graduated.

To top that shocking news, Austen said you were going dancing this weekend at some Iranian or Middle Eastern bar? It always amazes me how the little sister knows more than the parent. I must ask: Do you want to get blown up? It's the fifth anniversary of 9/11. In the Middle East, what do they blow up? Usually restaurants and dance halls or bars. The easiest places. Why? Because you can kill the most people at once. It's already started in Europe and India, so it's just a matter of time before suicide bombers become a staple of the evening news. You know one of the first targets will be New York. Oh well, perhaps we are all going crazy. People seem to think this terrorist activity is going to go away. How long did the Crusades last? Close to two hundred years? These conflicts are going to extend beyond your college years, probably through your entire lifetime. I know you have that youthful attitude: if it's my time, it's my time. Besides, what are the chances? One in a million? Still, think of my dad. Mistakes made in college can happen. Oh well, I have spoken my peace. Regardless of my rambling, we support you.

Just not in an exploding restaurant or bar.

Babbo

9/10/06 Half Ready to Die?

Dear Skyler,

    For my life, I have refined several goals and dreams to reach before my demise. One of them came true yesterday. You may have been part of the inspiration. What was my dream? Nothing earth shattering. I wanted Austen to compose a song, write lyrics for the song, and sing the song. In sixteen years, she had never done it. I know it's selfish on my part—like my wanting you to write your high-school novel in a single month when your closest friends were gone for that month. Nothing is better than a parental dream where the child does all the work. Well, Austen created another of her many original piano compositions, and then, to our surprise, put lyrics to it and sang it for us while she played the piano. It was a really, really good song. Plus, it's her first rocker, fast paced with rapid chord changes. Rather catchy. The words, and story, were cool. At the end of her rendition, I proposed that some pop group should record the song, but she axed that suggestion. She said that only one person could do justice to that song. Her! Now, can you guess the content of the song? It was about her distaste for all of the female drama in high-school life. Pure teenage angst. If you think the theme was a surprise, you should hear the lyrics. Maybe when you are home at Thanksgiving? Of course, she will share that song only with you, not with your friends. Still, it was a landmark day. For now, I am a happy man, ready to die. What type of demented father depends on his kids for his happiness? Far too many parents?

    Now, how about jumping from one man's dream to one man's nightmare? You would not have liked the scene for my meeting yesterday with my parents. I was probably not the best of sons. After they presented at our door, with my dad trying to drop off this strange, mean lady, and after I led them back to their house, I lost it. I unloaded on my dad for his treatment of my mom, and I unloaded on my mom for her even worse care of my dad. She's constantly belittling him for every memory lapse, for every misstep. But the biggest shocker? I confronted both of them, for the first time in my life, on the secret of my dad getting my mom pregnant in college and being forced into an eloped marriage, and I confronted both of them for their lack of integrity, never having told the truth to my sister or me for the past sixty years. They were shocked, horrified, and embarrassed that I knew the truth. For me, it was relevant to discuss their shared mistake because that buried issue is triggering my dad's anger and agitation. What a mess. It is still ongoing, as my mom is sleeping in the second bedroom because my dad keeps regressing into his dementia, convinced that my mom is hired help and should be fired. When I tell him she's his wife, he stares at me in utter disbelief: "Impossible. I don't even like her! And she's so mean!" I am in the middle of all of the conflict, physically and emotionally drained. Be glad you are away. I even told the truth to Austen today. Now, she thinks she's going to write another song on how unfair it is that you cannot pick your family.

Got to love that girl. Got to love you, too.

Babbo

9/18/06 Forget the Cup? Enjoy the Coffee!

Dear Skyler,

We received the following bit (below) from a friend, and we thought you might enjoy it more than another dose of my so-called wisdom.

A group of alumni, highly established in their careers, got together to visit their old university professor. The conversation soon turned into complaints about stress in work and life. Offering his guests coffee, the professor went to the kitchen and returned with a large pot of coffee and an assortment of cups—porcelain, plastic, glass, crystal, some plain-looking, some expensive, and some exquisite—telling them to help themselves. After all the students had a cup of coffee in hand, the professor said: "If you noticed, all the nice-looking expensive cups were taken up, leaving behind the plain and cheap ones. While it is but normal for you to want only the best for yourselves, that is the source of your problems and stress. Be assured that the cup itself adds no quality to the coffee. In most cases, it's just more expensive, and in some cases even hides what we drink. What all of you really wanted was coffee, not the cup, but you consciously went for the best cups. Now consider this: Life is the coffee, and the jobs, money, and position in society are the cups. They are just tools to hold and contain life, and the type of cup we have does not define nor change the quality of life we live. Sometimes, by concentrating only on the cup, we fail to enjoy the coffee."

So, forget the cup and enjoy your coffee.
    Babbo

9/21/06 Props to Your Own Vision

Dear Skyler,

Over this first month of college, since you and I flew back one month ago, I have experienced my share of down moods and a sense of loss. When you think about it, a lot has transpired in your first four weeks of college. But as the dust settles for this new experience, I must admit that I am developing a greater and greater appreciation of your own vision for your future. You saw what you wanted in college, realized what you could have at NYU, and you made a decision that was *your own decision*. At the beginning, before we flew back to NYU, and before we moved you into your dorm, I still had my doubts. Those doubts started to fade on your first day, and they have disappeared at this point. I think you made a great choice for college, and you should be applauded for your vision. Too many adolescents are dominated by the directives from their parents or even their friends. But you? You never went against your own instincts and judgment. Some say self-rejection is the biggest sin. Again, I congratulate you on your capacity to be yourself and stick to your own beliefs. Nothing is more important.

In retrospect, I do not think the other colleges had much of a chance. Manhattan and New York University are great fits for you. You have been to a play, *Wicked*, a concert by the Who, and a ton of New York–only activities. What campus is going to beat the excitement of your neighborhood? To top it off, you are diving on a collegiate team as a freshman. You may have seen that possibility, but I never did. I never saw you diving in college. Learn from these early steps. When you have a vision for yourself, follow it with all of your energy and passion. It just may turn out great, even if others do not share your vision. I am proud of your growing sense of self, and respect you more than ever. You are indeed making that transition toward adulthood, and I think you will do great living life, loving life, and finding your own niche. Like so many parents, I just need to get out of your way so you can take flight. So, despite my constant flow of advice, do your best to remain independent of my own opinions and my own deficiencies.

When I talk to one of my physician cohorts and hear about his son's fifty calculus problems per night or his thirty-five hours of homework per week at MIT, I think of my own college experience, where I worked way too hard, shortchanging myself of time for other pursuits, including better friendships. If you can remember that image, which you shared with me, of a man carrying a laundry bag, packed with the personality features he had to leave behind so he could be successful, that image would be me. Constantly working, dragging his better character features behind him, no longer active, no longer even visible. For you, I see more wisdom and better judgment at your age than I see for myself at a much older age. Mind you, I still think it's important to work hard, and I still think it's important to contribute to the quality of the world. But I have seen too many workaholics disappear into the night. I think it's a mistake to do anything if it means you lose parts of the real you. *The real you* represents your best chance to make a contribution to our world and, more importantly, your best chance to enjoy our world. Kudos for staying intact, balancing the competing components, and going forward as a complete person, not some shadow of who you could have been.

No worries, just applause.

Babbo

10/01/06 Hey, How About a Surprise Visit?

Dear Skyler,

Last night we went to Disneyland, eating dinner at the restaurant in California Adventure. Disneyland was decorated in Halloween style with tons of new decorations. Austen took several photos for you, as she observed you would not be able to see the decorations during your Christmas break because the Halloween decorations last only through October. That made her sad. I think she is going to e-mail you her pictures. Just pretend you can discuss the pictures next weekend when you have more time. After dinner, Austen and Mom were going to choose the Haunted Mansion, but I steered them toward Pirates because it had a shorter line. Plus, I told them we would come back this next Saturday night and view the Haunted Mansion. They seemed fine with that plan. Austen likes to go for short forays on Saturday evenings, as she seems able to ignore school and relax, forgetting her homework or tests.

At this point, everything is set if you decide to come for the surprise weekend. Austen has to sing at the Bowers museum on October 7, Saturday, for the Italian Embassy, but that is the extent of her obligations. She will also have homework for Sunday, but she will feel better completing it with you around. I am planning to give her encouragement to complete some work on late Friday afternoon, telling her I will have more free time over the weekend because of my Friday trip to San Francisco. Actually, that's the truth. Right now, I have nine cases to write up, which will take me six hours, which will have to be part of Sunday. Next Friday, I have to fly up to San Francisco to meet with a health-care company, trying to solidify consultations on the company's difficult cases. I hate leaving home, but it may work out, as I won't be picking up new cases for this coming weekend since I will be at an all-day Friday meeting. Plus, my return from San Francisco and your surprise arrival from New York would be perfect timing with us arriving at the same Long Beach airport, even around the same time.

So, I think it would be a great weekend to come home for this once-in-a-lifetime surprise for Austen and Mom. After you do it the first time, they'll be wary after that. If you fly home on October 6, it will have been six weeks since your departure, and it will be six weeks before your return flight for Thanksgiving. That would be perfect timing for a minibreak to prevent any California-withdrawal symptoms. This coming weekend would be short, but you would get three nights of sleep in your own bed. If any of your other college friends were around for this weekend, you would have a green light to meet with them at any time. Even with our evening trip to Disneyland, you know Austen will want to head home early so she can get her sleep. If you want anyone to come along or meet us there, you could stay even later. There are many options for your possible visit. Just let me know what you decide.

    Plus, a surprise visit would probably slow down my e-mails.
Babbo

10/12/06 Reflections on Your Surprise-Visit Weekend

Dear Skyler,

I am sitting here at my office, eating a peanut-butter sandwich and working through lunch, with a stack of charts spread across my desk, needing to complete a number of medical reviews for one of the local hospitals and their unfunded patients. See? I am helping the less fortunate. Before me, I see requests for radiology, orthopedics, dermatology, and even endocrinology consults, plus the usual psychiatry consults. My mind is going in other directions. I am thinking back to one week ago when you and I were texting each other throughout the day, mapping out your surprise visit on Friday evening. Back then, I was hoping we would pull it off, and we did, secretly meeting at the airport and driving home together. Do you recall the sequence of events as clearly as they are edged in my mind? I loved how you called Mom from our driveway, pretending to still be in New York, and how you rang the front door bell as you chatted, forcing Mom to open the front door while she was still talking on the phone. Well, Mom was about as stunned as I have ever seen her. And Austen, who was watching TV on the sofa? That was about as happy as I have seen her. So, thanks for the surprise visit, and thanks for your sacrifices.

In the future, please know you have a green light for flying home for weekends if you feel the need or desire. It is hard for us to judge the time you need for your activities and your classes, so it's all going to be your call. I will attest that six weeks seems about as long as Mom and Austen can last without you, at least at this early stage. So when you come home for Thanksgiving and then for Christmas, those will be manageable intervals for us. For your second semester? Who knows? Please don't feel pressured to come home at spring break, but just know the door is open. From the movie *The Man from Snowy River*, just remember the line, "You are welcome at our campfire anytime." Again, do it as suits your needs. Only you can judge your personal sacrifice with the long flight, the time-zone-change fatigue, and the subsequent squeezed study time. For us, there is no pain except for the sadness of saying another good-bye. For Mom, Austen, and me, your visit was worth that price. After you left, they both begged me to surprise them on some future weekend. Ah, such dreamers.

No other news to report, just know what an important part you play in our family. You really are the energy force that helps drive all of us. In high school, we had moments of disagreement. But even in those moments, you provided a certain energy that is often lacking in the family. Austen and I just drag from work to work, and Mom just shuffles from task to task. We appreciate you in more ways than I could possibly express. On that note, please take care of yourself in New York and on your trip to Washington, DC. If you can keep us apprised by texting and calling, that would be appreciated. This coming weekend is going to be tough for us, as we will keep reminiscing about last weekend and the joy of having you home. A big adjustment for us. From heaven back to earth. A typical parental day. We are counting the weeks to your Thanksgiving return. Mom and Austen discussed putting up our traditional chain of paper ringlets, one for each day, on the kitchen wall. They love cutting them down, just like we used to do for our annual summer Maui vacations. To enjoy life, we all need to live in the present, but it is uplifting to be able to look forward to something so enjoyable.

Me? I will survive, thanks to my many idiosyncrasies.

Babbo

10/28/06 Ready for a Parent-Weekend Gift?

Dear Skyler,
    As I sit here on a Saturday night, I wish I could be three thousand miles east, enjoying your parent weekend. I would have enjoyed flying into New York, exploring the Village with you, watching you dive, treating you to a couple of good dinners in the evenings, and sharing your life at NYU. Right now, as I glance at the chain of rings in the kitchen, which are counting down the days to your return, my mind jumps to November 22. I am really looking forward to your return for Thanksgiving, and it's not because of the feast. It's because I can't wait to learn more details of this semester. In appreciation of your calls, we want to send along a gift. Something for the parent weekend we are missing. Something to make up for our absence. I struggled to come up with an idea for a gift. I drove to our storage unit, retrieved your old baby book, and decided to type the first letters we ever wrote to you. You have always loved Halloween and scary stories. You have a special reason. Because, in 1987, on Halloween, that's when you were thawed and brought back from the frozen test tube. That's when you rose from the dead to join the living, when you crossed from darkness back into light. That's the date, Halloween, when you beat the odds. Changed our lives. Maybe that is why you have such a fondness for horror films? In any case, here are our very first letters. For now, consider it a parent-weekend gift from two absent parents.

Dear Skyler,
    From the moment I learned I was pregnant, I had a good feeling about you! I was most concerned about me. I was thrilled and excited with the pregnancy, but at the same time I was worried about what type of mother I would be. You gave me no trouble at all during the pregnancy with hardly any morning sickness, a twenty-one pound weight gain, no edema, and generally good health. It must have been the daily walks (Balboa Island on the weekends), the nightly stretching, the good food, and the weekly sushi. But, of course, the labor was not so easy. When you entered the world, no words could

express how I felt the moment I saw you, nor the moment I first held you. It was one of the best moments of my life. Another great moment followed, the first time I breastfed you. I was giving you something no one else could give you. We bonded immediately. We were a team. Someone once said, "You don't know love until you have a baby." And that person was right. Never had I felt such joy and love until you came along. I would go through the whole experience again just to relive the moment and see your precious face. I love you!

Love, Mom
7/24/88

Dear Skyler,

Six years of infertility, a conception on 6/08/87 in a test tube with my sperm and Mom's eggs, four months of suspended animation in CryoFreeze, a thawing and insemination on 10/30/87, a positive pregnancy test on 11/17/87, a normal amniocentesis report on 2/19/88 to prove all your genes were perfect, then thirty-eight hours of labor, a suction device, metal forceps, and a cord wrapped around your neck, but with our first look at you, we knew it was worth the long wait and the long ordeal. Love at first sight? Some people say it never happens, but for us, that's all it took. Just one look. God, how we loved you. To us, you were beautiful, almost angelic. What a surprise with brown hair and my features. For starters, that would have been my first wish: that you did not have too many of my features! Let's give you, our little lady, a chance. In truth, it did not matter how you looked, and it does not matter what you become. I love you now, and I will love you always. You have made us a family, and nothing is more important. Perhaps that is what I hope to teach. Feeling love, establishing a family, and having time to share life's experiences: that is what counts the most in life. The task will not be easy. There are setbacks and other demands in life. But persistence and perseverance are the secrets to staying true to your family. I hope I can be supportive to you in that process, both as a father and as a friend. My dad, in the good old days, used to call me "his best buddy." Maybe I can be that to you someday. As I write this first letter, it's only been a week since your birth, but already, our time together seems so precious. Whether it's washing you on the kitchen counter, changing your diaper, or cradling you in my arms while trying to sing, those moments have all been a delight. You have been a delight. You have been cheerful, energetic,

cooperative, and inquisitive to life with hardly a cry or whimper. Skyler, welcome to our world. I love you so much!
   Love, Dad
   7/23/88

After all these years, we couldn't say it any better.
   Babbo (and Mom)

11/04/06 Dad's-a-Changing? Maybe?

Dear Skyler,

It was fun to hear the account of your Halloween activities and Halloween choices. Should you go to the New York Halloween parade or stay in your dorm room and write your essay? And the next morning, after you had enjoyed the Halloween parade and gone to bed without writing your essay, should you skip your first class to write the essay or wake up at some earlier hour? A year ago, when you were still in high school, I would have argued for your staying home, forgoing any Halloween pleasure, and obtaining a high grade on your essay. After all, I am the wonderful father who would repeatedly send you off to school half-dead. A sore throat and a temperature of 102 degrees? *Off we go, young lady. I am sure you will feel better in class.* Nausea and periodic vomiting with the flu? *Don't worry, young lady, just make sure you finish taking notes before heading to the bathroom to throw up.* Great dad, yes? Well, this parent is changing, at least a little.

I applaud your decision to choose fun and friendship over work, and I applaud the decision to skip class and complete your essay versus getting minimal sleep and waking up early. Really, how much education can you miss in one class? Is one essay going to change your life? Isn't sleep far more important than any single grade? Do you want that "A" or a higher risk of cancer? Do you want DNA repair or newly formed mutations from the lack of sleep? Remember the line from *Freaky Friday*? "Make good choices." Well, I have reached the point where I think you are making good choices, even if they are not the choices I would have recommended a year ago. So, what has changed? First, when I speak to you, I can hear how much you are enjoying college and your new friends. That alone says you are making some good choices. Second, with your absence, and my loneliness from your absence, I have been forced to look at my parental habits and realize my multitude of mistakes.

When I look at my life, what do I see? I see an overload of work for the past five years with less time for leisure than I would have liked. I think of all the weekday nights when I buried myself in the computer room, completing medical-record review after medical-record review, all for additional money to help pay for college when I could have been enjoying more family time. The other night, after working all day at my regular job on medical-record reviews, what did I do? I came home, inhaled my dinner, and then retreated to my computer desk to work on even more medical records, this time from around the country. Yes, the money was needed. But when I had finally finished those cases around 11:00 p.m., everyone was asleep, and I was alone. All I could do was slump in front of the TV and watch the sports report on the earlier Lakers game. I had nothing left in the tank. I spent the entire day with no family interaction. Did you know that the average father spends only four to twenty minutes a day one-to-one with his child? What a mistake. Instead of family connection, it is just work and more work. Have I been making the most of life? Not a chance.

What's my point? Well, like so many people, I have gained insight but have not changed my behaviors. I am still working far too many hours with too little family time and too little fun. But thanks to you, I am committed to making more of a change, and perhaps helping other people to change. The quality of our life is the quality of our relationships, not the financial amount of our portfolios. To obtain quality, you have to establish more quantity. You can't have great relationships without sufficient time. In fact, those moments of high quality stem from high quantity. Here's my new advice. Make relationships the core of your life, and your life will be wonderful, regardless of everything else. I might propose the following litmus test when you start looking for a career. In which field will you have the best relationships? In medicine, everyone is always working. Get a group of physicians together and listen to the complaints. No free time. But what about the film or TV industry? Is it more of a family feeling? Is there more time for relationships? More time to work together as a group? More time for laughter and fun? I don't know the answers, but those would be my new questions. Don't follow my behaviors. Follow your instincts. Skip that evening homework. Forget the grade. Have some fun. Make your own good choices.

Does that sound like the same old me?

Babbo

1/10/07 A Belated "Good-as-Gold" Christmas Gift

Dear Skyler,

    First and foremost, I want to thank you for blessing us with your company over the past three weeks during your first college Christmas holiday. It was not only great to have you home, but it was wonderful to re-experience the Skyler style: spontaneous exits with your Honda zipping down the street; late-night returns while we were sleeping; unexpected people joining us at restaurants; and unexpected friends showing up at our door and staying for hours. You are quite a character and quite a life force. All three of us stand in awe of your *style*. On my part, I was only sorry that I did not have more time with you. But much of that was my fault, secondary to my bout of the flu and secondary to my work. Once again, I wish I did not have to work so hard, and once again, I wish I had more time with you. Isn't that what almost every parent says? Of course, I need to follow my own advice. Each person needs to refrain from judging and blaming. Each person needs to focus more on accepting and appreciating. That goes for assessing oneself and others. Forget any self-criticism. Erase any regrets. Expand gratitude for the present. In that spirit, thanks for sharing yourself as much as you did. All of us appreciated your time.

    Now, as to your belated Christmas present. Is it the cash I slipped into your wallet before the trip to the airport? Nope. This is better than money; it's as good as gold. What is better than gold? My advice, of course, which I promised to bury. Listen up. Think back to your four years at high school. Remember how you went through each year carrying your written goals in your pocket? Remember how you achieved those written goals? Well, I am recommending you consider reviving that habit of written goals, if you have let it slide. But not for grades. No, for those things that are far more important! I recommend you spend some time thinking about what you want to happen over the rest of your college career. Things that matter to you. Things that occur outside of the classroom, not just inside the classroom. I recommend you write down that list and tack it to a wall by your bed where you can glance at it on a daily basis. Then just start completing that list of goals, day by day, year by year.

Are you shaking your head in disbelief? Babbo has gone mental. Again, listen up. What if you wrote down a list of ten desires and goals for college that were balanced and covered the full range of possible activities you really wanted? For example, think about the possibilities. This list is probably off target, but it will give you a glimpse of what I'm suggesting. Would you like to get into a specific residence hall or get your own apartment? Would you like to attend certain sporting events or additional concerts? Would you like to join any new clubs? Would you like to find a few more new friends who could become lifetime friends? Would you like to invite several of your friends to visit you during the summer? Would you like to be hired for a movie-industry intern position? Would you like to spend at least one semester abroad? Would you like to see part of the world while still attending college? Would you like to get into the best physical shape of your life? Are those the wrong goals? You get the point. It's your goals and your desires. Just write them down and go for them over these next four years.

You've heard the spin, so here it is again. In that study at Yale, 3 percent of the class wrote down their goals. Twenty years later that 3 percent had more wealth than the other 97 percent who had not written down their goals. Writing down goals helps, even when they are not focused on money. Ideally, they should be balanced, with some focusing on your health and personal development, some focusing on areas of passion and interests, some focusing on extracurricular activities, and some focusing on relationships and friendships. They do not take away from any spontaneity. They do not take away from fun or excitement. The written goals prime the pump, leading you toward the more positive things you want in your life. At least that is what I have read from the experts. Of course, I am just another parent, pretending to be an expert. It is what we do.

Why am I offering this recipe at this time? Because college flies by at the speed of sound. You are already one-eighth of the way through college. Did the first semester slip by in a flash? It will be the slowest semester of your college career. To make certain you do not find yourself at graduation saying, "I wish I had done this activity, or I wish I had attended that event," why not reflect on your desires and goals right now, why not write down some balanced goals right now, and why not duplicate the success you had as a high-school student? Don't you remember how you wrote down, at the start of your freshman year of high school, how you wanted to receive all As? Was becoming a top student in your class a coincidence? No. Of course, those goals came from me, not from you. Still, written goals work, especially when they are your own. You are in a wonderful city. You are in a marvelous college. I encourage you to take control of your path through written-down goals, as it would add to your personal development. Anyhow, that is my belated Christmas present. Written goals with the quote that "no wind favors he or she who has no destined port" (Michel de Montaigne).

So, would you have preferred a scarf?

Babbo

1/15/07 A Toast to the Family

Dear Skyler,

    As you get ready to start your second semester and your second long stint away from the Courter household, and as I sit here in the quiet computer room, sipping your Christmas gift of delicious New York tea, I want to offer a new observation: how much I love our family. By saying I love our family, I mean the four of us: you, Austen, Mom, and me. When I was in college, being driven to some mixer in a two-seater sports car, I was asked an unexpected question by a good friend from Williams College. Who do you love more? Your father or your mother? I do not remember my response. At this point I like my dad, even with his dementia, far more than I like my mom because of the way she has been treating him. But love one family member more than the other? That is not a thought that had crossed my mind. Love is not quantifiable. Well, when I apply the same question to *our family*, I have a new perspective. I cannot say I love one family member more than I love any other family member. That would be impossible. I love you each as much as the other, but perhaps in different ways. But I can say I love *our family* much more—a zillion times more—than I loved my initial family with my mom, my dad, my sister Sherry, and me. Does that statement hold true for others? Is it natural to love the family you create more than the family that created you? I do not know the answer to that question. I know only one thing: as a parent, nothing beats our family.

    When I look around at my cohorts at work and see how so many doctors have poured money into their homes, upgrading and expanding them to add to their material wealth, I am cognizant of how I have taken a different path. I have not steered our money into our home. Instead, I have directed our finances into our vacations and experiences. Mom has been great in understanding and agreeing with that approach. She has sacrificed having a nicer kitchen and a better-decorated living room. For us, the reason is simple. We wanted our family time more than we wanted a nicer house, especially since I work so hard and since my family time is so limited during the week. We wanted our family time to be special. I have always loved the days when the four of us have been together on a planned trip. Hawaii has been perfect for us. Right now, I am especially pleased we are going to Maui this summer, and I am crossing my fingers that we can take that Europe trip at some point in the future. You can probably guess. Yes, it is one of my *written* goals, posted on the back of the door to my computer room. That will give it a better chance of coming true, yes?

It is my hope that we can continue to take our Courter family vacations for years, even decades, even after you and Austen move out into the world and even after our family expands with new members, new significant others. Whenever I reach retirement, I am going to continue my pattern. I am going to direct a sizeable portion of my saved money toward bringing everyone together for shared, regular Courter vacations. If that means paying for you and some lucky guy, or if that means bringing along a couple of families to a fun destination, then so be it. My goals are unchanged. I want our family time to continue, and I want our family to merge with your future family—and Austen's future family. Today, I toast the Courter family, *our Courter family*. It's a wonderful, bit zany, varied-personality family, but clearly it's the best thing in my life. Over the years, I hope it remains one of the better things in your life. Maybe we can be like one of those large families at Christmas. Everyone gathered together in some memory-filled house, each person seeming to enjoy the others. Or does that only happen on film? Oh well, I am going to list it as another of my written goals.

Have a great start to your second semester.
Babbo

2/28/07 An Unexpected Death? Any Lessons Learned?

Dear Skyler,

    Earlier tonight I spent ninety minutes sitting with my dad—or at least what was left of my dad. He died at 4:45 p.m. this afternoon. My mom called me before his death, letting me know he was beginning to gurgle as he breathed, and it looked like death was imminent. Unfortunately, I was stuck at work. I was also scheduled to pick up Austen after school, and I was not going to leave her alone on the street corner so frequently populated by the homeless. Consequently, I was not able to get to him before he died. However, my mom was nice enough to delay calling the local mortuary until I arrived, thereby giving me ninety minutes to spend with my dad's body with it lying in his bed as if he were still asleep. It was ninety minutes well spent, as I silently told him, although dead and pale white, about my love, my admiration, and my sense of loss. I recommend taking those moments when it's your time to share in one of those life events.

    When I arrived, the chaplain asked about the good times in my dad's life and when my dad had been the happiest. I was not sure how to answer that question, but I am sure he was miserable for the last years of his life. He had become a lost man, no longer immersed in any clear, specific passion and devoid of any sustained joy, especially considering the conflict with my mom. If I could rewind the clock and speak to him now, I would tell him to forget all of the conflicts and to stay focused on the real value of life, including those activities and friendships that gave him moments of bliss—or at least the memory of those moments and friendships that had given him his greatest pleasures. For him, I think some of his happiest moments came when he was constructing commercial centers, like building parts of Los Angeles (Century City) and building parts of Portland (John's Landing). Those passions keep you living, not dying. Those passions make you yearn for another tomorrow. Those passions are far more important than any money associated with the pursuit. Passions and purpose, combined with connections with people and friendship are the pillars for a happy life.

    That is my main message to you with this e-mail. I think everyone needs to find a special purpose in life, and when you find that purpose, that's when you reach a higher level of happiness. Sadly, for most people, it never happens. At some stage in your life, you will discover a passion that sparks your career. At another stage, you will find a core group of lifelong friends who can be part of your passion. At another stage, a handsome man will fall in love with you. At another stage, you may start your own family. The key is not the specific purpose; the key is finding those passions, grabbing those passions, and making them a core part of your life. Although truth be told, you do not find those events. They find you. As you progress through these stages of your life, including your current transition from an adolescent into a young, beautiful woman, keep yourself open to all of your passions, leaving the pursuit of money out of the equation. The key to life is your passion, purpose, and connection, not your wallet. More accurately said, happiness is the real wealth of life.

Now, at this point, I can hear your thoughts. You are probably asking yourself if you should fly home to attend my dad's funeral service. My dad did not want a service. All of his closest friends have already died. He remarked, more than once, that he had already attended too many funerals. My dad will be cremated, and at some point in the future, we will have a ceremony to scatter his ashes. That will be in the future, not now. We will look forward to your arriving home next Wednesday, as planned. If you want to do something for my mom, give her a call and offer her your condolences. Or send her a card. You can pay her a visit while home. Just ignore her usual negative and critical remarks. I recall how you and Austen, when you were children, used to count the number of insults from my mom, wondering who would win with the highest tally. Remember, with any period of grief, those types of behaviors are likely to grow worse, not better. She will become more, not less, bitter. For now, as always, we can rise above them. Less judgment. Less blame. Less anger. Sometimes, that is not so easy for me, as my mother and I could not be any more different. Sometimes, the lady drives me crazy. Stick to the plan of arriving home as scheduled. Back to *your* parents.

Live life and embrace it while it lasts.
Babbo

3/03/07 The Funeral Service for My Dad

Dear Skyler,
   We had a small service at the mortuary that lasted all of thirty-five minutes. Since there was only a pastor, my mom, Ace, me, Austen, and several of my mom's friends, I suddenly decided I wanted to say a few words. Rather abruptly and unprepared. But everyone seemed to appreciate my remarks, and I brought tears to Austen's eyes. After the ceremony, one of my mom's friends took me aside and encouraged me to type my remarks and give them to my mom, as my mom might want to mail them to her friends. I decided to take the high road, obliging the request. Thus, here is an attached copy of my remarks, just typed right now.

A Tribute to My Dad

For this service, I had not prepared, nor planned on making any remarks. But when I arrived at the mortuary, it just did not feel right to remain quiet, especially in view of everything my dad has done for the family and me over the years. I have only been to two funerals in my life, my sister Sherry's and my dad's. So, I was not sure what to say today. My dad always preached that you never learned anything while talking, but I think he might have made an exception for this occasion. I thought I would start by sharing some memories, which unexpectedly surfaced over the past few days. At first, the memories seemed strange, random, and insignificant. But after reliving them over these past three days, they have gained more significance and have become much more cohesive and telling.

When my dad died, my mom did something very special. She waited to call the mortuary until after I arrived. That gave me a chance to spend ninety minutes with my dad, where it was just my dad's body, my mom, and me, alone in that room. It was a wonderful experience that meant a lot to me, and it greatly eased my own pain. On that night, on the way home after the mortuary had retrieved his body, I had a sudden memory, a memory long since forgotten. I remembered myself as a young kid, throwing up on the side of a winding mountain road. I must have been five years old, and I am guessing the road may have been on the drive to Lake Arrowhead. I remembered how my dad pulled the car to the side of the road, how he opened the back door to let me out, and how he led me to a spot of dirt where he helped me throw up. But with that memory, I have no recall of exactly where I was, nor any recall of the events before or after that incident. But I have a clear memory of how my dad's hand reached around my waist, how he held me close so I would not fall over, and how much comfort I felt from his hand. It was the comfort and security from my dad's hand that stood out. Nothing else.

Later that night when I was trying to fall asleep, I remembered another long-since-forgotten memory. The incident occurred when I was probably nine years old, when we were living in San Marino, California. I remember I was driving with my dad, sitting in the front seat, when he suddenly slammed on the brakes, skidding to an abrupt halt, just as a car whizzed right in front of us, crossing the intersection through a red light. I have no memory of where the incident occurred, and I have no memory of the events before or after that incident. But I have a strong memory of how my dad swung out his right arm, how his hand pressed against my chest, and how his hand prevented me from flying forward into the windshield. Most importantly, I have a memory of how his hand felt. How its strength gave me a sense of safety, a feeling of protection.

Earlier today, as I was driving to this service, I had another sudden memory. It occurred a decade later in my adolescence. I remembered the time when my dad and I were body surfing on Poipu Beach on Kauai. We were treading water beyond the breakers, waiting for the next big wave. Suddenly, we saw this fin, this shark, in the water, probably ten yards from us, turning directly toward us. I remembered my dad's hand reaching out, grabbing my hand, and yanking me back toward the shore. Instantly, we kicked like mad, perfectly caught the wave, and surged toward the safety of the beach. With this incident, I didn't remember what happened next, except how the beach had to be closed. But when I think back to that incident, I do not think of the approaching shark. Instead, I recall the strength and comfort of my dad's hand, once again offering me help, once again offering me protection. And that's how my dad was through his life, always offering me a helping hand.

In life, I have a very simple philosophy that I have tried to teach Skyler and Austen, perhaps ad nauseam. I believe each person is special, each person has special gifts, and one of the purposes of life is to find your special gift, develop your special gift, and share your special gift with the world, making it a better place. My dad was the best athlete I've ever met. To be the captain of three teams in high school and to be captain of a football team in college, especially to be captain of a football team still regarded as one of the college's best, that's no easy feat. When my dad graduated from college, he had an offer to be an assistant football coach. I think he would have been an outstanding coach. It could have been his calling. When the time came to make a decision, I think he realized he had a more important purpose: to provide for his new family.

Over the next sixty years, my dad stayed true to that purpose, making sacrifice after sacrifice. When he was a young executive with Alcoa and had to travel four days a week to help with recruiting, he made that sacrifice. When he worked for Alcoa for thirty years and moved from city to city, leaving behind his friends, he made that sacrifice. When he helped build Century City and had to work most Saturdays, he made that sacrifice. When he started his commercial development project in Portland and had to fly there on Monday morning and return to Southern California on Friday evening, he made that sacrifice. Over and over, time and again, he made those sacrifices to provide for his family. From my perspective, he was a wonderful success. He gave us a fabulous life. We lived in the East in Pittsburgh, we lived in the South in Louisville, we lived in the Midwest in Chicago, and we lived in the West, our favorite, in Southern California. It was a good life and a life of opportunity, all thanks to my dad's lifetime of sacrifices.

Even in retirement, and even after he was no longer making an income, he stayed true to his purpose. For the past five years, I have been going over to my mom and dad's house every Saturday morning to help pay the bills. Well, my dad hated to pay the bills. It was probably the angriest I have ever seen him, signing those checks. He hated to have the money going out to someone else; he wanted that money saved for the family. Even with his dementia and his transfer to Aegis dementia unit, he hated the idea of spending money on his own care. He wanted that money to be spent on us, not him. I do not think it was a coincidence that he died on February 28. It saved my mom from spending money for another month of care. At the end, he wanted to give that money to us more than he wanted to keep on living.

From my viewpoint, my dad was a wonderful man, and from my viewpoint, my dad stayed true to his main purpose in life, providing for his family for over sixty years. So, I wanted to take these few minutes to pay a tribute to his sacrifice and his hard work and to thank him for his helping hand. Whether I was a young kid vomiting by the side of a winding mountain road or a grown man buying a house, he was always there with that helping hand, ready to offer support. He was always ready to give, always ready to sacrifice. He was a fantastic father. I loved him dearly. I will miss him dearly. And he *was a really, really good man. If there is a heaven, if I get into heaven, and if my dad is not there, well, I ain't staying.*

Thank you.

You did not miss much except my own sentiments. You were there in spirit! And, after the ceremony, we even talked about you, including the pastor. You received praise for your courage to go to a college so far away from home.

As if you did not know that already.
Babbo

3/18/07 Thank God You Survived the Car Crash

Dear Skyler,

    At this instant, you are flying Jet Blue Flight 212, with the flight screen showing you are just fifteen minutes from your landing in New York, back from your spring break with us. And at this instant, Mom and Austen are watching TV while I am sitting in front of my computer, flanked by my dad's ashes. What type of dad writes his collegiate daughter just after placing his hand on the ashes, saying a little prayer, and thanking his dad as if he had a role in keeping you alive? Not many, I suspect. That is my feeling tonight. On one hand, I am sad you have left because our house is never the same without you, and on the other hand, I am so glad you survived your car crash over the holiday with only bruises and arm burns from the air bags, especially since you totaled your Honda CRV. It could have been worse, so much worse. For many parents, it's the call we fear the most. Your child has been involved in a car accident. Your child has crashed into a tree or another vehicle, and suddenly your child's voice is gone, never again to be heard and never again to be cherished. Remember our shared tears on the drive home after the crash? After you declined the ride in the ambulance to the hospital and elected to come home with me. Do you remember on the drive home how you apologized for totaling the car, claiming you would find some way to pay back the cost? With me saying I was just glad you were alive. Forget the loss of the vehicle. I couldn't care less about the car or the money. Focus on our luck that you are alive. That is all that matters.

    That's why my constant refrain of "Be safe; be good; be you" always starts with your safety. Between now and the end of the semester, let's turn around our recent bad luck and let's get back onto the track of the living. Dare I repeat our setbacks? My dad's death. Your car collision. Plus, your lost iPod, your lost cell phone, the abrupt eruption of warts on your hands and feet, the dermatologist's liquid nitrogen treatment and your subsequent multiple blisters, the mold in our vents, and the construction work in our attic. They are thankfully behind us. As I sit here with my dad's loss, I am aware I can handle that loss. I can place my hand on his ashes and feel a sense of comfort. Could I have placed my hand on your ashes? Not a chance. That I could not have handled. That would have killed me. A child can bury a parent. A parent cannot bury a child. Your life lies in front of you, and I want you to have the chance to enjoy all the great parts of that life. Your friendships. Your passions. Your personal triumphs. The different phases of your life. You and Austen are the best two things I have done with my life. Thanks, of course, to Mom. Again, live life to the fullest, but live safely, OK?

Anything less would kill us.
Babbo

3/24/07 The Art of Driving a Parent Crazy

Dear Skyler,

If you thought totaling your car would *drive* your parents crazy, you have found a better way. Mom has been pacing around the house all afternoon, muttering to herself, "It would be the most stupid thing she has ever done!" What have you done to cause a meltdown in your mother? You have her convinced you are going to buy a pet—for New York during the school year and for our house during the summer. Better yet, I shared how I told you, "Hey, why not a cat? Mom, with her allergies, could just take a Benadryl pill each day." You should have heard her response. Quite humorous. She keeps telling me I have to talk to you because you are *my* daughter. Like that's going to help. Good luck with your choice of a cat. I liked our hamster and all his multiple tunnels and sleeping bins. I had a blast switching all the tunnels and activity cages, as if he had a new living quarter with different toys every few days. I have also loved having Paris all these years. Every family should have a dog. Before you do anything, I would take care of yourself. With Mom saying you have bedbug bites the size of quarters, I have this image of your car-wreck bruises, the air-bag burns on your arms, the warts on your hands and feet, the varied blisters from the liquid nitrogen, and now these bedbug bites on your arms and legs. Sorry, but it does not make for a cuddly image. It's more of a boyfriend repellant, if you were to ask me. Of course, a parent would be the last to know.

Speaking of driving someone crazy, and much more than usual, I am not having much luck with my mom, who seems more and more bitter, plus more and more selfish. Today, when I was helping her with the bills, she was talking about buying herself a new car. She wants a two-seater red Mercedes, and since Dad's not around to curtail her self-centered materialistic nature, anything goes. I told her if she buys a new car, maybe we could buy her old car so you could use it during the summer. If my dad were still alive, he would have said, "Oh, that's a great idea, but we'll just give the car to Skyler." My mom's response? She quickly shot down the offer of us even buying her car, saying she would get more money with the trade-in value, as if she needs the money. For her, it's just an excuse; she's allergic to giving. Always has been. Always will be. Now I have tried to refrain from judgment, but it is still sad. There is a saying: "You are rich from what you give, and poor from what you keep." Emotionally and spiritually, my mother is so very poor, and worst of all, she does not even seem to know it. So, in terms of your car, what are the realistic options for the coming summer? Buying a used car at the start of the summer and selling it at the end of the summer? Or perhaps I can buy Mom a new Honda Accord, and then give Mom's old Accord to you? I am not certain what we will do, but don't worry, you will have a car. Like my dad always held out his hand for me, I will hold out my hand for you. Some parents do it; other parents don't. Everything will work out for the best. Your summer will be a delight.

Until then, just keep driving your mom crazy.
Babbo

3/25/07 More Reflections on Life

Dear Skyler,

One of my physician cohorts sent me an e-mail last night, lamenting the quality of his contribution to the world. His starting point? With the world strife, he addressed his minimal role and limited contribution to society. For the sake of sharing, I thought I would pass along my response and recommendation to him. Just so you get to know your dear old dad a little better. For me, the more time I sit with my own mom, the less I seem to know her. I do not want the same with you. Even with our geographic distance, I want you to know me more and more. From my perspective, that is a good goal for any point in a parent's life, but especially an important goal while the son or daughter is attending college. It can be done from a distance! It can be accomplished through e-mail correspondence. Now, for the below e-mail, when you read lines about my future goals, the specific goals are not well delineated in this exchange. But Mom and I have a list of goals that involve time, fun, and traveling. Of course, as previously stated, with the entire extended Courter family, not just for the two of us. Anyhow, here is my e-mail to my fellow physician.

In my journal on April 12, 1999, I wrote: Where has the time gone? Again, it's the consulting work I bring home and my pursuit of money. So stupid, so wrong. Last night I told Priscilla, "It's amazing how smart I was and how stupid I have become!" Instead of doing the things I love, I am doing things I don't even like. Spending hours and hours reviewing medical records. Attending innumerable administration meetings day after day. Wasting every Saturday morning at my mother's house, listening to her endless series of negative comments, complaints, and criticisms. Do I have time to listen to my audiotapes for self-education and personal growth? Do I have time to write a second draft for my first novel? Which has been sitting in the garage for years? Do I have time to start writing my second book, a planned nonfiction book? No. But we are building a pool this summer, and we are heading to Maui for a two-week vacation in June. Yes, the material things. I am paying the bills, providing a richer life for the family. But have I gone astray, trying to give the loved ones a better life? Am I giving them a better life? Or is it just a richer material life? A more superficial life?

So, my friend, you can see we have some parallel issues, trying to measure the value of our life and our contribution to our family and our community. Trying to find a more satisfying direction for our life. For me, it was true a decade ago, and for me, it is still true today. Right now I have fourteen private consulting cases to dictate, plus a pair of Medi-Cal Appeal charts to complete. A good Sunday ruined. Another marble spilled from the jar of life. One day of my life wasted, which I will regret on my deathbed. Did I need that money? Did it contribute much more than the extra income for the family? In your case, my friend, you contribute high-quality work to a number of hospitals, plus you offer your own private consulting work. You provide assistance to your parents and your brother's children, doing much more than anyone else would expect of you. But is it all that you want? I think it is time for both of us to break free, to return to our passions.

Do I have any specific advice? Get used to the doubts, as they do not get less as you grow older. Get used to the criticism from others, as that seems to last a lifetime. But there is a light at the end of this tunnel. Death? No, my friend, there is hope before death. In Hinduism, they preach we go through four distinct phases: pleasure, achievement, personal development, and liberation. You may be at one of the crossroads. Over the next year, your level of achievement and financial reward may skyrocket, but maybe you are feeling the tug for more personal development? Or perhaps a tug for more liberation from the career treadmill? Freedom is a good thing. Perhaps you have an image of a different path? A path toward a potential slice of heaven. They are opposing forces with contrary results, so it's unavoidable to have these moments of indecision. How much wealth do you want? Or how much achievement do you need? And how much would you prefer a quieter place on some island? Or some foreign location? Or a life filled with more time for your real passions? Tough choices with no easy answers.

In Hinduism, they recommend a geographic move when you retire, where you can shed your old identities and where you can start anew for your final phase of life. Good advice for parents who are losing their children to college. I do not think we will move geographically, but I am hopeful we will move emotionally, for lack of a better word. I expect to retire from work as soon as it is financially acceptable. I know. There's a contradiction right there. For retirement, I hope to clarify my real passions, my real goals. I hope to pursue those passions with vigor. Happiness, to repeat, comes from pursuing a passion, not from making an income. Happiness comes from friendships, not working alone in an office. As a starting point, I have been creating a list of all the things I want to do before I die. It's not a bucket list of destinations. It's more of a personal mission statement. Some of the passions include the possibility of contributing to the world through more writing. Many actions simply focus on personal satisfaction. Listening to more educational tapes. Reading more novels. Getting into better physical shape. Being more available to my family. Exploring more cultures. I may not reach all of my goals, but those goals help, as they give me a future road map with a sense of direction.

My final recommendation? In down times, I turn to my list of goals. When I hit bottom, I sit here at the computer and stare at the list, imagining a better future with those activities adding joy to my life. Of course, I am the guy who has my dad's ashes set next to my computer where I can reach out and touch the urn. It is surprisingly heavy, and in more ways than just weight. What's that often-posed question? Who's the bigger fool? The fool, or the man who follows the fool? If you want to follow my lead, take time to start a list of activities you want to do before you die. Maybe it will give you a new direction, a new level of clarity. Maybe even a new destination. To reach those goals, how much money and achievement do you need? How much personal development do you need? How much freedom do you need? Are you moving toward those goals? Or are you moving away from them? Maybe there will be an epiphany at some point. It has not come for me. But my own mission statement helps, at least with my day-to-day survival and my hope for the future.

So, Skyler, did this e-mail, written eight years ago, reveal anything new about me? Or offer any changed perspective on my usual advice? Or did the material sound remarkably consistent with my usual literary outbursts? Either way, that perspective applies to me, to you, to each of us. We all need to make major decisions as we advance through life. For you, you have plenty of time, especially if you use these next four years to full advantage, and especially if you utilize the first decade of adulthood to explore your possibilities. College can be great, but the twenties can be a decade to clarify some changes in priorities, some changes in direction. But I still like to repeat my motto: discover your passion and create a purpose. Today? Tomorrow? Just sometime! In some ways, despite the chaos of the world, life can be just that simple.

Care to give it a try?
Babbo

4/20/07 Another Update on Family Conflicts

Dear Skyler,

    I have grown weary of my visits to my mother. She has become progressively more denigrating. In the last few weeks, she has attacked Mom for her Mexican and Spanish heritage, saying Mom was beneath me. She criticized Mom for not working as a nurse all of these years and for being just a-stay-at-home mom. She attacked you for not having to work for your new car, even though we wanted the car for you because you *would* be working this summer. Maybe it's part of the grieving process, or maybe she is just showing more and more of her true colors. Seriously, if my dad ever had a choice, I do not think he would have married my mother. He always gave; she always took. He wanted to hide his hard-earned wealth; she liked to showcase it through her possessions. Strange, especially for a woman who never worked a day in her life. Her only success came from capturing the right man, a loyal man, my father. In those heated, Saturday conversations, I always hold my ground, sharing how much I love *our* mom, how smart *our* mom is, how she was a great nurse, and how she has always been such a great mother to you and Austen. I share how hard you two work and how well you two have done. My positive comments never seem heard. The lady talks, but never listens. She is the exact opposite of my dad. So sad.

    It's strange. I know how I should respond. I know I should ignore her remarks and try my best not to judge or criticize or blame. I know I should ignore her attacks on our family, not taking any of them personally. I know I should keep my distance from her poisons. I know I should focus on just our positives. But, wow, is it a challenge. With the people in her life, she presents such a different side. Over the years, I have seen her up close and personal. Her friends think she is a fun, entertaining woman. After all, at one party at our house, when it was growing late and no one would leave, she just dropped to the living room carpet, spread out, and announced she was not getting up until everyone left. To me, that takes some spirit. Yet, when the door is closed, and the spotlight if off, she is so markedly different. She was so demeaning to my dad during the final days of his life, and she has become equally demeaning to all of us. Oh well, I will try to utilize my insights. Please underline the word *try*. Instead of shrugging off the negative remarks, I usually hit a point where I return the friendly fire, although it progresses to a point where it is not so friendly. For me, she is like one of those diamonds: sparkling on the exterior, but showing plenty of flaws when you turn the microscope to its inside. No judgment? No return criticism? Sorry, but that is not how those mornings typically end.

After our confrontations, I just disappear and head back to the sanctity of our home, where there are no arguments, no criticisms, just love and respect. Which brings me to some family news. We had a meeting with the dental surgeon, Dr. Cummings, who announced that Austen's surgery would have to involve cutting through her upper jaw and her lower jaw, something I was trying my best to avoid. The length of her underbite was apparently too large, just over one centimeter, for surgery on just her lower jaw. Her June 20 surgery will be a maxillary and mandibular osteotomy, which will be more difficult and more problematic, with more potential side effects. Plus, it will include six to eight weeks of her jaw being wired shut, meaning she will have to survive by ingesting soup and liquids with a straw along her gums for those two months. It sounds awful, but Austen is pretty brave and pretty persevering. And the operation has to be done if she is going to be able to enunciate clearly and sing all of those operatic songs in college. Sacrificing to be better at your craft. What a concept.

It's so nice to focus on *our* family.

Babbo

5/13/07 Thanks for the End-of-Freshman-Year Rendezvous

Dear Skyler,

    I thought that Mother's Day would be a good day to express my thanks for our rendezvous in New York. It was a wonderful experience to fly to New York, meet you in your dorm, help you move out, and return you back to our home. It was great to gain a snapshot of your life, minus the chaos and mess of your dorm room and the time it took to peel the tape off your walls. It was fun to meet your friends, explore different restaurants, especially Ninja, and see the city sights. I was struck by your maturity, self-sufficiency, and further emergence of your sense of self. You are becoming your own woman. I may have been wowed by next year's dorm, the Palladium, with its gym and pool in the basement, but I was most impressed by you. Your personal growth is visible, and remarkable, to all of us.

    At this point, it is great to have you home. We may go our own ways for much of the day, and you may arrive home after 3:00 a.m. to parents who are not too happy with the late hour. Still, it is a great feeling to have you as part of our daily lives for another summer. Last night I awoke at 4:00 a.m. and stole a peek into your room and Austen's room. I cannot describe the warmth it brought to my soul. The two of you, and Mom and me, back in the same household. Nothing is more important than having good relationships within your family. Mutual respect. Mutual love. Full support. Any good parent will say the same. Here's to hoping we can remain close friends as you move through this important transition of your life. For some young adults, it's a fast good-bye to one family and hello to a new family. For me, I hope it's a slow transition with just the addition of more families: our family, your friends, your future work-related teams, and eventually your own family. Let's make the best of life by joining these families into a great extended family, with each family focused on what really counts in life: one another.

    Cheers to our shared future.
    Babbo

SOPHOMORE YEAR

8/25/07 Another Year of Missing You

Dear Skyler,

It's Saturday afternoon. Your plane is flying back to JFK airport with lucky Mom as your companion, and I am sitting here at the computer as Austen puts together binders and notebooks for her senior year of high school. I am feeling much like I did last year when I returned from New York after the move-in for your freshman year. I am feeling sad but proud. I am sad because you will be sorely missed. Despite our complaints of your late nights, it felt great to write you, over the course of the summer, those notes, setting them by the foyer lamp, to welcome you back home after a night out with your many friends. Simply put, it felt great to have you back home. Again and again, you light up our house with a spirit and energy level that disappears when you leave. We may howl at periods of excessive energy or questionable habits, but we love you, and we love having you home. We will miss you dearly. Already, the place does not feel the same. I find solace in the fact that you are only a sophomore, so you might be returning home for several more summers. Think of me. With medical school, I returned home for the summer until the age of twenty-five. A parent can dream, can't he?—about your returning home during the summers and staying for extended periods of time. So, here's hoping you always find our home worthy of a return.

I also feel a continued sense of pride as I watch you make the transition from high-school adolescent to young college woman. Over the summer, I shared my viewpoint on the parental situation for John Lennon and Paul McCartney. In my opinion, part of their success was due to the death of their mothers and the freedom from any parental restraints or parental expectations. Now, since Mom and I are not too keen on jumping off some cliff just to improve your future, I want to try to do the next best thing. When it comes to your finding your passion and path, I want you to remain free from parental restraints and parental expectations. Remember what I said in last year's first e-mail? I quoted Garth Nix in *Sabriel*: "Does the walker choose the path, or the path choose the walker?" I still do not know the answer to that question, but I want you, not us, to choose your path. I want you to maintain your freedom from my constant flow of suggestions. I do not care what courses you take or what major you select. It does not matter to me whether or not you stick with the diving team. It does not matter what outside activities you pursue. I just want you to feel free to make your own choices, find your own passions, and create your own path.

For me, my sophomore year at Williams College was a turning point. Once I had successfully completed the required freshman classes, I felt tremendous pressure from my parents to major in chemistry and solidify my plans for medical school. In many ways, I felt more pressure than I felt when they pushed me toward selecting Williams College over Stanford. The result? My path was chosen by them more than it was chosen by me. Worse, it was chosen for social status and finances, not for any love or passion on my part. I cannot escape my accountability. I cannot just blame others for that path. I did not have sufficient strength of character to push back on that parental pressure. But I do not want any pressure on you. I want you to have a college experience with no interference from us. So, embrace this freedom and enjoy it over these next three years. I will still offer more than enough parental advice—some habits are difficult to break. I am not expecting you to follow my suggestions; frankly, I just like giving them. Like any parent, it makes me feel good. For you, I want you to see your unrestrained spirit, energy, and passion. I wish you the best of luck as you start your sophomore year. Even if it is Mom flying back with you to New York. Even if it is Mom—not me—helping you move into your dorm.

Now take care of Mom, as we all need her. Especially me.

Babbo

9/03/07 Easier, But Still Sad?

Dear Skyler,

How has returning for your sophomore year compared to starting your freshman year? Is it a little easier, yes? And a little more fun? I think we find ourselves in the same position minus the fun part. Last year when you left home for the first extended time, it was a massive challenge for us. The house felt like a tomb. Austen walked around for weeks, mumbling: "I miss Skyler!" This year? We still miss you just as much, and the house will still feel just as empty, but emotionally, it is a bit easier. Maybe it's because we have been through the experience and already survived the upheaval once before. Maybe it's because of this past summer with your work and late nights where we went days without seeing much of you. Maybe it's a carry-over response from Austen's jaw surgery and our ten straight, horrific, never-going-home nights at the hospital's surgical ICU, working hard each night to help keep her alive through her post-surgery abscess, second surgery, wired jaw, and multiple complications. Maybe those nights toughened us? Our suctioning 150 cc of blood per hour, through a tiny tube slipped along her gums, as she gurgled, trying to breathe through blood and phlegm? Who knows, but the start of your sophomore year has been easier for us. Despite that observation, it is still sad, and we still miss you. The house still feels "not whole" without you. I think it always will, to some degree.

Our separation from you during your freshman year was helped by your frequent telephone calls. With those calls, you still felt a part of our daily lives. I do not expect you to call as frequently, but any calls are much appreciated. Another part that helped us was the sending of our frequent, twice weekly cards. It felt good to mail you a constant stream of cards, sharing our wishes for you. Old school. But watch for those cards, as we have already mailed three of them. Our collective e-mails also helped. My own e-mails? Well, as you can tell by the extended length of my e-mails, my letters have helped me feel connected with you and your experiences at NYU. So, expect the same onslaught for your sophomore year. Lest I forget, your class schedule also helped. Last year we had it posted at home, and I had it posted at work, right above my desk. Hour by hour, day after day, it felt good to visualize your daily activities. So, when you have a chance, please send us your class schedule for the first semester of your sophomore year.

Enjoy your sophomore year, follow your own passions, and ignore any perceived restrictions from your parents. You are well on your way to, how shall I say it, reaching your potential. Now that word should bring a flood of memories. In our high-school arguments, I used the word frequently. As I remember, you did not particularly like the word. But you do have such wonderful potential. I mean that across the board. You are primed for a great time in your twenties. You are approaching a special time of life when you will transition to a full adult, starting your path toward some career and eventually, at some later point, experiencing the wonder of falling in love. The twenties were great years for Mom and me, and I expect them to be equally great for you. Although, we all have to admit it: you are facing a far more challenging, toxic world than we faced at your age. The world may seem to be turning faster, but I am guessing its chaos is going to slow down your transitions. The world's global, financial, religious, and ethnic conflicts will impact much of your life course, creating havoc at many corners. My only suggestion? Be patient with yourself. The world will have its turning points, and you will have your own turning points. Yours will come of their own accord and at their own timing. Much of it will seem out of your control. You can only be receptive and ready. Success and sustained happiness will just take time. But life is going to be good—hopefully great. Best wishes for taking the next step. Enjoy the journey, and don't rush the destination.

And keep ignoring your intrusive father. Who?
Babbo

9/11/07 What? A Letter from You?

Dear Skyler,

The terrorists may have hit New York six years ago, but I sure loved talking to you tonight. More importantly, I really appreciated the e-mail below from you.

Hey Babbo—

So it's late over here, and I'm just about to get ready for bed, but I wanted to let you know how much tonight's conversation meant to me. First, I love how I can call you anytime and talk to you about these things, and get your advice and opinion. As I mentioned last year, a surprising amount of students don't have that relationship with their parents, which is so sad because I value our conversations so much. Second, I can't tell you how much your faith in me means. Sure, I have faith in myself (most of the time, anyway), but it feels infinitely more amazing when you have someone behind you, believing in you every step of the way, believing in the choices you're making and the road you're on. So many of my peers don't even have enough belief in themselves, which I think is the beginning of their downfall. How is anyone ever going to be successful if she doesn't believe in herself? It's a ridiculous concept. It also makes me so happy that, in hindsight, you understand the choices I made in high school. It's such a relief for you to know that I was never throwing away my future, but rather embracing a different one with a different set of priorities. The choices we make now, I think, will reflect the choices we make later on in life, so I chose to start making the right ones early. With any of our choices, we are going to face questioning and doubts, which in turn can influence our own self-confidence. But talking to you tonight, in a way that words can't really express (although God knows I'm trying here), reaffirmed my confidence in myself and in my future in a way that I never really expected. So thank you. I love you so much, and I sincerely love our conversations. They have always been good ones, even way back when. Maybe one day we should take a road trip—that way, we would have hours of brilliant, life-affirming conversations.

I think a lot of it has to do with how we're raised. Tina and I, while we were on our fabulous day of Soho-filled fun, were talking about how we seemed to be the only two people in our clique that seemed to have our lives together. By that, I mean that we aren't messed up. All of my friends continually make poor choices, whether it's in choosing majors, drinking excessively, doing drugs, cheating on boyfriends, working too hard *in insignificant jobs, blah, blah, blah, etc., etc. Neither Tina nor I feel any inclinations to do any of these things, and basically end up looking at each other, laughing and going, "**Why**??" We know who we are and where we are going in life. We have people in our lives who love/care about us unconditionally, and love us for who we really are. Coincidentally, all of my friends also seem to come from broken or dysfunctional families. Seriously, though. They always seem astounded at my relationship with you and Mom. I have to admit—I **love** that. I **love** breaking the mold when it comes to parental relationships, and being able to talk to you guys all the time. It's pretty much awesome, and I hope that, one day, I'll be that type of parent to my kids.*

Well, I'm leaving now to get some rest for my busy, busy day. Even though words can't really, truly express how much I loved and appreciated our convo tonight, I hope I conveyed the general sentiments well.

I loved your e-mail, and it warmed my heart. As I will repeatedly say, I am so lucky and proud to be your father. It is one of the best things to happen to me in life. God was kind to me.

I hope God is as kind to you.
Babbo

10/14/07 Ready for Some Distortions?

Dear Skyler,

    I applaud you for how busy you have been with classes and diving, but you are now interviewing for film internships? In Buddhism, they often talk about how each person sees life and other people through his or her own individually distorted lens. I think that is a good metaphor to keep in the back of your mind as you progress through the interviews, because each person will see you differently. And if someone does not like you or does not hire you, it may be because of his/her distorted lens, not a reflection of the real you. So, what can you do? Just be yourself and present your own view of yourself, including your path, your dreams, and your hopes for the future. Trust me, after years of interviewing people, I am amazed by how much distortion can occur. If the hiring is done by a committee, it is also amazing how many of those interviews can result in so many committee members having different opinions.

    From my lens perspective, I see you as someone who is a people person, someone who gains energy from relationships. I see you as someone who is energetic, outgoing, positive, almost always happy, and fully engaged with people. I also see you as someone who is very smart, and especially smart with problem solving. In that context, I see you as a leader, ready to lead others through any problem-filled enterprise. With those skills, I see you as someone who would do well with any pursuit, but especially a pursuit where you have to work with a team or lead a team. You were not born to be an island to yourself; you were born to be part of a group, and a central part of that group. That was true when you were a child in grade school, and it is equally true today. I also think it will be one of the defining characteristics of your career and life.

    I also see someone who seems to get better with the bigger projects, like your early school assignments in grade school; your longer essays in high school; writing your novel in a single summer month, even when it was not your choice or passion; and finding a college that suited your dreams. When the issue was sizable, you always seemed to rise to the task, even if we did not always know it as soon as you knew it. I see someone who is not derailed by setbacks, someone who will probably go through life without many regrets. I see someone who will be looking toward the future—not the past—yet brings the people of the past with her into the future. I see someone who will choose to face many sizable challenges when others would have chosen to avoid those challenges. I see someone who will help others survive through those challenges. For you, I think it will be a blast. Of course, that is always the parent's hope.

When you have those interviews, I would discard all of my perspectives and all of their distortions, and I would present yourself as how you see yourself. In interviews when hiring physicians, I often asked the doctors to assess their own weaknesses. Many of them struggled for an answer to that question. From my perspective, I do not see any glaring weaknesses in you. But as you progress through life, it is worthwhile to know your own limitations. Maybe your limitation is that you do not do as well when the work is not aligned with your passion, that you do not work as hard when the work is not aligned with your own goals. In truth, that may not be a weakness; it may just be a guidepost to keep you on track, to keep you aligned with your purpose. Good luck with the interviews. Just remember, you are interviewing them as much as they are interviewing you. They have to match your requirements and meet your high standards. Lastly, don't be like so many of your classmates, who seem to be constantly lowering their standards to keep within the herd. Maintain your high standards, and keep raising those standards, even if it creates some distance from your peers.

Don't settle for less, professionally or personally.

Babbo

11/25/07 Thanksgiving Gratitude

Dear Skyler,

 When we hugged good-bye today at the Long Beach Airport, I felt a tear welling from inside, but I held it in check. You know me. I cry easily in movies but almost never in real life. I cried when I was told my sister had died, but I did not cry when my dad died. I felt sad, and still do, but I did not cry. Why am I mentioning this self-observation? Because I want you to know, again and again, how very much you are missed. You can never tell anyone *enough* how much you love him or her. I certainly felt that love, deep in my core, when I hugged you good-bye. Do you remember, when you were probably six years old, you told me I hugged "too lightly"? You deserve a big, warm, power hug. You are the one who injects the most love, the most energy, and the most life into our family. I hope you never lose that quality, as it is really special, just like you. The family of the future? The *next* family, who brings you into their daily life, through work or marriage, will be a lucky family. I consider us the luckiest family. We have already had you for twenty years. Thanks very much for coming home. It boosted our spirits. You have always been and remain a family godsend. Thanks for any visit, now and in the future.

 We are at cross-purposes during this transitional phase of life. You are rushing toward a wondrous future, and I am trying my best to hang onto our past. To what do I want to return? Take a deep breath, and get ready to forgive me. High school and even grade school, when you were not so independent. Just strong willed. I loved the time when it was just the four of us, heading to the park or a dinner or a movie. Or Disneyland. Or Sea World. When we did not have to say good-bye for anything longer than a few hours. When I saw you for each breakfast and each dinner. At least we always ate those meals together, which is something more families should do. As I grow older, I suspect I will look back at those years and claim them as my favorite time, the good old days—with more free time, more family time, for all of us. God, I loved those years. I thank you and Austen for being the cornerstones of those memories.

Of course, you have to go through some incredible periods to reach those good old days for yourself and your own family. You have to progress through college, finding a career, falling in love, starting your own family, and raising your own family. I do not want to deny you any of those great periods, each with their own joy and excitement. I am happy you are transitioning toward those wondrous periods of life. Enjoy them to the max. As I am sure you will. It does not get much better than having kids and your own family around you. In retrospect, I could have eased off on many parental concerns and many goals, especially the academic push. But hey, I have already moved beyond that phase. I remember only the good parts with the four of us. And, lest I forget, our annual vacations to Maui. My God, they were special. That is something I recommend for all families. Not Maui. We had Maui because we lived in California. Maui was just one simple flight. I recommend more family time with more vacations for all families. Those vacations do not have to be expensive. After all, the key currency is not money. The key currency is time together.

Mom and I could not be any luckier. You and Austen are a perfect pair, each equally endearing. You are the yin and yang of our lives, balancing each other and our family. While you were claiming you were fine, even with a broken elbow at age eight, Austen was waking up at age six reporting she had ruptured her spleen or broken her clavicle. How perfect is that. I did not even know she knew those words. You were each a delight, and you each had your own style, which we would never change. Yes, we could not have been luckier parents. Better parents, yes. Luckier parents, no. I have no reason to bemoan the passage of time and your departures back to college. Instead of focusing on any sense of loss, I will try to appreciate the present. I applaud your progress toward becoming a beautiful woman with a fabulous life waiting before you. As always, be safe; be good; and be you. That is, and will always be, more than enough for me.

Thanks for being our daughter.
Babbo

11/26/07 Wow! Another Letter from You?

Dear Skyler,
   Your letter made my eyes water! I am the lucky one!

Dear Babbo—
   Thank you so much for your e-mail. It made my eyes all watery! Just so you know, I loved every minute of being home. It was wonderful to spend time with the family, even though you guys are all crazy :). Especially going to the beach with you—that was a real treat and something I will remember for a long time to come. I could not have asked for a better ending to a phenomenal week home. You always tell me how lucky you are, but Austen and I are the lucky ones. I get back into the city (and despite how much I miss home, that skyline still takes my breath away), and talk to my roommates, and all they can say is how excited they are to be back. How they had been home for too long (four days). How getting back to school is a welcome respite. All I can talk about is how wonderful being home was and how excited I am to go back in three short weeks for Christmas. Growing up with you as parents, it's hard for me to understand and relate to these kids who tell me horror stories about their own parents. It astounds me how much conflict, tension, and sadly, hatred arise in these situations, and again makes me thank God for you. It's because of you both that I am the way I am.
   On another note, I cannot thank you enough for tonight, Babbo. Tina's roommate (her name is Kate, she is the fifth roommate in the single in the suite), was really, really scared from her trouble breathing, to passing out, to the chest pain. But after I talked to her, and conveyed your words to her, she really calmed down. You really saved the day. Again, you have no idea how glad I am that I can turn to you, no matter what, and know you'll be there for me. Plus, I know I always joke that they switched the test tubes, but I can see how much I get from you. One is a level head and the love/need to take care of people. After I talked to you, I made sure Kate drank lots of water, took Benadryl for her allergic response, then I ran to Food Emporium to get her something to eat, came back, and made sure she ate two minibagels with chamomile tea to calm her down. I'm able to do all of this because of you and Mom. On a more practical note, I know sometimes being a doctor is hard, but it has its dividends. I'm not sure if you appreciate how medically well-educated I am, thanks to you. Instead of being panicky and confused, I

most often know the right course of action to help my sick or injured friends. So, there's one advantage to your job. Now, if you can find others…well, that's a different story. :)

Basically I wanted to let you know that I am blessed to have such a spectacular family. When I have children, I hope I can raise them half as well as you raised me. I love you very much. In closing, I will leave you with a little story from tonight: I was talking Kate down, telling her that you said her chest symptoms were not indicative of a medical crisis, and that you would be happy to reassure her personally over the phone if she needed. I mentioned how smart and helpful you typically are in situations like these, and Tina chimed in. She mentioned how good your advice had been when she'd had mono. Kate takes a breath, and goes, "Your dad sounds really great." And I just kind of smiled and went, "Yeah. He is."

I love you. I miss you. I'll see you soon,
Skyler

I would like to take credit, but your ability comes from within. You have always managed to keep a level head, regardless of the situation. That was true when you were in diapers, running across playground apparatus, and crashing into some protruding piece of equipment. You never panicked, never erupted into tears. You just picked yourself up and kept going. It remains equally true today.

You have been, and always remain, an absolute joy.
Babbo

12/09/07 College and Finances? Want Some Advice?

Dear Skyler,

    As I thought about your pursuit of that possible job where they pay you to watch and critique TV shows, I had a fear you were following my current path of doing things primarily for money. I have not always been that way. When you were born and when Austen was born, I took time off from work to enjoy your first days. In fact, in the history of the healthcare agency, I was the first father who requested a paternity leave. I did not receive an income, but my administrative position was held open for my return. When you were growing up, prior to high school and college, I eschewed work in favor of family. I gave up many opportunities for extra work and extra income. Those were great decisions, and they gave me much happiness. My own personal struggle has been over the past five years when I have focused on maximizing my income to pay for the college expenses. Too many of my dad's plans, discussed at length with me, have been undone by my mother. My dad spent seven years paying an attorney and setting up the transfer of their house to me. With no mortgage, the value of the house was significant. When it came time to sign over the house five years ago, he had started to show some signs of early dementia. He still wanted to complete the house transfer, even signing the forms, but my mother would not cosign the form, so the house transfer was never accomplished. My dad's financial plans for me were undone. For him, I think his disappointment hastened his death. For me, it meant I was forced to scramble for additional income.

    That is not all my mother blocked. With my dad's life insurance policy, he had listed me as the benefactor. The insurance was worth quite a bit. It would have paid for your college tuition and Austen's college tuition. But my mother once again asserted the money was hers, not mine. She deserved the life insurance inheritance, not me. It did not matter that my father and I had discussed the matter numerous times. He had made his intentions clear. Remember those stories of how he was always holding out his hand to me? He planned the same gesture for his death. His plan was simple. I would receive the house before his death, and I would receive the life insurance money after his death. I would be able to retire early, pay for your college experiences, and be free to pursue my own passions. Talk about a giving, loving father. If his plan had worked, he would have been so satisfied with his financial contribution to my happiness. That was just my dad. That was not my mother. I paid back all of the life insurance money. She got the house and the inheritance. Worse, since those financial components did not break free from the Courter Family Trust, I could not touch anything that was already half mine. My mother was delighted. It made her feel wealthy. My money was in her pocket. My unexpected financial challenges? It did not matter. I did not fight her. I knew she would never budge. I knew she would just become more problematic. Instead, I just focused on increasing extra work and extra income. Why so much extra work over these past few years? I did not want you and Austen to have student loans. I wanted to hold out my hand for the two of you like my dad held out his hand for me.

I have learned from this setback. I was fortunate in that I could increase income through outside private work done at night and on the weekend. It is not any different from what millions of parents are forced to do. But my extra income, although necessary, has not translated into greater personal happiness. My best choices in life, such as living in Spain to write, taking time off at your births, postponing the second job as long as possible, have all involved saying no to more income. Those decisions gave me more time with Mom in our romantic years, more time with the two of you in your early development years, and a greater chance to have an impact on you and Austen during your formative years in grade school and middle school. My schedule, when I started two jobs, matched your tough schedule. When you hit high school and encountered your abrupt increase in homework, that's when I started my second job and achieved my abrupt increase in work at night and on the weekend. For both of us, there is a lesson to be learned from our deluge of extra work. When you are overloaded, it is often easy to go astray from your true passions. As we go through life, let's both keep that in mind.

So, what is my point? I would caution you against decisions made for increased money. I would encourage you to embrace the college years, and all those years have to offer, without chasing the dollar. At this point in your life, you cannot earn enough money per hour to justify what you are giving up. Equally importantly, the money is coming, just give it time. For example, for Europe, I will plan on sending you more money than you are currently receiving. We will add additional money for your London semester. You do not need to focus on the pennies at this stage. Try to do those things to change your life, not your wallet. You might be feeling as if you need to relieve my financial burden. You cannot. I will tell you how you can help: you can help by making choices to maximize the benefit of college. That will make me feel far better, and those positive feelings will help keep me healthy. Give some thought to forgoing extra income, and give some thought to what is best for your future. Make it as good as possible. That will make any parent feel better about his or her own sacrifice.

So, keep the strength to say no to any financial chase.

Babbo

1/06/08 My Sunday Morning Blues

Dear Skyler,

    I awoke this morning around 6:30 a.m., struggling to open my eyes to escape an upsetting dream. My dream involved a family trip to Las Vegas, but it was weird, distorted, and confusing. The airport seemed to be in the center of town. Mom and I had to push an urn of ashes, and somehow, as we were reaching the hotel, we realized we had lost our luggage and, most importantly, we had lost you and Austen. I was mortified. Acute depression might be the best clinical term. Now, I am no psychologist, but it does not take much interpretation to realize that my dream reflected the sense of loss that came with your return flight to New York. Yes, on the way home from picking up Austen from study time with her friends, all three of us, Mom, Austen and me, commented on how much we miss you and how depressed we felt. The same feeling is there today. Awake or asleep. I think we could take a poll of which families miss their students the most, and our family would be the winner. I cannot think of anyone else at NYU who is missed by his or her family as much as you are. We love you and we really miss you. Do I say that too often? Surprisingly, the feeling has not decreased with each new semester. Instead, it is the one constant in our new kid-in-college life.

    However, the "awake" part of me is the realist. You know my perspective. Do not let guilt or other people's feelings, no matter how long they last, derail the course of your life. Keep following your path, and keep enjoying your life. We, of course, hope your path leads back to Southern California. But our presence here, as stated before, should not be a factor. As much as I loved my father, my own return to Southern California was not based on my father's presence; it was based on my love of this area. In these e-mails, I will lament your absence and mourn your departure. Take it as a positive reflection on how much you are appreciated by our family. Do not take it as a signpost saying Come Home! Our biggest happiness, ironically, would come from watching you find your own happiness along your path, no matter where it leads. So, stay on your own path. Enjoy that path. Don't let anyone sway you from your path. Including me.

At the same time, just be careful on that path. That is the most we can really ask. Right now, you are getting ready to fly to Miami for varsity diving for a week of twice-daily sessions. My hope? Ignore those college divers who are trying for a future place on the Olympic team. Instead, just be careful with your diving. We want your happiness more than we want your success. We couldn't care less what score you receive on any dive. We just want you to be satisfied with your progress. The score of your diving does not reflect our admiration for your effort. We admire you for following your own interests, your own passions, and your own pursuits. The same holds true for how we view Austen. The success along any route is secondary. It really is the journey that counts, and the fun you find in that journey. Most importantly, it's the love that finds you along the journey. Love will find you. You are too special for love to *not* find you. My viewpoint is simple: If you want to find love, keep sending out your love. Your outgoing love will come back to you. It's one of those circles of life. One of the truths of life.

So dive toward life, not just toward water.

Babbo

1/13/08 Can I Stop Myself from Giving Advice?

Dear Skyler,

I am writing this e-mail on Sunday morning. If I understand your Miami diving practice schedule, you are flying back to New York right now, ready to start this next semester. Despite all of my efforts to restrain myself, I still offer way too much advice. How can I possibly stop myself? Am I just your typical parent? Or am I addicted to giving e-mail advice? Oh well, for a change, this advice is not mine! Here are some words from George Carlin (below). I think they were made shortly after his wife died, and they reflect his view on life and our society. I thought they captured the true value of life. Here's hoping you find and establish long-term balance between all of your activities and an appreciation for what matters the most. Welcome back to New York. Welcome back to my e-mails. It is Babbo, still crazy after all these years. But my sanity is not the question. The question is how much you are going to enjoy this semester. And how much we can all respect the wisdom of George Carlin.

A Message by George Carlin

The paradox of our time in history is that we have taller buildings but shorter tempers, wider freeways, but narrower viewpoints. We spend more, but have less. We buy more, but enjoy less. We have bigger houses and smaller families, more conveniences, but less time. We have more degrees but less sense, more knowledge, but less judgment, more experts, yet more problems, more medicine, but less wellness. We drink too much, smoke too much, spend too recklessly, laugh too little, drive too fast, get too angry, stay up too late, get up too tired, read too little, watch TV too much, and pray too seldom. We have multiplied our possessions, but reduced our values. We talk too much, love too seldom, and hate too often. We've learned how to make a living, but not a life. We've added years to life, not life to years. We've been all the way to the moon and back, but have trouble crossing the street to meet a new neighbor. We conquered outer space but not inner space. We've done larger things, but not better things.

We've cleaned up the air, but polluted the soul. We've conquered the atom, but not our prejudice. We write more, but learn less. We plan more, but accomplish less. We've learned to rush, but not to wait. We build more computers to hold more information, to produce more copies than ever, but we communicate less and less. These are the times of fast foods and slow digestion, big men and small character, steep profits and shallow relationships. These are the days of two incomes but more divorce, fancier houses, but broken homes. These are days of quick trips, disposable diapers, throwaway morality, one night stands, overweight bodies, and pills that do everything from cheer, to quiet, to kill. It is a time when there is much in the showroom window and nothing in the stockroom. It is a time when our technology can bring this letter to you, and a time when you can choose either to share this insight, or to just hit delete.

Remember, spend some time with your loved ones, because they are not going to be around forever. Remember, say a kind word to someone who looks up to you in awe, because that little person soon will grow up and leave your side. Remember, give a warm hug to the one next to you, because that is the only treasure you can give with your heart, and it doesn't cost a cent. Remember, say, "I love you," to your partner and your loved ones, but most of all mean it. A kiss and an embrace will mend hurt when it comes from deep inside of you. Remember, hold hands and cherish the moment for, someday, that person will not be there again. Give time to love, give time to speak! And give time to share the precious thoughts in your mind. AND ALWAYS REMEMBER: Life is not measured by the number of breaths we take, but by the moments that take our breath away.

Good advice from a wise man, yes?
Babbo

2/02/08 Austen's Historic Day

Dear Skyler,

As we have previously discussed, relationships are like the tides. With any relationship, there are times when the water rolls inward, sometimes overwhelming, and there are times when the water seems to have drifted back out to sea, creating a little more distance than you would like. One of the keys to any relationship is staying true to your love of the person and letting the tide run its natural course. Too many people go chasing the tide when they should be letting the tide roll back to them. That's true for relationships at any age, but I suspect it is especially true for relationships in college. Relationships probably shift, week-by-week, semester-by-semester. My suggestion? When you find yourself in a future intense relationship, I have confidence that you will stand solid and enjoy those fluctuations of love, embracing the shifting tide.

The same types of fluctuations also apply to the intensity of missing someone. Trust me; there is not a single day in this household where one of us does not mention the fact that we miss you. But I want to share—for this week—the missing of you has been especially intense. First, it was a historic week, and second, it was a week of much joy. And you are the master of joy. When you heard the news of Austen's early acceptance, with a full Presidential scholarship, in the USC Thornton School of Music, you had tears on the phone. For the rest of us, we just walked around in shock. If the Lord has been watching from above, he would have observed a family struggling to accept their good fortune, struggling to release the joy. Your presence, and your ability to release that joy, would have helped guide us through our own stupor.

Last night we celebrated Austen's admission at Orange Hill Restaurant, with its wonderful mountaintop panoramic view of Orange County, but it felt incomplete without you. What is the point of this e-mail? First, to tell you how much you are missed, especially when fate brings the tide back in with some out-of-the-ordinary experience or some more-emotional-than-usual events. Second, to tell you that we have realized how nice it would be for us to be near you and Austen as we grow older. It's one thing to experience those historic family moments; it's another thing to be able to share them with the ones who matter the most in your life. For us, that translates to a successful transition from the usual parent-child relationship to adult-adult friendships. That is a challenge for all parents. May we find our own special path toward that wonderful destination.

One of your challenges? It's to not let us impact you too much. As previously stated, I do not want you to come back to SoCal just because we want to be near you. So, beware. I think we have realized that if we need to move to be nearer to the two of you later in life, then we will do that. Over these next two years, we may remain at a geographic, but not emotional, distance. But in time, we will reduce that geographic distance. Tides always swing in and out on their own accord. But we might as well move to be close to the water (metaphorically speaking, of course), and we expect to do just that! So, we are missing you intensely this week. We are hoping you are well despite your toe injury from hitting the diving board. Thanks for sharing part of our experience despite your own challenges. And we are already mapping plans on how to best follow you for the rest of your life. How's that for *breaking news*?

Now try diving out from the board. Maybe toward us?
Babbo

2/18/08 Yep, Still Struggling with My Mother

Dear Skyler,

You know my standard Saturday schedule. Despite my disagreements and conflicts with my mother, I am still spending every Saturday morning at her house (although, I could say *our* house), helping with paying bills, fixing broken appliances, and running errands. Why am I still doing it? It comes from a sense of responsibility as the remaining child, and to my promise to my dad to take care of my mother. When I was visiting my dad in the latter years of his dementia, I still enjoyed our conversations, even when fragmented with irrational statements about the past. With my mom, her constant chatter gives me a headache. If the average man says three thousand words a day, and the average woman says ten thousand words a day, my mother must say twenty thousand words in a single morning. She talks constantly about her friends with money, elaborating on their good looks, their material possessions, and their expensive trips. She never talks about their character or their values; she only talks about their appearance and wealth. It's so shallow. My head is exploding by the second hour of my visit. I carry Advil in my pocket at all times. I have even considered stuffing my pockets with Valium.

Every once in a while, I have a moment of triumph, but it does not change her one bit. Let me give you an example. In high school, there was one guy in my class who was the son of her best friend. But her friend's son was a horrible person. With his good looks, he attracted his share of girls. He would sleep with them, brag about his conquests, and then ditch the girls. Most of us, with some sort of moral compass, could not stand him or his exploits. When I tried to explain to my mother those behaviors, she would defend him, saying, "But he is so handsome. He is so nice. Something must be wrong with those girls." Wrong. My mother thought only of his good looks and his future wealth. Well, here is the update. My mother's best friend just died this week, apparently found dead in her living room chair beside her evening glass of wine. With her friend's unexpected and unexplained death, my mom promptly wrote a letter to the handsome son, asking what had happened to his mother and asking when there would be a service. I told her, based on my knowledge of the guy, she would never receive an answer from him. She asserted I was stupid. Of course, he would answer her letters, explaining everything about his mother's death. After all, he was so attractive and such a gentleman. He never responded to any of my mother's letters with even a single response, not by phone or by letter. He never had a service for his mother or placed a notice in the newspaper obituary section, and he rapidly sold her house, took the family money, and disappeared, heading back to his third wife in Las Vegas. My mother still did not get it. Even with her disappointment, her opinion of him did not change. How is that possible? She figured something must have gone wrong with the mail and her letters. Once again, she was looking at all of the wrong characteristics.

I remember one of the times when I was trying to convince my dad that my mom was his wife, and he blurted out to me, "How could I have married her? There's nothing there! Nothing!" Truth be told, I am seeing her more and more clearly. When my dad died, I was flooded with memories of how he had helped me. When my mom dies, I wonder if I will be flooded with any memories of her or any memories of any helpful interactions with me? I am worried it might be zero. She was always busy cleaning the house, making it more attractive. Or she was off with her friends at some garden club meeting or some cultural event. I have no memories of her making an effort to spend time with either Sherry or me, unless other families were present. Did you know she placed her own mother in a personal care home for the last fifteen years of her mother's life, and that she never visited her mother over those fifteen years, not even once? Maybe that is another reason why I am so committed to trying to help you and Austen. I have seen the other side of parenting from my mom. Self-centered, materialistic, and preoccupied with her own personal treasures, she has missed the real wealth of life. She missed the opportunity of building a close relationship with her two children, and she has missed the chance of creating a close relationship with her grandchildren. You can't have a close relationship with a family member when you constantly criticize that family member. My mother remains, even to this day, unchanged, with no personal growth and no new insights into her character.

For your college experience, I think you can learn from her mistakes. When she attended college, there was one primary goal: find a husband. There was no focus on her education or any personal growth. There was only a focus on catching the right man. In today's world, where marriage comes so much later, I hope your classmates can expand their goals. College should not be about finding a husband; it should be about learning and personal growth. Learning classroom material is obviously important, especially if you are learning a set of skills for your career, but a student's focus should also be on learning outside the classroom, trying to upgrade your character and solidify your values. It's strange, but when I was in college, I never had any thoughts about improving my own character. I only thought about improving my grades. In some ways, my goal for grades was no better than my mother's goal of obtaining a husband. There is so much more to college, so much more to life. Are there any courses at NYU that focus on improving character? Any courses that focus on developing the correct habits? After thinking about how my mother wasted her college career, and how I shortchanged my own college career, we both could have benefited from some of those classes. In the meantime, beware of my future e-mails and their focus on better habits.

Reading my e-mails. Now, that is a good habit, yes?
Babbo

3/02/08 Are We All Working Too Much?

Dear Skyler,

It is late Sunday night. I am dead tired, as I was up until midnight last night working on my taxes, and I worked through much of today completing those taxes for myself, my mother, and the Courter Family Trust. Right now I want to slip my head onto the pillow and disappear into a hundred dreams. To my left, sitting on the floor, I still have a stack of six medical charts, which need to be reviewed. I could work all night and not get all of the charts read or my reports completed. This weekend was supposed to be my vacation weekend, as I stopped work this past Wednesday so that I could spend Thursday and Friday with Austen at the USC Explore weekend, which was wonderful. But, alas, work is always waiting to be done. So, why am I staying up later than I would like? Why not put my head on that pillow? Because of my desire to give you my perspective on workloads, both yours and mine.

I worry about your current workload. If I have learned anything from my career, it is the following: it is very easy for a person to disappear beneath a heavy workload. It does not happen overnight, but it can creep insidiously into your life, ending up hard to control and harder to decrease. As I understand from your last telephone call, you are now working twenty-five hours a week for your film internship. My question is simple: Can you fit in twenty-five hours of internship and your schoolwork? I know internships are part of the core of NYU life, but I would still not miss out on college classes or your chance to learn interesting course material. I would not give up that once-in-a-lifetime chance for classroom learning for something as common, and lifelong, as regular work. Trust me. You are never going to get that chance at classes again. You will miss the education quality of those college classes when you graduate. Please, make the most of your classes over these next two years. Not for grades. Just for the experience. Sitting with friends. Learning interesting topics.

I am not suggesting you give up any internship. I am making a case to sit back and ask yourself if the internship would be better if it were fewer hours. If it were really up to you, and if you could have the ideal number of hours of internship, would it be fewer than twenty-five hours per week? If the answer is yes, then you might want to raise the issue with the film company and reduce your time. You may want to let them know that there are days when you may have to decrease your hours because you will want to attend a course or a lecture. In other words, I am encouraging you to take control of your time before it takes control of you. It happens quicker than you can ever imagine, and it's a road that you want to avoid. Just look at me. Too often my work intrudes. Too often the workload controls me, not the other way around. The time to start is now. You don't want to find yourself buried beneath a stack of work, unable to get out. Life is much too short.

Tell me: Was this message worth my missing thirty minutes of sleep?
Babbo

3/29/08 How Much Are You Sharing?

Dear Skyler,

 It was another one of those nights when I climbed into bed, stared at the ceiling, and kept thinking about you. So, I slipped out of bed, without waking Mom, and came down to the computer room to send off another late-night note. I kept thinking of what you had shared last week. If I remember correctly, you were sitting in your bedroom when the girl, with the connecting door, called out your name, and asked for your help. You promptly stopped your work, opened the door, and stepped into her room, finding her sitting on her bed, razor blade in hand, cutting on her wrist, and mumbling she "could not stop." You did not panic; you calmly asked for the razor, and then you helped clean up the blood, while stopping the blood flow, and convinced the girl to go with you to the hospital. Did you say it was her second admission of the semester for a suicide attempt? I kept thinking about it, not just to clarify my memory, but because you handled it so well, and because you were able to share it.

 It seems that in this day and age, so many college kids attempt suicide. Even on our initial NYU tour, didn't that guide say five students had tried to jump to their death while in the library? So many of those students get lost, are distraught, and are ready to end their pain. They do not reach out for help. Equally true, the college friends who help them often do not share the experience, wanting to keep it quiet. I want to thank you for always sharing these experiences, as upsetting as they might be. Even if the call comes in the middle of the night, waking us up. For these college years, we need to stay connected. That means student to student, but it also means student to parent, especially when there is a great distance between college and home. I want to commend you for maintaining your connection to us. I also want to commend you for maintaining your connection to your prior high-school friends. You have had so many high-school friends visit you at NYU, and you have made so many visits to other schools, such as your trips to Washington, DC. At the start of school, I was worried. Not anymore. I think those visits to the other schools, as well as our communications, keep you grounded, knowing you have a group of individuals ready to support you at any moment. That poor girl must have lost that feeling. I wonder: Do you think her parents were aware she was struggling with those feelings? Do you know if they made any attempt to help? I know it is easy for me to say, but I would have caught the first plane to try to help.

Here's hoping you never experience that feeling.

Babbo

4/09/08 Sixtieth Birthday Wisdom and Advice

Dear Skyler,

As I celebrated my sixtieth birthday, I had another one of those revealing conflicts with my mother. After giving me a present, a sweater, for my birthday, she asked for help with the remote controls for her TV set. She has to use two of them, and she is always hitting the wrong buttons. With today's tutorial, and with writing down all directions on a separate sheet of paper, she stared at the remote controls, stared at my written steps for their correct use, and asked with all seriousness, "How do African Americans and Mexicans work these things? Surely, it must be too hard for them." I could have blasted her for her racism, but what's the use? After all, this is the lady who has always frowned if I mentioned a friend and his last name happened to be Jewish. I do not want to stereotype all Germans by acknowledging she is part German, but I think she could have been friends with Hitler, except he was too short and not sufficiently attractive. Plus, she has never liked Mexicans. Yet has she ever had a single friend who is Mexican? No. Isn't it strange how people hate what they do not know?

With the African American and Mexican comments, I tried the intellectual approach. My mother is many things, but she is not stupid. I explained how people's skin color is not reflective of who they are or reflective of either their intelligence or their character. I explained how skin color is reflective only of the latitude of their ancestors. I encouraged her to watch the next Olympics, especially the opening ceremony, trying to guess the latitude of the country by the color of the skin of their citizens. As a physician, I explained how people in Ethiopia needed dark pigmentation to reduce the penetration from damaging rays of sunlight, and I further explained how people in Finland needed pale skin with no pigmentation so they could better absorb vitamin D from the sunlight. In short, the changes in the color of skin occurred, through evolution, to help maintain the health of a group of people living at a certain latitude.

At the end, I could not resist. I offered my own hypothesis. I told her if we took all the people in Germany and moved them to Africa, and if those people could not migrate for several centuries, their skins would grow darker and darker. I told her, if we moved her to Africa, and if she could live to several hundred years, her own skin would grow darker and darker until *she* was black. That was a bit of a lie, as DNA mutations do not occur that quickly. Still, I wish you could have seen the look of horror on her face. My mother with black skin? Now, when I arrived home and shared the story with Mom and Austen, Austen asked me how I could have grown up with her as my mother, and how I could have grown into someone who was just the opposite. I echoed some of the sentiments that I have shared with you. I have learned from her mistakes. I have learned the value of character, not wealth or appearance. I have learned the value of contributing, not just consuming. As often happens, the conversation led me back to one of my lifelong questions: What have I contributed to the world? My mother has contributed nothing. But how much have I really contributed? Not as much as I would have wished.

Later in the evening, I told Mom there are only four things I am really proud of in my life. No, it was not going to a good college or medical school. Or having a career as a physician. Or any work-related accomplishment. I am proud of marrying Mom over my mother's protestations; I am proud of creating you and Austen; I am proud of our time together—in particular, our annual vacation; and I am proud of the wisdom and advice I have been able to share. Those four items are my contributions and my legacy. So, let's make the most of my mother's failures. Let her life, and even some of my mistakes, form the foundation for our better judgment. Be tolerant. Be accepting. Be giving. Be loving. When swimming against the current, be independent of the opinion of others, and keep doing all of the above. Trust your own values, your own beliefs. Don't let the actions of others distract you from your own plans. Trust your own self-assessment, not someone else's assessment. Believe in yourself. Believe in your view of the world, at least the way the world should be. That perspective beats any other approach.

How's that for advice on my sixtieth birthday?
Babbo

5/23/08 Thanks for the End-of-Sophomore-Year Visit

Dear Skyler,

It is a reflection of my life that I am writing you on 5/23/08 to thank you for my trip to New York from 5/11/08 to 5/13/08. Right now, before starting this e-mail, I glanced at Yahoo and there was an article on what countries work the hardest. It appeared that South Korea was the hardest-working country, with its average worker laboring seven hours daily, with only three vacation days per year. However, our country was ninth in the world, so we are all working long hours. Despite my delay, I want to thank you for the visit to New York. It was a delight to see your dorm room, to meet your friends, and to visit your apartment for next year. It was an equal delight to step away from work. Your life seems pretty well set, at least in terms of college offering you many excellent options. For you, these are good days, so enjoy each of them, and enjoy these next two years as you make that transition from student to professional.

With each New York trip, I always enjoy our one-on-one meals and our enjoyable conversations. I loved the Indian food and the Chinese food, but my highlight will be our expensive dinner at that Tavern restaurant. May 13, 2008, will be a date I remember, as it was our first meal where they served you a glass of champagne with you still underage. Before we know it, next July 15, 2009, you will be twenty-one years old and able to drink legally. It was fun to share a drink of celebration. You have reached the point where you can manage your life and plan your future, so you certainly have reached the age where you can drink. Mom would appreciate that sentiment. As she has often joked, "I am not drunk; I am just *me*!" The best part of the trip is always seeing *you* in a clearer light and celebrating the emergence of the real *you*, as you are clearly developing into a woman of her own vision. I raise my glass of champagne and toast you, "You are truly a remarkable woman!"

Many congratulations for completing your sophomore year.
Babbo

JUNIOR YEAR

8/17/08 My Salute to the Junior Year

Dear Skyler,

It was bittersweet taking you back to New York. We were excited with your apartment, and we were delighted to help put together your bed and bureau, plus watch you and your roommate paint those walls. It was even fun to retrieve all of your belongings from your storage unit, although I thought we were going to be forever lost in the bowels of the Lower West Side of Manhattan. After that hour in cramped, dark quarters (can you remember its smell?), it was a relief to deposit everything in your bedroom. At the same time, it was fun to have dinner at the top of the skyline and attend the play *In the Heights*. A good stay for us, even though it was short, with four nights at the Giraffe Hotel. We were sad to leave you on Wednesday and sad we would not be seeing you until the parents weekend at USC. Yep, that's the parents weekend at USC, not the parents weekend at NYU. Mom and I wish we were closer to you so we could attend some of the New York University events. Alas, we will have to make do with what is realistic. Your flying home to LA, arriving to participate in Austen's weekend, is much appreciated. Not fair, just another of your sacrifices.

For us, these two weeks have been a double whammy, as we are now scrambling to get Austen ready for her moving into USC on Wednesday,

August 20. Bittersweet, once again. Having you gone is one challenge; having Austen gone is another challenge; but having you both gone? Well, that will be a huge challenge for Mom and me. Our house will go from your high-energy level and Austen's high-entertainment level, with her music and funny, sarcastic remarks, to a quiet morgue. As for me, I just work, and work, and work. I told Austen that college won't seem that much different, as we are so busy we just pass one another in flight. It is sad how time flies by for all of us, gobbling up our freedom and sending us rushing toward various assignments. Is that equally true for all families—or just American families? We ask ourselves what have we accomplished with our nonstop activity? Simply stated, the two of you. Our contribution to the world, to date, is just you and Austen. For us, that is perfectly OK.

That statement sounds like hyperbole. But it's the truth. It has been immensely rewarding to have raised you and Austen. We are two lucky parents. Incredibly blessed to have you two as our children. Our persistence through those seven years of infertility paid great dividends. Ironically, tonight, we watched the *Friends* episode on infertility. We persevered where others gave up. My God, were we rewarded. If our contribution to the world is just the two of you, we are more than satisfied. We are thrilled with our good fortune, and it is still quite an achievement. I suspect most parents share the same feelings, especially around these college years, as they see the results of their years of parenting. For you, I hope these are four great years. I hope you enjoy your college life to the maximum. I hope you make and keep great friends. And I hope you find your own passions, focusing on what makes you happy. If you can complete those tasks and create kids who are half as good as you and Austen are, you will have an amazing life—a life well worth living, despite the growing chaos in our world.

I know you dream of a big house with plenty of family and friends. Maybe that dream will come true. But make your real life as big as that imagined house. Make your life into a wonderful house, full of interesting rooms, all connecting into an amazing maze. They say the most important script you will ever write will be the script for your own life. Take your time to write that script, trying your best not to give in to other people's expectations and trying not to give in to your own view of your limitations. Although with you, there do not seem to be too many limitations. While you are forging your own path, keep sight of the balance that is crucial for traveling any path: a balance that includes good physical health and solid emotional health. Those two pillars will establish the framework for your journey, the foundation of your house. You cannot create a great life without health. Austen will attest to that truth. After her jaw surgery and brush with death, she seems to have adjusted her own priorities. It will be interesting to watch her transition into her freshman year at college and see how she prioritizes her activities. For your junior year, I wish you friends, laughter, extracurricular activities, new experiences, great classes, and a life with balance so you can set a solid foundation for your future. I salute your junior year.

May your junior year be another of many turning points.
Babbo

9/01/08 Are We Sinking Toward Davy Jones's Locker?

Dear Skyler,

 I think that these past two weeks have been some of the toughest of my life, rivaling even the ten days when Austen was struggling to stay alive last summer in the Medical ICU. For these past two weeks, I have averaged two to three hours of sleep per day, while working, trying to help Austen to change her room assignment. Apparently, you are not allowed to start that process until you have been at the school for at least two weeks. You know me. I am not someone who waits when there is a problem. I battled administration to obtain an early room change, garnering Dr. Goh's assistance (her ENT specialist) to establish medical rationale for the room change (I wrote the four page letter, and he signed it), and then taking time off to move Austen from one dorm to another. Right now, we are getting ready to take her back to USC and complete that move to Fluor, her new dorm. On Friday, we gave up moving the last of her belongings around 5:00 p.m., and it still took us three hours to drive through traffic from Los Angeles down to Orange County.

 It was good to get Austen home, as her mood promptly improved. In short, there is a long road ahead with many obstacles. Her problems were simple but difficult. First, she had a roommate who belonged on a psychiatric unit, which is more of an observation than a condemnation. Second, Austen is now starting late in a new dorm where everyone else already knows one another. Third, despite her beautiful voice and years of vocal training, she has already realized, after two just weeks of classes, that she does not want to be a professional opera singer. Worse, she is stuck in music vocal classes, surrounded by peers who love opera and want to pursue that career. She has no one like herself: a real musician who happens to be a remarkable singer but wants a different, broader path in music. Like you, she is going to have to muster the courage to find her own sense of self and create her own distinct path, regardless of the opinion of others.

 You may ask how she decided so quickly about an opera career after all those years of singing through grade school and high school. I once read how leaders make decisions quickly but change them slowly. That leaves out most of our politicians, yes? For Austen, it was a sudden realization of the life of an opera singer. Having teachers who were once professional opera singers, and having them share their many life stories. Well, reality made an impact. Constantly traveling the world without a set home? Singing in different performances on all of the continents? Staying up late night after night for each package of shows? Plus, it was the realization of who would be her associates. She was surprised at how many divas thrive in the opera world. She saw those personalities in her performing arts high school, but she was hoping those personalities might be aberrations. She was hoping, at least, for a little decrease in those character traits as the singers rose into the adult world. Apparently not. I also do not think she could tolerate the idea of working with those divas in show after show, year after year, having to wait, and wait, and wait as they slowly learned their lines. Lastly, she was surprised at how few of her fellow classical singers played the piano, the guitar, or any other instrument. They had learned one instrument: their voice. Worse, many of them did not seem to appreciate the role of the other instruments. Can you imagine her horror? And disappointment? Sometimes, you do not know a career until you are in it. Ah, the reality of life.

As for the room situation, I feel responsible for the initial setback. I encouraged her, as a Presidential scholar with a financial scholarship, to select the dorm that was set aside for the Presidential scholars. I should have known better. Intelligence is great. Graduating at the top of your high-school class is great. However, those academic achievements are overrated. Other characteristics, like compassion, kindness, and the ability to connect with others, are far more important attributes. Her original roommate, like Austen herself, may have been an academic whiz, but her original roommate was paranoid. Her roommate began locking the bedroom door at all times, leaving multiple, repetitive Post-its for Austen: "Lock the door whenever leaving." How would you like six of those notes spread across your bedroom door? When Austen went to the bathroom in the middle of the first night, the roommate locked her out, knowing Austen had not locked the bedroom door and not taken her keys. Poor Austen, she was stuck in the hall, knocking on the bedroom door, and having to wake up the junior proctor because her paranoid roommate would not respond to her knocks to reenter the bedroom. Me? At that age? I would have strangled the roommate, but Austen just went back to bed, feeling annoyed, confused, and alone.

With such a roommate, what can a parent do? Since USC was so close, I was able to jump into action. If it had happened to you, I would have been a basket case, as I would not have been able to help from such a distance. So thanks for opting for a routine but enjoyable dorm with normal students. Your choice was right, and your wisdom remains appreciated. On that note, I want to ask you to keep supporting Austen. Tell her that college gets better, not worse. Tell her how people are confused at the beginning, and how they often remain confused through the first several months. Tell her how many other people have experienced rough starts, terrible roommates, or classes they do not like. I remember your freshman English class. For most of that first semester, you skipped the class and just sat in on the art history class in the next room. How many English classes did you actually attend? Just the written tests? Give Austen some encouragement to speak to her songwriting teacher so she can ask about other options in the music industry. I think support from you goes a long way in helping her find her own path. Parents can only do so much, as you have witnessed well from me.

Lastly, do not forget to keep us advised as to how you settle into your classes. Good news is much appreciated, but honest news is valued more. That goes for Austen, and that also goes for you. Let us know your class schedule and how much you like or dislike your individual teachers. It sounds as if you have liked almost all of your teachers, except the teacher of that redundant English requirement. Keep us informed as to how early you have to start registering for London for next semester. You have an exciting future for next semester and for Spain next summer, but enjoy Manhattan while you can. Lastly, if you are pushed for time, your communications with Austen trump your talks with us. Pray for a change in the recent Courter climate, especially for Austen and USC. We desperately need to catch some fresh wind. Otherwise, this vessel might sink. Not Austen—me! Austen seems to always find a way back to the surface, back to the top. I guess if you have breathed through phlegm and blood for day after day, you have learned how to tolerate most anything.

Let's avoid Davy Jones's locker,

Babbo

9/18/08 Let's Hit the Road? And Say We Didn't?

Dear Skyler,

    For a father who has sworn off giving advice, it is amazing how often I try to give advice. No wonder Austen deletes so many of my e-mails. Let's just call it what it is: a parental addiction. But I have no remorse or guilt. I am like the addict, pulling out the next syringe. Here we go. If I were a junior in college, I would work hard this semester, taking the best possible courses while still making the most out of my New York experience. For next semester in London, I would take a different approach. I would take the easiest courses and place my priority on enjoying London while launching myself into as much of Europe as possible. Where will it lead you? I think of the line at the end of the movie, *Dan in Real Life*, where Dan ends his newspaper column with the statement, "Prepare to be surprised." That is how it is with life. We are constantly surprised by your decisions. Film major. Art history major. Two majors? Two minors? Honors thesis? I would never have guessed. At this point, there's no point predicting where your Europe adventure will lead you. Go for it. Get out of that classroom. After all, how many times are you going to have a chance to explore Europe? Some people go a lifetime without that opportunity. Besides, where are you going to learn more? Inside some collegiate building or out on the road?

    Now, was that advice so bad?
    Babbo

10/03/08 Ready to Step off the Conveyor Belt?

Dear Skyler,

    Congratulations on being officially accepted for the London campus next semester. Four months in London? What a treat. Do I need to repeat myself to steer clear of those classes that would lock you into your dorm room? I would take interesting classes, but classes that would allow you greater time, especially for the possibility of a three-day or four-day weekend. Wow! Would that ever give you time to explore Europe and expand your own vision of the world, plus possibly expand your vision of your own career and work options. If your homework consists of reading and writing assignments, that would be perfect, as it would allow you to complete the essays on the train. Lord knows you will not write once you hit some new destination. Either way, congratulations. Lucky you. It will be an experience that will stay with you forever. Like Spain for your mom and me, when we were much, much younger. I wish everyone had a chance to create some free time before he or she steps on the career conveyor belt of life. I think they would live better, happier lives. Maybe this London semester is a chance for you to step off the college conveyor belt and see what the world really looks like?

    On another note, we just received Austen's schedule for the year. She completes classes on May 1, and her finals finish between May 6 and 13. When you have the time, please check your schedule for the spring semester, and please check your schedule for summer in Madrid. I would like to clarify your summer dates as early as we can, at least by Christmas, so that we can start mapping our European rendezvous. You will need to look at your schedule, and see when you would like us to visit you in Spain. Personally, I think it would be great for us to tour Europe as a family after you finish your stint in Madrid. I want this vacation to be different from any previous vacation. All vacations have been planned by me. I want to give you free rein to plan the entire month-long vacation. All flights. All trains. All hotels. All small excursions. You will be the European expert. You will be our tour guide. What do you think? Can you do it? Regardless of your decision, it is going to be a great year with new experiences for all of us. As always, as you head into London and travel through Europe, I hope you always hear my voice in your head…"Be safe; be good; be you."

Say hello to the Brits.

Babbo

11/09/08 Where Did You Learn These Skills?

Dear Skyler,

I just want to share how impressed I am with how well you have managed your time. You have had back-to-back visits from two friends, John and now Brandon, who stayed with you in the dorm, sleeping on the floor I presume, and you have still been able to fit in your diving, tons of homework, multiple midterms, and several long papers. That takes impressive time-management skills. I guess I do not have to offer any additional advice on that skill set. I suspect you already know you should never start the day before you finish the day. I imagine you have heard the phrase "Plan your work and work your plan." You obviously know how the things that matter the most should get placed at the top of your to-do list, and the things that matter the least should get placed at the bottom. You probably also know how few people set aside any time for planning their life. They plan their vacations but never plan their life. So, what can I say to offer any advice? Nothing. I am just going to assume you are already an expert at time management and life management. We can move on to other, more important topics, right? Wait a second. Are there more important topics than time management and life management?

Seriously, I cannot address all of the areas of your life where I have been so very impressed. That would take too long. I am proud of your capacity to focus on your own priorities; I am proud of your solid sense of self, sufficiently strong to withstand the pressure from any peers or professors; and I am proud of your growing maturity and ability to make prompt decisions. With those surprise visits from high-school friends, most students would have panicked. You did not. You gave them a good time, and you managed to complete what needed to be accomplished. Want to know a secret? In college, in my junior year, I had a girlfriend (and she was not even a close girlfriend) who drove three hours, with one of her roommates, from Boston to Williams. Apparently, her roommate was visiting her boyfriend on his birthday, and my so-so girlfriend decided to surprise me with a knock on my door at 10:30 p.m. Only it was Wednesday night, and I had a chemistry midterm exam the next morning. I was already in bed, trying to get to sleep so I could wake up at 5:00 a.m. to study, as that was my habit for all exams. I was not very happy with her arrival. The girl was put to bed on the sofa without even a kiss, which is where she would have slept anyway, and the next morning, to be nice, I had to drag her around to breakfast and the library before my test. With significantly reduced time to study, a drop from five hours to two hours, I received my lowest chemistry grade, a C, on that test. I had to get an A on the final exam just to receive a B+ for a final grade. That was not satisfactory. But for our similar incidents, you succeeded where I failed. More importantly, the quality of your two friends was much higher than the quality of that rather presumptuous girl. She was one-tenth the quality of your mom. Glad I kept to my own high standards.

Now, with three semesters left in college, I hope you continue to show me how time and life should be managed. Since I know you will follow your own compass and your own clock, let me switch my focus to your upcoming Christmas vacation, return to New York, and flight to London. We would love to have you home after your final exams in December until January 11, giving you several days in New York before flying to London. We also support any earlier return back east if you want to join the diving team for the annual Florida training session before you head to London. We respect your decision of not needing any assistance for that trip to London. What a change from your arrival as a freshman at NYU where I was your typical helicopter father. Again, that reflects your growing self-confidence, your expanding independence, and your comfort in your ability to solve any unexpected crisis. On all three components, you are so far ahead of me at the same junior-year juncture. I was a study machine, trying my best to keep up with some very smart students. I was resistant to my forced parental direction but not successful in my opposition. For me, like for any student, that translated into "forced" studying in an area where there was no passion. I was not capable of handling unforeseen distractions with any grace. Kudos to you.

Back to your Christmas visit, which we can discuss over Thanksgiving, we will accept whatever time you have for us. That is going to be the MO for the rest of our lives. You have broken free of the nest. You just need to know you are always welcome back at the nest, at any time and for as long as you want or need. A father can dream of having his daughter back home now and then, can't he? That perspective applies to what you do after graduation. I am ready to support you in any endeavor, even if it has nothing to do with future work and everything to do with following some crazy dream like surfing or scuba diving or living in a foreign country. I love watching your life unfold. It is so much more entertaining than anything I could have planned for you. Stupid me. I never knew your life was going to be so exciting and interesting. You give us all a wonderful sense of wonder, even when we are just the bystanders. We will do our best to get out of your way and let you be...well, you. Ah, what an amazing person you have become. On the flip side, it makes me wonder. At that age, who the hell was I?

Congrats on your ongoing transformation.
Babbo

11/30/08 A Bite of Turkey? Then Taking Flight?

Dear Skyler,

    Thanks for coming home and making our Thanksgiving so special. It is always a special treat to have you back as part of the on-site, active family. Repeatedly, you give us a lift in energy, a surge in conversation, and a boost in joy and happiness. If you were a drug, you would be illegal and in high demand. We always feel lucky you are part of our family. Thanks, too, for sharing your junior-year college schedule in such detail. For me, this semester has been a blur, lost in our activities to help Austen make a successful transition to USC. Your New York schedule showed us all how much of a load you carry, how packed your life is on a daily basis, and how hard you must have worked, without any prodding from us, to juggle a ton of activities and a steady stream of assignments. We came away very impressed with your ability to handle everything so well. All we did, as stated before, was learn to get out of your way. If more parents would follow suit and let their kids find their passions, select their own paths, and create their own futures, I think there would be more success stories. I also think there would be less depression, fewer suicides, and fewer tragedies. With you, we do not have to worry about any of those negative consequences. Thank God!

    I want to thank you for your wonderful relationship with Austen. You are the extrovert, and Austen, like me, is the introvert. You gain energy by interacting with others, while Austen and I restore ourselves with down time when alone. Even Mom falls into our category, as she loves to read—always energized by a good book and a bit of solitude. How did we get so lucky? Two daughters so different yet able to be so close. I have no recollection of you two fighting except when Austen bit you when you were two years old. Your relationship with Austen warms our hearts. If Mom and I can take any credit, it is for one habit we established early in our family. At the beginning of each summer, we took that two-week family vacation to Maui. The location did not matter. The cost of the trip did not matter. What mattered was the extra time we spent together. It was not just important for our parent-child relationship; it was equally important for your sibling relationship with Austen. In personal relationships, quantity gives you a chance for quality. Year after year, trip after trip, we grew as a family. Our love for one another grew. Our tolerance for one another grew. We each grew in our own unique fashion. If I can offer yet another recommendation, when you have your own family, create a habit of regular family vacations. Didn't that tradition help create a solid foundation for your personal growth? I will defer to someone much smarter, but my vote is easy to guess. I think all of that family time was crucial for each one of us.

For now, stay healthy. Keep up all the great experiences. Stay safe in your diving. For your classes, learn what you want to learn, regardless of the grades. Come home safely so that we can enjoy you for three weeks for the Christmas holidays. And then onward to London and your experience of living in that city and touring through Europe for four months. Do you know that to be a taxi driver in London you have to take courses for three years, know one thousand historic sites, and pass an extended exam? Do you know that in New York, you only have to know ten historic sites and pass a short series of questions? What does that tell us? Probably nothing. Except Europe may be a bit more complicated than New York. Maybe it might also be a bit more dangerous. There may be some hidden risks in Europe, so do not ignore those risks. Pickpockets. Crowded bars. Intoxicated, self-serving young men. Enjoy your days and nights. Make the most of them. But avoid the pitfalls and mishaps as much as possible. If there *are* mistakes, do not crash and burn. Crash and learn. If not for your future, for *our* future. I do not know how we could live without you or without your positive impact on all of us.

You are the heart and spirit of this family.

Babbo

12/14/08 Sorry, An Alcoholic's Slip

Dear Skyler,

 No, I did not hit the bottle. You know me. There is no hard liquor in our house. Never has been. Never will be. But my recent slip was like the relapse of an alcoholic, abstaining for two years and then buying a bottle of vodka. What did I do? When we were talking on the phone, and you were discussing all of your deadlines for this week, I was dumbfounded by how you could fit in a weekend trip to Washington, DC, to see your best friend, right in the midst of finals. I guess I just lost my focus. Before I could stop myself, I was arguing for your staying in New York, at least to properly prepare for the finals. How stupid! When I know, thanks to you, how experiences outside of a classroom are more important than the experiences within a classroom. I did not stop myself until five minutes into our argument (you do stick up for yourself!), and I am sorry for my misstep. At times I think I am improving as a father, gaining some wisdom. At other times, I think I have taken a step backward, reverting to old habits. That must be the toughest lesson for all parents: to develop the habit of letting go of how they did things in their days, and to maintain the new habit of allowing their child do things her own way, without the parental interference.

 With just that one verbal conflict, it has been a depressing day for me, realizing how my shortcomings can return with such a knee-jerk reaction. The world is growing increasingly competitive. You do not need me to add to your stress. At least I am aware of my deficiency. By nature, or by my own upbringing, I have been far too competitive for my own good, and for the good of you and Austen. I mean, it's OK to ruin my life, but it is not OK to ruin your life. But you corrected the situation with your prompt opposition and effective confrontation. You put me in my place. Good children do that; they help parents become better parents. Do not ever feel reluctant about helping me see reality. It's a good thing, not a bad thing. Short-term, the discussion can result in fireworks. Long-term, it helps to improve our relationship. In the future, I will try to catch myself whenever I see myself relapsing, whenever I notice myself trying to steer you in any direction that is not of your choosing. Of course, that could be daily. On the next telephone call, let's get back to focusing on your chosen path and your happiness, not my old demons.

Congrats on your new double twister.

Babbo

12/14/08 Whoa, Another Letter from You?

Babbo,

I really appreciated your e-mail, but there is no need for an apology. Now, I'm going to keep this short since I am so excited to catch up with you on the phone after my DC trip. But you should know that your relapses are few and far between. Stop protesting. You are an incredible (I didn't say amazing, now did I?) father, and I am so lucky to have you in my life. Actually, to be perfectly honest, quite a few of my friends are jealous of me because I have you as a father. You have given me more than anything I could ask for—and that's aside from our lifestyle. The freedom to choose my major, the freedom to choose my areas of interest. You have provided endless support and constant encouragement. You'd be surprised how many of my friends' parents don't *give them any of that. I can never say thank you enough. Yes, you may have pushed me in high school, but look what heights you've pushed me to. Look where I've gotten because of it. The focus on grades in middle school and high school got me into the school of my dreams, NYU, which is* exactly *where I'm supposed to be. So don't beat yourself up about your recent relapse. And while you're not perfect, let's be serious—I'm about as far from perfection as you can get. I'm not the easiest daughter to raise. I can make rash decisions, and I can certainly fight back. But I think that our flaws help shape us. We don't need to be perfect. And I think as time goes by, the two of us, recognizing our imperfections, can work to be better people. Sounds like a win-win situation to me.*

I love you so much, it's ridiculous!

Skyler

1/08/09 A Father's Additional Confession

Dear Skyler,

As you start to get ready for your flight to New York and your flight to London, I thought I would share my memory of my six months in Europe. Mom and I fell in love. I wanted to try to write a novel, so when my residency was done, I arranged a rental of a small villa, right on the beach in Marbella, Spain. Since it was October through March, the villa cost only $125 per month. The owner, whom we had met in South America, liked me, and offered us a great deal. However, that was the good part. The bad part was the reactions of our parents. My dad exploded, claiming he would not have wasted all of his money on my medical education if he had known I wanted to write. My mother was convinced I was just lazy, not likely to amount to much of anything. Mom's parents were worse. Her dad said he would hang her by her thumbs if she ever lived with a man before marrying him. Worse, he warned her, for years, she should not marry two types: a bum or a doctor. Clearly, I was both. We went to Spain with no support from any parent. There was not a family member who was hoping we might succeed. Everyone was betting on our failure, hoping we would return home, begging for their forgiveness.

They were right and wrong. I wrote a five-hundred-page, first-draft novel, titled *The Cure*, which I never submitted for publication. It still sits in the garage cabinet, waiting for a second draft. They were right with their definition of failure. However, they were wrong with a broader, and more valuable, assessment of the overall experience. Mom and I spent 24-7 with each other for six straight months, plus additional time in our traveling before and after the rental. We fell more in love. I proposed on New Year's Eve, and we came back engaged, ready for a September wedding. When I wrote my mother and father in January, announcing our engagement, I did not receive any words of support. My mother continued to refer to Mom as "that Mexican" (even though she is part Spanish, with heritage from Spain through a wandering minstrel). In her response to our wedding announcement, there was my mother's prompt response, encouraging us to elope while we were in Spain. It was unspoken, but my mom did not want to attend a wedding of her son to a Mexican. Imagine her disappointment when we invited some of our Latino friends, great people, to our wedding. Nothing but disgrace from my mother's perspective, and this viewpoint comes from a woman whose only success was her ability to get pregnant at the right time with the right well-to-do young man. Now you can see why I have such distaste for those parents who put their desires above the needs of their children.

What is my point? I want to reexplain why I was so disappointed in myself with our argument before your finals, and why Mom and I want to support this year abroad as much as possible. In our six months in Spain, we learned more about life and ourselves, including our priorities, our values, and our dreams, than I ever learned in college or medical school. Embrace the world outside of the classroom, not just those rows of seats and four walls inside the classroom. The goal of these next two years is to prepare you for the world, not to excel in the next course. Within that context, please feel free to share everything about your European experience. Even if you skip a class. Even if you end up incarcerated for a night. If something goes wrong, we want you to feel free to call for help at any time. It could be for that get-out-of-jail card. It could be an urgent need for an emotional vent. It could be a desire for a little Southern California sunshine. It does not matter. Unlike my parents, especially my mother, we want to be more than supportive. Without prejudice or bias. Without judgment. We want to be part of your life. With me, did I ever share much of my college life, or any part of my life, with my parents? Not really. When I called home from college, I remember my mother talking and talking, but rarely listening. I knew all about their life, but they did not know much about mine. But with you? We will listen. We hope you share everything, at least everything you want to share. There are some things so personal they are not meant to be shared, but some of those things are the best part of life. Keep those to yourself.

Now go enjoy this adventure of yours.
Babbo

1/10/09 Flying High? Without Drugs?

Dear Skyler,

   Neither Mom nor I slept very well last night. Mom was up several times before the alarm went off at 5:45 a.m. Me? I awoke at 2:30 a.m. and came downstairs for Advil, plus a small bowl of cereal—not the best path toward good health, as you should not snack late at night or during the night so your body has a chance to rejuvenate and heal. I awoke before the alarm, ready to rush you to the airport. I guess we were too wired for your departure. Right now, we are cleaning the house as you fly to New York, periodically checking your flight status on the computer. It looks like you will be arriving early around 4:30 p.m. EST. I will make this e-mail short, but I want to thank you for spending so much time with us. It was a great Christmas vacation, with multiple dinners, multiple trips to Disneyland, and multiple fun times. Austen claims you stole all the Courter happy genes. It may be the case, but do not change. Stay just the way you are. As always, you lit up the Courter household more than our Christmas tree. More than all of those lights hanging from our first floor and second floor gutters. Your "light" was much appreciated, and much needed, by each of us.

   Many thanks for your assistance in so many areas. A special thanks for setting up our computers so that we can Skype with you over the Internet as you spend the next four months in London. Were you secretly thinking more Skype would lead to fewer e-mails? Can't blame you. But the key, for all of us, is to still stay in touch. Too many parents do not stay in touch. So far, we have not lost any of the closeness of our connection, and we want the trend to continue over these final semesters. We wish you the very best for your trip to London and your European experience. When flying to London on Tuesday, do what you did today. Cram as much as possible into your two suitcases and pay for the overload. It would be so much easier to have everything there when you arrive, so you can get settled without so much hassle. Do what you have to do. You might have to purchase some things like new towels. I have one request: keep up our dinner agreement. It was one of my better ideas for college. In London you have my permission for one expensive dinner, on me, each month, treating one or two of your friends. Please don't wait too long to get the new cell phone for Europe. Call us anytime. News is always appreciated. In any case, we miss you, we love you, and we wish you a great adventure.

Everything else is secondary.

Babbo

1/13/09 Soaring to London?

Dear Skyler,

 January 13 is one of those landmarks days in your life: the start of your new adventure and your semester abroad. I want to wish you the best of luck for a safe flight over the Atlantic and a safe transition to your London dorm. As fathers go, I rank near the top for offering unasked for advice, but I want to repeat the one piece of advice that will always hold merit—"be safe; be good; be you." I want to underscore the safe part. That refrain goes for all your days in Europe, not just your landing and arrival. The world seems to be getting less and less safe with each passing year. If, during your travels, you hit a part of some city that feels unsafe, do me a favor. Pull out the family credit card and find yourself a better and safer accommodation. If you are ever the target, God forbid, of some assault, remember my own MO. Take action from the start. You are the better athlete. Do not wait and let the odds increase against you. If I can kill someone in the eighth grade, you can do what you have to do. Your safety and your life are worth any cost. Our lives would never be any good without you. I may joke about your staying in New York after graduation, as I think that will be the site of your future, but you will be alive and still part of our lives. That is all that any parent wants.

 Now, as to my own story, I was playing a round of golf in the summer after eighth grade. On the fourth hole of a public links course, I hit the best drive of my life. It soared and soared, traveling forty yards longer than any previous drive. I looked in wonder until I realized the ball was heading straight for an old man in the middle of the fairway. A bit late, I screamed, "Fore!" The old man jerked around just as the ball landed smack at his feet, missing his golf shoes by inches. He paused, seemingly OK, then dropped to the grass. It was a heart attack. When I arrived at the scene, two of his buddies were hovering over his body while the fourth member was running for the clubhouse for assistance. No cell phones in those days. My ball was eight feet from his body. Awkwardly, I asked the older men, "What should I do? Play through?" One guy, as stunned as myself, just nodded. Without moving the ball, I pulled out my four iron. I blasted the ball high over the water, and I watched the ball hook into the green and roll to within six feet of the hole. It was, after having played that course for two years, my first birdie on that hole. Right after killing the old man. Poor guy. The newspaper reported that it was his second heart attack. His doctor had recommended retirement and much more golf for better health. Well, I ruined that simple prescription. But there is a point. Regardless of what happens, you have to be prepared to take action. And you do not have to always yell, "Fore!" Sometimes, people are better off without a warning.

Just be safe.
Babbo

2//08/09 Miss Gutsy Lady? Who Knew?

Dear Skyler,

I want to congratulate you again on becoming such a gutsy lady. It worries Mom, but I am very proud of you. Since I heard the story second hand, let's see if I have this story straight. You failed to get onto the school's two-day Stonehenge and Bath tour. Rather than give up, you booked a one-day private tour through a separate tour agency to get you to Bath on the same day of the school's tour. Then, on your own and with no back-up plans, you left your private tour and found your college tour. You were able to blend into one of the groups of the college tour as they entered the hostel; you were able to find an empty, unmade bed in one of the many rooms; and you were able to make up the bed with some pilfered linen, blankets, and a pillow from the hallway closet, depositing all of the stuff on the bed, as if it were yours. Now, did I get the sequence correct? At least some of it?

Then, after a two-hour spa, bath, and pool experience, you were able to find an open restaurant and have a great meal with your new classmates when everyone else claimed the restaurants were closed. You led the group? The following day, after slipping away on your own to attend mass at the famous abbey, you snuck onto one of the two college buses, waiting through four counts and recounts of the "heads" on the two buses, as the tour director, growing more confused with each new count, kept tallying one too many students. Finally, taking a deep breath, you summoned the courage and went up to the tour director. You explained the discrepancy in the count of one extra "head," and then you asked if you could sit in the free seat on the bus for the drive back to London, so that you would not be stranded in Bath. So far, reasonably accurate? Pretty damn gusty, if I say so myself. You proved Wayne Dyer's point: with the right effort, there is always another chair. At a conference. On a tour bus. In life itself. Your courage is another of your wonderful qualities, which is going to bring much joy into your life. I am so proud of you. In retrospect, over the course of my life, I wish I had broken more rules.

Once again, you are my hero.
Babbo

3/02/09 Keeping a Journal? Finding Any Answers?

Dear Skyler,

You are keeping a journal of your travels? Have your travels helped clarify what you want to do with your life? I do not expect any answer, but I think it is something to tuck away in the back of your mind. Maybe it is something to include in your journal? When I look at my life, I see a fork in the road where there was a choice between wealth and the security of being a physician versus the long-shot chance of becoming a writer. I made one attempt at becoming a writer; I felt that the novel was not sufficiently good; and without submitting the book for possible publication, I retreated to the work of a physician and the security of a health-care agency. Yes, there were some intermittent attempts at additional writing. Those sideline attempts included five screenplays with Dr. Joe Hullett, and he successfully turned a number of those scripts into good plays. He was an outstanding writer who stuck to his goals. Me? There are several truths. I lacked the courage to say *no* to Williams College and *yes* to Stanford University, I lacked the courage to say *no* to security and *yes* to attempting more writing, and I lacked the courage to say *no* to wealth and *yes* to the possibility of greater happiness. I only had the courage to swing at that golf ball beside the dead man in the surrounding chaos. Trust me. Security is the lowest form of happiness. I wish I had more of your courage. You have always been willing to stand up for your passions. You have always been willing to take the risks. To accomplish anything great, you have to be willing to embrace risk. With that sentiment. I wish you continued courage.

As long as you are following your heart, right?
Babbo

3/04/09 Time? Going, Going, Gone?

Dear Skyler,

    I must admit, your life seems pretty exciting. Prague today. Budapest tomorrow. That's pretty cool. I wonder how you will react when you finally return to New York after spending a summer in Madrid. Will New York seem as exciting? Will you like it more or less? Regardless, I think you are making the most of this junior-year opportunity, exploring Europe and gaining a better view of the world, and maybe a better view of how you want to fit into that world. When I was much younger and falling in love with Mom, I would stretch beside her and keep telling myself that this was *our* time. In the history of the world, with all the people who had lived and died, and with all the people who had not yet been born, these moments were *our* time in the grand scope of history. That philosophy helped me appreciate how lucky we were to be alive and to have each other. The same perspective can be applied to you. I am not suggesting you settle down beside some strange fellow. But this is *your* time. You are lucky to be alive and young with the world awaiting your future. It sounds as if you are feeling much of that same spirit. Embrace *your* time! Before it disappears!

    On the flip side of the equation, I want to say I was sorry to learn about the theft of your Canon camera and its telephoto lens, and the loss of hundreds of pictures of Europe. It was clearly an inside job. If your camera went into one end of the museum's scanning machine and failed to come out the other end, it was a planned theft. I suspect they pull the stunt on young travelers with easy-to-sell items when they know the individuals will not be able to stay around to press charges or push for an investigation. It is sad, but it is another one of life's lessons. You have to let go of your anger, accept the loss, and move forward. There is a saying that you are not punished for your anger; you are punished by your anger. It eats at *you*, not at the real culprit. So even though I am once again breaking my code of restraining myself from giving advice, I would purchase a new camera, buy a couple of disks, and resume your photographic journey without another thought of the loss. Letting go. Moving forward. Accepting setbacks. Facing risks. Maintaining your appreciation of life.

Keeping your own lens focused on what you want to go right, not on what's gone wrong. It is amazing how many people get stuck because they lose more than their camera; they lose their own focus.

Forget the bad. Appreciate the good.

Babbo

3/15/09 A Father's Woe-Is-Me Lament

Dear Skyler,

    I shortchanged you during your first semester of your junior year with decreased e-mails because of my initial focus on trying to help Austen make the transition to USC. With this semester, I have also shortchanged you because of my time commitment with Mom's foot surgery. At times like these, when a man's wife is incapacitated for her normal activities, a husband realizes how much she actually does. With her sidelined, I have been helping her with her morning shower, as she needs a special wrap on one leg to prevent water from leaking into the foot wrap. When that task is done, I make our oatmeal breakfast, feed Paris some dog food, and clean up the kitchen. Then I make my own breakfast and lunch before rushing off to the office. When I arrive home after a usual administrative day, I help make dinner, clean up the kitchen after dinner, feed Paris again, and walk Paris. By the time I get down to my work, it's about ninety minutes later than normal. On the weekends? Today, I drove Mom to Vons to help her buy groceries, took her to Petco to buy dog food, and then we went to another grocery store for some additional items. That was in between carrying loads of laundry up and down the stairs. At night I picked up our dinner. I am working two jobs plus covering Mom's equally important, equally time-consuming responsibilities. Piled together, I am working harder and staying up later than ever. It is 11:30 p.m. on Sunday, and I am just finishing my charts and my consulting work. I could also mention the hours and hours I just spent preparing my taxes, and then the hours and hours I spent preparing my mother's taxes, but it is late at night, and I will stop. Tonight's theme would be "woe is me," but self-pity is not attractive. Still, I want to apologize again for not e-mailing you more often. Just enjoy your freedom from my constant e-mail clutter. As you grow older, there are times when the word *freedom* seems like empty rhetoric.

    For now, embrace freedom in every form.

Babbo

4/06/09 Wait, a Letter from Mom?

Hey Skyler, my love,

It was so good to hear your voice today from Nice. I pretended you were here. You sounded great, and I bet you looked great! I am glad you are having a fantastic time with no major glitches and that you are safe and healthy. The time seems to be going by very quickly. Does it seem that way to you? I enjoyed hearing about your exploits and the beautiful Italian coast. It probably feels good to be alone. At least for a few days. It gives you a chance to rewind and see where you've been, what you've learned. A time for some reflection, looking at things from a different perspective. Catch your breath and enjoy the scenery, perhaps over a cup of coffee. I'll go for that! Wish I were there. I am also glad you had a nice visit with John. He has been such a good friend to you.

By the way, my next foot appointment is a week from Tuesday. Everything looks great. Still a little black and blue, a little swollen, and a little tender, but I am walking in a tennis shoe, and I am out of that boot! Before I know it, I will be back walking with Nancy. And I will be fine by Europe. You will be in Rome on Easter Sunday, correct? All I can say is be careful. *There will be a billion people, and it will be crazy. Don't let anyone steal your camera, pick your pocket, or pilfer whatever you will be carrying. When you are all squished like sardines, standing to view the Pope, that's when the pickpockets get to work. Evil even lurks in heaven. So be on guard! And let us know when you are safely through the experience. I miss you so much that I can't stand it! Oh well, I'd better go. Keep texting to let us know you are safe.*

Avec beaucoup amour,
Ton Mare

4/17/09 Remember Kafka's Burrow?

Dear Skyler,

    It seems like forever since we have talked. I hope we can Skype this weekend when you safely return to your tiny dorm room. Only one month to go in London and you will have completed your spring semester abroad. Mixed feelings? Sad to see it end? Or glad to be heading back to New York for your senior year? Or are you focused on your summer Spanish course in Madrid? Just be glad of your many experiences. While you have been traveling across Europe, I have been traveling Saturday mornings to my mom's house, helping her with the upkeep of the house. Over this past week, she drove through a red light and was pulled over by a policeman. He asked her what she had done wrong, and she answered, "I drove through the red light." He responded by saying that was the first honest answer he had heard all day, so he would not give her a ticket. Ah, if he only knew her. However, he offered the suggestion that she might be getting too old to drive, that she might be better off giving up her driver's license, and that she might want to consider some retirement residence for her safety. Of course, that is what I have been telling her for the past two years.

    Through all of our discussions, my mother has repeatedly insisted that she could not possibly give up her possessions: her clothes and her jewelry. I have never added up the number of clothes, but I would bet she has 150 sweaters, 150 blouses, 150 pairs of pants, and probably 100 pairs of shoes. She is like the rodent in Kafka's burrow story: so preoccupied with her possessions that she cannot move forward to enjoy the best parts of life. For your final month in London, and for your upcoming time in Madrid, I hope you keep in mind the value of experiences, not possessions (or loss of possessions). When I visit my mother, I feel as if I am getting an example of how *not* to live your life. There is no positive attitude, no focus on contribution, and no attempt at any connection with anyone outside her small, wealthy group. I think the best of life is buried when you focus on what you can possess, not what you can experience. So, enjoy these last two periods in Europe, first in London and then in Madrid. They are great experiences. They will be with you much longer than any possession. Unless you are like my mother, who has kept every item she has ever purchased. That's just not my idea of life.

Ready for Madrid?

Babbo

5/28/09 Madrid? How's Your Spanish?

Dear Skyler,

Congratulations on making it to Madrid. I hope you love your homestay and your new family for the next six weeks. I hope you embrace Madrid and all of the experiences, and I hope you enjoy your Spanish classes. I am delighted, as I was with London, with your class schedule. Having your Spanish classes Monday through Thursday opens up Friday, Saturday, and Sunday for traveling. I would utilize these initial weekends for exploring Madrid, but I would use many of the weekends for traveling to different cities in Spain. We loved Granada, Seville, Cordoba, and all the neat Spanish villages. Keep us informed as much as possible. We will live vicariously through you. I was wondering if you can use your computer at the homestay. Or do you have to use it only on the college campus? In any case, I want to ask you for your suggestions on what flight we should fly from Los Angeles to Madrid. Is that something you can look up on your computer and offer an opinion?

Right now, Mom, Austen, and I are planning on flying directly from Los Angeles to Madrid on one long flight. We would like to arrive in Madrid on July 9. That would give us two nights in Madrid to readjust to the time difference before we start the *Skyler European Tour* with our flight to Venice. Most likely, we will be useless on those two days in Madrid, tired from the flight and the time change. So, for those two days, plan on having some end-of-the-semester fun with your classmates. A party or two? A good-bye outing? For us, I just want to make the travel arrangements from LA to Madrid, but I am leaving you, as the worldwide traveler, to make all of the other travel arrangements, including our flight to Italy and our return flight from England to New York. Once in New York, I will have arranged for our rooms at the Giraffe Hotel, and we will probably be there for the four nights so we can move you into your senior-year apartment. Wow. What a friggin' vacation. For us, it will be culture shock. For you, it may be "same ol', same ol'." But at least we will have your company for four full weeks. How can we beat that? Our longest family vacation has been only seventeen days. Will we ever be able to beat, in our lifetime, the feat of a month together? I want to be a dreamer, but part of me knows this trip will be one of those once-in-a-lifetime experiences.

Worth every penny, even if I have to work a little harder.

Babbo

6/11/09 You, Our Tour Guide? Have I Gone Bonkers?

Dear Skyler,

It is midafternoon, and I am working on some chart review while listening to Enya's *And Winter Came*...CD, and I had a sudden flash of memory of my reading *Sabriel* in the middle of the night, listening to Enya. When I think of my favorite reading experiences, I think of *Sabriel* and *Lirael* by Garth Nix, and then I think of my first reading of a copy of *Knightfall*, of course, by Skyler Courter. You have given me some of my favorite reading moments, just as Austen has given me some of my favorite music moments. As I think of your many contributions to the Courter family, I want to thank you again for taking on the burden of organizing our vacation. I do not know any other twenty-year-old who is currently managing her family's vacation. That is a true role reversal. I mention it at work and my coworkers think I have gone bonkers. They ask, "You trust her with planning your entire trip? With determining your finances? What if she spends *too* much?" But they do not have such a mature daughter, and I wonder if those parents have truly stepped aside, allowing their children to grow? There is nothing I can do for them, so I might as well enjoy how you have blossomed. We will love the trip and whatever you put together, and we will trust your own financial wisdom. Besides, after thinking of the recent Air France airplane crash, we all need to enjoy life as much as possible. Our time together should never be taken for granted. Life can disappear in a second. Until then, let's enjoy one another.

In the meantime, enjoy this summer semester. I know you will be busy with school and equally busy on the road. I also realize you will be communicating most with Mom via Skype, probably before I get home from the office. If you do not hear from me directly, just know you are in my thoughts and prayers. We still think about you daily. I suspect we always will—a parental affliction. Have fun with all your trips, including the upcoming scuba diving in the Mediterranean. I do not know how much there is to see beneath the surface, but it will be another body of water you can check off your list. I enjoyed my scuba dives at your age, even when a ten-foot shark circled above me as I stayed hidden for about fifteen minutes, buried in the thick kelp off Catalina Island. For that trip, the best part was eating the raw fish that was served once we had returned to the deck. My first sashimi, sort of! Maybe that will be true for your dives. Some new experience. Some new thrill. But the best part will be the camaraderie with your friends when you are safe and sound. Have a drink, and a toast to life, on me.

Stay alive so you can keep booking our flights and hotels.
Babbo

8/04/09 Should I Break My Pledge? Give a Grade?

Dear Skyler,

    I awoke in the middle of the night, thinking of you and our just-completed trip through Europe. Can you guess my favorite part? No, it was not relaxing on Santorini, although that was a beautiful island. It was not bracing ourselves for the onslaught in the bazaar in Istanbul, even though you, Mom, and Austen handled that challenge with ease. It was not even our wanderings in Venice, which is easily the most interesting city I have ever visited. The highlight of the trip, for me, was our celebration of your twenty-first birthday. I will always remember how Mom and Austen collapsed into their hotel beds, dead tired from our sightseeing in Florence. I will always remember how you and I stole our way up to the hotel roof. One *mojito* after another, one hour after another. Such a delight. Worth repeating in this e-mail! But best of all, I had the privilege of experiencing one of life's golden moments. Feeling as if I had risen above the bustle of life, I was able to pause and appreciate the beauty of Florence and the beauty of my daughter, now a grown, independent, and lovely woman. By giving up income, by diverting myself from other responsibilities, I had created a memory that was, as they say, irreplaceable. I had created something special, something worthy of a legacy. Truly an amazing evening. Unforgettable. My heartfelt thanks!

    Now, as to postponing the verdict? Not a chance. You deserve a standing ovation. As for your tour directing, I was impressed with how well you handled major multitask challenges, making all of our flight, train, and hotel reservations, plus handling all the dinner arrangements, tour arrangements, and the never-ending bills. Your choices, from flights to hotels to dinners, were outstanding. We did not have a bad hotel or a sour meal. What was more impressive was your ability to accept and embrace all of those adult responsibilities. You are an amazing traveler and a woman with many skills. You have grown from the curly topped girl with tons of energy and chatter to a wonderful, gorgeous, energetic, and hard-to-throw-off-your-smile woman. As I repeatedly say, you are going to make an extraordinary woman and an amazing wife. Please, no rush for the latter. You have developed all of the necessary tools, wisdom, and beauty. I am very, very proud of you. I cannot vouch for the quality of each and every one of your college classes, but I can vouch that NYU has prepared you well for life. Either that or you did it all on your own.

Now, are you ready for an actual grade? I admit, I promised to steer clear of any grades. But how about one final grade? Not for the tour, but for your entire college experience? I give you an A+. Even though I am unclear as to your plans after graduation, I love your idea of surveying the film industry terrain, selecting the best path as it presents itself. No hypothetical situation. Just keeping it real. Too many people rush headfirst into poor choices, restricted paths, and dead ends, where they live years of unfilled promise. I am confident you will never end up in that predicament. I am confident you will always make the decision right (which is different than making the right decision), and not worry about the adjustments, which are always necessary for moving forward. I think you should always try to grow, but never change your inner self. Do not lose any of your confidence or your buoyant nature. Do not lose your energy or enthusiasm. Do not lose your love of people or your ability to easily interact with those people. As I say ad nauseam, you just need to focus on being yourself because being you is already pure gold. Pour those ingredients into your future cauldron, and life will reward you with excitement and splendor. As Robin Sharma once said, "Become the architect of your future." From my perspective, you are successfully following his advice.

That's his advice, not my advice. Congrats!
Babbo

SENIOR YEAR

9/05/09 Your Senior Year? Are You Ready?

Dear Skyler,

    With your roommates now ensconced in your apartment and your senior year about to commence, I want to wish you good luck with this last year of college. The year will fly by, as if gathering speed with each passing month. With gravity, when falling, you are supposed to reach a maximum rate of descent. Those same laws do not apply to time, especially to the days and weeks of your final year of college. Stop and smell the roses. Take time to enjoy these days, each one of them. That is one of the challenges of life, reminding one's self to appreciate each single day—easy to proclaim and difficult to accomplish. Keep a daily gratitude list in some small journal. Each night, write down three things for which you are grateful, trying not to repeat yourself. It will keep you focused on the positive moments of each day. Enjoy the start of your classes. Enjoy the start of your internship. Enjoy the start of your last year of collegiate diving. Enjoy all the people who populate this last year. Some of them will disappear into faded memories. Make them last as long as possible. Make this year great with surprising interactions, unexpected activities, and unpredictable fun. Lastly, try to keep the focus on the present, not the future, as the future will be discussed more and more as you approach the date of your graduation and entry into the workforce.

I want to highlight one other point, which might seem a bit contradictory. Tony Robbins used to say that one of the keys to life is asking the right questions. For your senior year, how about writing down a list of questions for your future? How much do you love films? How much do you love art? How much do you want those passions to become part of your career? How much do you love diving and scuba diving? How much do you want those sports to be part of your life? And where—east coast, west coast, or somewhere else—can you best maximize your varied interests? You know how I highlight long-term thinking versus short-term thinking. But since life flies by at an ever-increasing pace, maybe there is not as much difference between the short-term and the long-term as people think. How about settling on a middle ground? Focus on enjoying this senior year, but begin to ask the fundamental questions of how you can maximize your pleasure and happiness for next year. So, as your friends begin to shift their focus to jobs, you continue to keep your focus on your passions, on your happiness first, for this last, great senior year. Then, for after graduation. Good luck with both of these endeavors. Most of all, enjoy this last year of college.

Ready?

Babbo

9/07/09 A Special Post-Senior-Year Offer

Dear Skyler,

   As you progress through your senior year, and as the topics of conversation turn to next year and what you are going to do after graduation, here is my special offer. For the year after graduation, I would be willing to offer financial support, allowing you to take some time as you transition toward employment. How about six months where you could relax and explore your options without any financial rush? Many parents recommend against offering that type of financial support to your graduating son or daughter. Make your child grow up. That is their mindset. For you, I disagree. You are already a woman. You are already independent. At this point, nothing is more important than clarifying your personal path. Too many people select immediate work based on money and end up getting buried far from their dreams. I would like you to have a chance to follow your dreams with a little freedom. Maybe the freedom will lead you to a series of nonpaying internships at different film companies, either in New York or Los Angeles. Maybe it will allow you time to clarify which companies mesh with your own values, your own purpose. I just want next year to be as successful as this year. I want you to find a pathway to your dreams, but not a pathway to making money alone. From my perspective, money should be your lowest priority as you make that transition to employment. The high priority remains finding your passion and starting down the path toward happiness.

   There are some other advantages. You know me, I am a strong believer in taking time off for other pursuits. You already know the story of my writing attempt in Marbella. But do you remember how I took four months off from work, without pay, when Austen was born, seventeen months after your birth, so I could spend time with the family? You and I went to Disneyland three days a week. By the fourth month, even the train conductor knew your name. Our trips gave Mom a chance to bond with Austen, plus a chance to rest when Austen napped. For me, those four months gave me time with you, time with Austen, and time with your mom. Those breaks from work never earned me a penny, but they gave me a level of unsurpassed happiness. They also gave me a renewed perspective. It's a bit strange. The happiest periods of my life have all come when I have earned no income. That should tell us something. Give yourself the flexibility to create a future, separate from financial concerns, and give yourself the time to create a future without pressure to match your friends' starting salaries. As Carlos Castaneda once said, "All roads are the same... choose the one with heart." You can only be successful at that challenge if you have sufficient time to follow your heart.

Life should not be rushed.

Babbo

9/11/09 Now, How about My Future?

Dear Skyler,
   In four years, you have markedly changed. Me? I am not so convinced. I have the same idiosyncrasies and many of the same habits. I try to grow, but I just remain the same. When you started NYU as a freshman, I used to follow your moves, knowing when you were sitting in some class, when you were heading out for a Broadway show. I would always sleep better when I knew you were back safely in your dorm. Tonight? Four years later? From Mom, I learned you were heading out tonight to see Tina in Brooklyn. For me, that meant you would be returning late to Manhattan via the subway. I checked the Yankees game several times, noticing it was raining at the start of the game, and then raining again in the seventh inning with two rain delays. With the thought of the pouring rain, the thought of your ear infection, and the thought of your late-night return all alone on the subway, I found myself worried for your safe arrival back to your apartment. Just like four years ago. Yes, unchanged parental worry. Never gone.
   My insight has improved, but my behavior remains unchanged. Tonight, as I watched the reports of the downpour, what did I do? Just what I did four years ago—I texted you despite knowing that I would not receive a response. After all, I am the guy who is encouraging independence, including independence from your hovering dad. Right now, Austen is asleep, as she is home from USC for the weekend. Mom is asleep, as it's 10:45 p.m.—past her bedtime—and I am sitting before the computer with your wonderful photos of Europe sliding across my screen. Earlier, I tried to sleep, but my thoughts came back to you, your safety, and your future. Why is it that in times of concern, we want to express our feelings? Why do I feel such a need to e-mail late at night? By now, you are hopefully sleeping in your warm bed with the rain falling against your windowpane. I still send my love and prayers. May they ripple across the three thousand miles, knock at your window, and give you a pleasant dream. May God watch over you. With my emotions expressed and my spirits lifted, I am ready for sleep, although I will feel far better when I awake in the morning

knowing you are beginning a new day, safe and sound. Of course, I will still be thinking about you and your future.

Parents pretend to change, don't we?

Babbo

10/05/09 My Fear of You Slipping Away

Dear Skyler,

    I awoke at 2:00 a.m. thinking about you. Now, you might guess I was worrying about how you were managing your overload of a senior-year schedule with internship days on Mondays and Wednesdays, heavy class days on Tuesdays and Thursdays, and Friday morning classes from 8:00 a.m. to noon. Or you might guess I was worrying about how you were managing to handle all of your visitors, including LJ and Jake's recent stay with you through the weekend. You might even guess that I was worrying about your recent spider bites and the tennis-ball-size swellings. Well, I worry about all of those things, and much more, during the day. But not so much at night. No, I awoke thinking about how it feels as if you are slipping away, at least from home and us. For the past three years of college it was easy to imagine you coming home for vacations at Thanksgiving, Christmas, and spring break, but those illusions are disappearing with the reality of your status as a senior. The end of this transition, as wonderful as it has been for you and for us, is approaching, and there is nothing that will stop it, just like there is nothing to stop time itself. In daylight, I can laugh at the thought, even taking delight in your future possibilities. In the darkness, I feel more of a heaviness, a sense of sadness as further separation approaches.

    Are you ready to take my confession? You can be the priest, and I will be the person stepping into that dark, tight booth. My secret? As a parent, I preferred the emotional comfort of your grade-school years. Mom would drive you and Austen to school and pick up both of you. You and Austen were home every night and every weekend. The soccer games. The diving meets. The homework with Mom's consistent oversight. Her reading to you two every night, even until you were close to adolescence. Those were wonderful years. And, of course, the annual Maui vacations, starting off every summer with two weeks together as a family. All of those years were a true delight. Treasured memories. I will grant you that this summer's Europe vacation with four adults—not two adults and two children—was epic. It was the vacation that will always stand out as the very best. But I will admit I carry a hope for even greater, future vacations with all four of us, and maybe even with a significant other or two, traveling to other distant cities. Yes, I pray that many adventures await us.

Still, I am a man who tends to be bound to reality, and I tend to worry about the reality of your sliding away from us. As I struggle through these final transition stages, I want you to be aware of my misjudgments. I am the guy who told Mom I expected to work for the health-care agency for eighteen months. I have lasted over thirty years. My goal was to write for a living. But here I am three decades years later with nothing published. That means zero success from my earlier dreams and my lifelong passion. I admit I awaken some mornings and wonder, "How the hell did I get here? How the hell did I let myself drift away from following my own heart?" As I often repeat, forget my worries, ignore my never-ending ruminations. I will survive. That is what parents do. I will make it through these late-night awakenings and these repetitive worries. Am I so different from other parents? I think not. Push aside any concern about me, Mom, or even Austen. Just learn from my own mistakes, which is why I am sharing more and more of my life, my stories, and my feelings. Focus on what gives you the most pleasure.

That is the foundation for your happiness.

Babbo

11/08/09 The Distance between College and Home?

Dear Skyler,

    With Austen's sophomore year, Mom and I are realizing the significant differences between having one daughter attend a local college and the other daughter attend a college on the opposite side of the country. With Austen, we see her almost every weekend as either we drive up on Sunday to take her to lunch, or she comes home for a short stay. In addition, we get to attend the USC football games and some of her concerts. On Friday night, we drove up and saw her participate in the choir concert. With you, we do not have those same opportunities. It is our loss. But it makes your trips home that much sweeter, especially when you can add a few extra days like you did this Thanksgiving weekend. We appreciate your company. If you were asked about the distance away from home, I suspect you would answer how NYU is a perfect fit for you, how the distance is well worth the experience, and how your wealth of friends counterbalances any loss of family time. For you, you are right. But please know, for many parents, the distance between college and home does matter. For us, it would have been fun to be able to see you on some of the weekends, fun to be able to watch you dive in meets, and fun to be able to meet more of your friends. Thank God for your cell phone calls and the Skype sessions. Again, they have been much appreciated.

    Now, why is distance on my mind? Because I just wrote a birthday card note to my dad, planning to mail it tomorrow to my mom for his ninetieth birthday on November 11. My mother will probably not understand my impulse to write the letter, but that does not matter. What did I say? I wrote, *"Dear, Dad. Physically, you are no longer with us, but I am sending this card to your spirit to celebrate your ninetieth birthday. I wanted to reexpress my appreciation for having you as my father and reexpress my thanks for all that you did for the family and me. All of your sacrifices. Your many geographic moves. Your constant hard work. Your saving of money. Your financial support of my education and my first purchase of a house. You were terrific. You are greatly missed. Most importantly, I still feel your spirit, and it still gives me comfort. I hope you are alive in some spiritual world, and I hope we will meet again. Please know, on your birthday, we are still celebrating you and all that you meant to us. Love, Doc."* Will the letter have any impact on my mother? Maybe soften her a little? Who knows? To you, my point is repetitive. Geographic distance is difficult, but geographic distance does not equal emotional distance. You are in our hearts and minds every day. So, whether far or near, it will be more than enough to be part of your life. Thanks for giving us that blessing and for sharing so much of your time.

And, could you send me, dead or alive, a birthday card on my ninetieth?
Babbo

1/04/10 What, a Return to California?

Dear Skyler,

    I hate to repeat myself, but we want to thank you for coming home for these past two weeks of Christmas. Mom, Austen, and I love having you home. You are a shining light that illuminates our lives. We enjoy your enthusiasm, your energy, and your love of people. Our world would be much darker without you. Austen would be much darker without you. We appreciate you and who you are as a person more than you can possibly know. Now, all of those remarks have been repeated and repeated. How about something new? Well, we were delighted with your announcement of your decision to return to Los Angeles after graduation. That is worth a bottle of champagne. For us, it will be so great to catch you on the phone to hear about your day at work, to be able to see you on some weekends, and to get together for special occasions. It will be doubly nice to be able to share further vacations, spending time together as a family. As I have said before, and will say the night before you are married, the man who marries you has no real concept of how lucky he is, and how lucky he will be. Love and romance is one thing. A life together is something different. You really are our sun: always shining love, adventure, and passion. When you return to Los Angeles, don't change. Not one single bit, either at work or at home.

    Let me pause for a moment. At different points in these e-mails I have mentioned romance and marriage. I do not mean to place any pressure for that part of your life. You live in a different era. When my mom went to college, her sole goal was to graduate with a husband. She graduated from Barnard College still single. Is it any surprise, that in that first summer after her graduation and while my dad was still awaiting his senior year, she would set the trap, dropping her books before him, garnering a date, and getting herself pregnant? For you, marriage may be an issue that comes much later. As with so many things, we do not care. Your passions and your career take precedence. We support you in setting your own priorities. You know what I admire about you? In college you shared how your roommates were always encouraging you to lower your standards for dating. You never lowered your standards. To this point no man has met your measure. With a national divorce rate of 50 percent, lowering your standards would be the first step toward a divorce. Do not change your standards or your priorities. We want you to take your time. Focus on your career. The family part will come later, possibly much later.

Embrace this last semester, and then come home.

Babbo

1/25/10 Finally, a New York Parental Visit?

Dear Skyler,

I just want to share my heartfelt thanks for our visit to you in New York. We loved seeing your homey apartment, spending time with your roommates and friends, eating some fine food at a series of interesting restaurants, attending your diving meet (where we thought you were awesome), and most importantly spending time with you, in between your many parties, of course. As Mom says, "My God, she's still always going out!" But time is the most important currency, and we loved our time with you. We were impressed with your growing beauty (you are getting prettier and prettier), your constant enthusiasm for life, your love of people, your fun and outgoing personality, your intelligence and insightfulness, and your growing maturity. When you were a little girl, and when you grew into adolescence, I always saw that potential. It's no longer potential; it is there at your doorstep. You have blossomed into a beautiful woman. We can't wait until the movie industry meets a young Miss Skyler. You will stand out as someone special, right from your first position.

I also want to thank you for sharing your diving blog entries. I thought your summary of the training trip to frigid Florida was funny, and I thoroughly enjoyed your comments about the senior-year diving meet. You were kind to thank us for our attendance. But the treat was all ours. I wish we could have attended more diving meets and I wish we could have spent more long weekends in New York during your four years of college. But for the first two years we had Austen in high school with the responsibility of driving her to school every day. For her, alone, that drive to high school would have been a nightmare, but with me, and the car-pool lane, the drive took only thirty minutes. For this last year, with USC, our availability was crucial for Austen, as she needed the option of returning home on periodic weekends. One of your goals, as I remember, is to die with no regrets. I hope you achieve that goal. But I ain't going to reach that goal. I regret we did not visit more often while you were at NYU. However, the quality of this visit and the quality of last summer's month-long European vacation, overshadow any regrets. Better yet, your upcoming return to

Southern California further mutes any regrets. We love our time with you, and we are delighted with the thought of even more time together in the future.

With you back in Los Angeles, that's one goal we will achieve.
Babbo

1/25/10 Wonderful Weekend (from Mom)

Dear Skyler,

    I am finally home! I took Lynn to lunch at the Cheesecake Factory for her birthday. Then I went to Planet Beauty, Lowe's, the market, and then another market. Whew! I now have a headache. However, I really wanted to write you this e-mail to tell you how much I enjoyed our weekend in New York with you. First of all, I need to backtrack a little. I read your e-mail to us and it almost made me cry! You are the best! Thanks for the parenting affirmation! I can honestly say I did something right. You and Austen turned out great. It probably had very little to do with Dad or me. But I do see examples of horrific parenting every day. We are lucky to have each other. Secondly, I am sorry we did not go to New York more frequently during your four years. We would have loved to visit. But lots of factors were in play: cost, Dad's work, Austen's schedule, etc. It is what it is. I am just so glad we did it this time. It was a delight to see your friends (all great, by the way), meet your coaches, and get a glimpse at a little slice of your life, having great meals and great conversations with you! They all contributed to some wonderful memories! I had so much fun. I can't believe you are all grown up. Keep up the good work! You looked beautiful, and I am so proud of you. I am also proud of your diving. I was so impressed! You are amazing! Thanks for allowing us to share your life. Enjoy this last semester. I have a feeling it will fly by so fast. I can't wait until graduation. Take care.

    Love you forever.
Mom

2/15/10 Your Final Diving Meet?

Dear Skyler,

    I just want to wish you well on your final diving meet in Atlanta. I am so glad Mom and I visited for your home diving meet, as we both gained an appreciation for how good you have become at diving and how much fun you have enjoyed over these past four years. We also gained an appreciation of how much time that sport has taken. It was so much easier when I was in college. We just had a two-hour practice each day for each sport, and we had a different sport for each season. It is now so different. There's so much focus on just one sport. During the season, you have a morning practice and an evening practice, and throughout the year you hit the gym on a regular schedule to maintain strength and fitness. Plus, your meets take all weekend, not just a Saturday afternoon. If I had done that much athletic activity, I do not think I would have been able to maintain my grades. Your honor-roll grades sound fabulous to me, but I have forgotten all about your grades. How you manage to skip an entire week of your classes because of your Tuesday to Saturday national diving meet is beyond me. Really, that time loss would have been a death stroke for my chance at any decent grades. I had enough of a struggle keeping up, let alone trying to catch up for a missed week. Enjoy your last meet, and then get ready to experience a new college life with ten to fifteen extra free hours added to your weekly schedule. I love the way you have orchestrated your new free time for these final three months. It will give you a chance to enjoy the semester and your friends. Best wishes for a great ending to a great college experience.

    We would not have expected anything less.
    Babbo

2/17/10 Need Some Cheering Up?

Dear Skyler,

I almost labeled this e-mail "Need a Reality Check?" but after your difficult week of diving, I thought that e-mail would never be read. I want to offer a realistic but truthful perspective. In all your years in sports, from early swimming, to soccer, to diving, you were always in the top half of the athletes. But I have never had any coach walk up to me and say, "Wow! Your daughter is one of the best athletes I have ever coached." That compliment may have been delivered to my dad, but that compliment never happened to you or me. The divers who qualify for the Olympic trials are of a different breed. Just remember, you have something even better. I have experienced the unique surprise of having two of your teachers pull me aside to tell me you were one of the smartest kids they had ever taught. I think your SAT English 800 score verifies their perspective. From my own viewpoint, I think your problem-solving skills, your leadership skills, and your social skills are unbeatable. Now, why am I mentioning those points? If you can remember our many talks over the years, I have always accented one of the keys to life is to focus on the positives, not the negatives. To focus on your personal strengths and your special gifts, not your weaknesses. None of us is good at everything. None of us slips through life without numerous setbacks—which brings me back to your diving. For your final diving meet, I would remember the enjoyable moments with friends, not the scores, which were lower than what you wanted. If you enjoyed the process of diving over the past four years, the final meet's scores do not matter. What counts is not how well you did, but how much you embraced the full journey. Let yourself be free of the results, just like you should be free of the opinion of others. We are a society much too focused on results, and we are a society much too focused on public acclaim. That is not the best path for pursuing a high level of happiness. There are other areas where you will shine. Even then, it is still the process and your appreciation of that process that matter the most.

My personal concerns are always focused on health. Our lives are shaped by the quality of our health. You know how much I prescribed antibiotics when you were kids. Now I know better. But my dad's mother died when she was in her forties from a mitral valve heart defect. My own sister Sherry died when she was in her forties. A dental infection seeded into her mitral valve. Within two weeks she went from being able to beat me in a set of tennis to not being able to walk a full block without shortness of breath. It was out of her control. Antibiotics and two heart surgeries only partially repaired the damage. When I list my goals for all of us, health is always number one. You cannot enjoy the best components of life without your health. I ask you to give appropriate value to wellness as you emerge from college into the workforce. Use your diving practice as a springboard for setting your lifelong health plan. Set up an eating style and an exercise routine, and learn how to balance those activities with your work assignments. You will spare yourself from later illnesses. Remember the importance of maintaining those habits. Those habits are far more crucial than even your performance at the office.

Here's to your future health and happiness.
Babbo

3/15/10 Your Last Flight to New York?

Dear Skyler,

    We just returned home after dropping you off at Long Beach for your Jet Blue flight. Right now the Jet Blue status says your plane is taxiing, but I am going to assume that flight 204 has taken off, especially since it was due to depart at 8:55 a.m. Either way, we miss you. Each time you leave, it is like a piece of sunshine or a burst of energy disappearing from our family world. Fortunately, we can balance our sorrow with the realization that you will be returning, for good, in just a couple of months. In a way, this spring break was symbolic of your four years at NYU. With all of your friends and all of your activities, including arranging the flight tomorrow morning to Jamaica, you still managed to squeeze us in for four days of your vacation. Austen appreciated your time together, and Mom enjoyed her shopping with you. We consider ourselves lucky to get any of your time. In truth, this sharing of yourself is going to be one of the challenges in your life. You are going to have people wanting to spend more time with you, not less. Sometimes it is a tough balance, giving everyone sufficient time. Soon enough you will be back in SoCal for good. In the film industry, with all of the long hours and all of the late-night networking, your challenge will become harder, not easier.

    I also want to congratulate you on looking so fabulous. When you set your mind to a goal, you always seem to reach that goal. You told us you were going to get into better shape as we ate our way through Europe this past summer. You looked fit, and you looked beautiful. What a great combination. And great timing. It will be great to start your post-college adult life with great health and excellent fitness. Together, they will give you the stamina you may need for those initial long hours of employment, and it seems as if you have decided to start with a nonpaying internship at a Los Angeles film company. At the beginning of employment, each company always seems to work you to the bone. In fact, most companies work you to death over the course of several decades. At least you are well prepared for any onslaught of long hours. World beware: Skyler Courter is about to send her own seismic waves.

On that note, good luck on your spring break in Jamaica. You have my approval, as if you have ever needed my approval, for some cliff diving in Jamaica. I know you as well as you know me. If you find some cliff, you will be the first one to suggest that dive to the other girls. We have done it in Maui, and I am sure you will do it in Jamaica. Did someone discuss swimming with the sharks? If they offer that activity, I know you will be underwater before everyone else is even ready. Am I worried? Not really. I know how straight you enter the water from any height, whether you dive or jump. I know how quickly you can tuck, once entering the water, to avoid any rock. I know how well you can swim against any current. I also know how you maintain calm in any crisis. So, a couple of nearby sharks? I suspect your pulse will remain unchanged. Still, I will just look forward to your call at the end of this vacation, telling me you are back in Manhattan. Dive safely. Swim safely. Try to do both without any alcohol in your system! Just drink those pineapple rum drinks at night, deal?

Can't wait for all of the details.

Babbo

4/25/10 Ready for Your Final College Weeks?

Dear Skyler,

As the senior year winds down to a final closure, I should be writing you more, not less, frequently. However, with all of your extensive papers, including your senior honors thesis on horror films, I imagine you will have less time to read my e-mails, so I will try to limit my communications to give you more time. However, take a good look at your current assignments. Could you have handled the four twenty-page papers, the one-hundred-page honors thesis, and the upcoming examinations four years ago? I think not. You have developed a new level of capability and an expanded skill set. You have really grown from that caterpillar to the butterfly. Take one day at a time with sufficient breaks to recharge yourself. Do not even think about grades. Just focus on learning the subject and producing a level of work sufficient to satisfy yourself. See? We have both grown during your four years of college. You have developed new internal strength and new beauty. Me? I have grown older and changed my priorities from my passions to *your* passions, from grades to learning, from classroom to other activities. I suspect you will not need much assistance, but I will always be available to discuss anything at any time. In the meantime, take care of your sleep, your health, and your energy. Do not let the fun moments escape you over these final weeks. Lord knows I wasted too much of my college life studying too hard, and I have spent too much of my adult life working too hard. Look where it has gotten me. Still trapped. Still working. Satisfy yourself. Enjoy your friends. Reach graduation in great spirits. Sound simple?

Ah, life is never that simple.

Babbo

5/03/10 A Senior Honors Thesis on Horror Films?

Dear Skyler,

    Congratulations on finishing your classes and completing your thesis. Four years ago, looking at the young high-school graduate, I would never have guessed the topic of your thesis. If I had been forced to guess, I might have imagined a thesis on some classic literature or perhaps a dissertation on some famous artist. I would never have thought of the title *Blood, Bodies, and Bombs: Violence and National Trauma in Horror Films.* Nor would I have ever pictured the opening paragraph written below. It is included for my benefit, not yours. Where is the sweet, innocent girl who used to sing to Raffi? Where is the girl we took to see, and who thoroughly enjoyed, all of those Disney animated movies, including *Beauty and the Beast*, *Aladdin*, *The Lion King*, and *Toy Story*? Do I recall any horror films in our family outings? None, except of course *Alien* with Sigourney Weaver. So, how do I react when I turn to the first page of your thesis and read this:

A screen door slams. The young girl glances behind her, knowing she should leave but instead takes another hesitant step forward. "Kirk?" she calls, the panic rising in her voice as the camera follows her slowly making her way through the dark, seemingly abandoned house. Unable to see, she suddenly trips, careening headfirst into another room. At first, it appears as though she is lying in a thick layer of dust and dirt. However, it quickly becomes apparent that she is face down in hundreds and hundreds of human bones, teeth, and animal feathers. A live chicken clucks incessantly from a small cage hanging from the ceiling, accompanied by a fresh looking skull and human hand all swaying eerily in a breeze. The shot closes in on her face: mouth open in silent horror, her wide eyes flit back and forth—from the rotting cattle skull to the couch constructed of bones—trying to make sense of her surroundings. She doubles over, retching. As the hysteria sets in, she scrambles up, and it is clear that all thoughts of Kirk are long gone. Suddenly, a towering man with a grotesque mask of human skin appears behind her, letting out an unearthly yell as he lunges for her. Screaming in blind terror, the young girl sprints for the door, and tastes the sweltering summer air, before he grabs her and drags her back inside. She screams and thrashes madly against him, but to no avail: he easily carries her down into the basement, with its bloodstained walls and rusty meat freezers. Then, the screaming abruptly stops as he thrusts her flailing body onto a meat hook; she lets out a strangled sob in excruciating pain, arms raised in a futile attempt to free herself. The deformed man, however, has turned his attention to a teenage boy lying unconscious on the table. The sound of a chainsaw erupts, drowning out her renewed screams as he begins to dismember her boyfriend in front of her very eyes.

Now, before you scream, I know you well enough that you would not want me to judge your thesis and your writing skills by one opening paragraph. After all, that writing represents only a description of the action in one single scene. You probably don't even want it in this correspondence. After all, that paragraph does not represent your analysis of the horror film and the factors that impact the horror genre. You can relax. Unfazed by the opening, I settled down before my computer and I took my time reading the lengthy thesis. I must admit, I enjoyed reading your selection of films (*The Texas Chainsaw Massacre*, *The Last House on the Left*, *Saw*, and *Hostel*), your observations on those films, and your interesting point of view of how the violence within those films represents the real traumas of our world, as evidenced by the first two films during the Vietnam era of the 1970s and the second two films from the post-9/11 era. I think I understood the message of your thesis, but please correct me if I am wrong. Our world is growing more violent and chaotic, and those horror films reflect the escalation of violence and chaos. From that perspective, I especially liked the paragraph below, right before the conclusion, as this paragraph led me to an appreciation of how much you have changed through four years of college, and how your vision of the world has changed.

This paper has been occupied with exploring the horror films of the distinct yet parallel eras of Vietnam and the post 9/11 period. These subgenres of gross-out horror and torture porn, respectively, are both characterized by immensely graphic violence, minimal plot, and a disorienting aesthetic. They are undeniably disturbing and horrifying; they have been called "misogynistic, degrading, sick, and socially un-redeeming," (Thompson 1) and even "a degrading, senseless misuse of film and time" (Gross). Consequently, critics and scholars alike have cast them aside as unworthy of discussion. However, as I have demonstrated, the hyperbolic and sensationalistic violence in these films is not a reflection of declining taste. Rather, the violence emerges directly from the extremely chaotic and violent atmospheres of national trauma.

What was my reaction to reading the full thesis? It gave me an appreciation of how you have gone through a transition from a wide-eyed high-school girl to a grown adult woman during a troubling global time that cannot be so easy to assimilate. The world seems less predictable, less secure, and much more dangerous than when I graduated from college. With our economic, environmental, and world issues, your future work and career choices seem much more uncertain. That realization reconfirms my feeling that now, more than ever, each college student needs more, not less, support from his or her parents, and that each student needs to develop, more than ever, the right habits to be able to prosper through this difficult transition. The world may be falling apart—many families may be falling apart—but our family needs to stay fully intact. As for the future, I will do my part to make certain our relationship stays intact. For me, nothing is more important. Thanks for sharing your thesis. Hope you don't mind my tossing parts of it back at you. Thanks for reopening my eyes to the world that awaits you and your cohorts. Congratulations again on your personal growth, your understanding of the world, and your ability to educate even your own father.

    You are becoming my teacher. Now that was worth the price of NYU.
Babbo

5/09/10 Your Long and Winding Road? Coming to an End?

Dear Skyler,

What else can I say? It has been a long and winding road as you have weaved your way through four years of college. I am very proud of how you have developed into this resourceful and independent woman, I am proud of how you have transitioned into this adult, chaotic world, and I am proud of how you have developed the correct habits. You have never looked healthier or more beautiful. Beauty, in everyone, lasts only so long. But health, fitness, and vitality? Physical and mental? You need to shepherd these attributes throughout your life, as your physical and mental sharpness will be your foundation for facing all of life's challenges. As I think back over your four years, I am impressed with your adjustment to New York, your ability to develop so many friendships, your stream of extracurricular activities, your use of two New York internships, your commitment to four years of diving and two years of captainship, your courage exploring Europe while living on the London and Madrid campuses, and your capacity to problem solve through every crisis. In these past four years, you have become more educated, and you have become much more prepared to face the real world with a wide-ranging skill set.

If the religious world has become more problematic, if the political world has become more contentious, and if the security of any professional career seems more fragile, the world is still a place where friendships are crucial, accountability is demanded, and your future is of your own creation. Sorry, but I cannot refrain from some final words of advice. My focus will not be as wide as it might have been four years ago. You have taught me well. As you hit the world of employment, I have just three recommendations: Stay true to your values and standards. Stay true to your dreams and passions. Stay true to your purpose. May it be aligned with your employer's purpose. You will attract success, and by success I mean you will attract great friends and enjoyable, satisfying work. Much of what happens in your life is out of your control. Major corporations close. Good people lose jobs for no valid reason. Seemingly solid marriages can fall apart into messy divorces. Despite all of that chaos, you can still follow your dreams, your passions, and your purpose.

If I were to offer another piece of advice, I would frame it as more of a reminder. The luckiest people are not those who are the wealthiest people. They are the people whose work is aligned with their passion and purpose. They comprise a small segment of our society. Most people spend the majority of their lives in jobs that are not satisfying, trying desperately to grab some happiness on the weekends. I am certain you will create a higher standard of living. You just need to utilize all of your wonderful skills to your advantage. You need to find and stay on the right path, aligned with your interests. You need to focus on connection and contribution, giving, not just taking. In addition, being good means more than being good at your job or career; it means being good as a person and being good as a neighbor. Your New York University education may have been fairly expensive, but for me it was worth every penny, as it prepared you for the next phase of your life. On that note, we (all three of us—Mom, Austen, and I) cannot tell you how excited we are that your next phase of life returns you to Southern California, not three thousand miles away in New York. Welcome home to what we are certain will be an extraordinary and fabulous life. A couple of months from now, when you look up from your film industry position, don't be surprised if you spot three faces pressed against the glass of your office, looking inward. Yes, that will be your family members, stronger than ever, tighter as a family than ever—showing up at your office to lend our support, regardless of the disbelieving stares from your coworkers.

How lucky can you be, right?

Babbo

5/16/10 Graduation? A Day to Remember!

Dear Skyler,

All three of us want to thank you for a wonderful graduation week. Mom asserted she has one complaint. She wants to bring you home in her suitcase rather than let you stay in New York until your apartment lease has concluded. We had a great week. We enjoyed both graduations. Radio City Music Hall and Yankee Stadium were spectacular settings. The rain will always be remembered. Congratulations on closing your college career in spectacular fashion. We were impressed with the two majors and two minors. We were impressed with all of your friends. They seemed to come from everywhere, even from colleges in Michigan and Texas, just to be present at your graduation. That speaks volumes about you and the quality of your relationships. Thanks too for being your usual outstanding tour director. Ala Europe, you were superb. In Manhattan, each site, each store, and each restaurant was fantastic. Great food. Even better company. If you were not heading into the entertainment industry, you could run a travel agency. You are a gem at creating good times. You have our respect, our love, and our deepest congratulations. All three of us think you are exceptional, now better than ever, and ready for a successful return to Southern California!

We will be waiting at the terminal.
Babbo

5/16/10 What? My Own Graduation Speech?

Dear Skyler,

    At your two graduation ceremony speeches, you were told you were brilliant and should now turn that brilliance into action. The various speakers were good, but if I had addressed your class, I would have offered a far different message. Typical for your dad, yes? The man who repeatedly promised to give less advice cannot even resist the thought of giving more advice, not just to you, but to your entire graduating class. You can probably guess what I would have preached in my speech. So, go ahead. Think back to my four years of letters. If I had to summarize my basic tenets, what suggestions would qualify for a short overview? Here is your challenge. Write down a list of what I have tried to teach you and your classmates and see if it matches my imagined speech. I am betting you hit 75 percent of my speech. But what have you missed? Is there anything else I would recommend? Something you need to consider?

    I would have started my speech with a summary of Russell Conwell's sermon "Acres of Diamonds." I would have told the story of Ali Hafed, a Persian farmer who lived near the River Indus around the time when diamonds were discovered. I would have told them how Ali Hafed sold his farm, deposited his family in the village, and started his decade-long search for wealth. How he covered much of Africa, parts of Asia, and a wide path through Europe, searching for diamonds, but committed suicide in Spain, distraught and penniless. I would have explained how one year after his suicide, the new owner of Ali Hafed's farm stumbled across a large, unusual rock just beneath the top layer of dirt, and placed it on his dining table. A neighbor declared it had to be a diamond. The new owner laughed, saying that would be impossible because his farm, Ali Hafed's old farm, had acres of those rocks. Well, those rocks were indeed diamonds, and that single plot of land produced one of the world's largest diamond mines. I would have highlighted the moral of this true story and how it relates to the graduating students.

    Each of NYU's students is like Ali Hafed. They are leaving the farm, New York University, and venturing out into the world. Many of them will be searching for money, traveling to distant locations and working long hours. Here is the hidden truth, one of the keys to life: You do not need to travel the world to find wealth. It is right beneath your feet, buried within yourself. Buried within your friends and your family. Your real wealth is not your money, your fame, or your acclaim; it is your level of happiness. How do you establish your happiness? One clue. It's not an acquisition; it's a skill. I have a simple belief that each person is born with a special gift. You need to find and develop that gift, and you need to share that gift with the world. It sounds simple. It is not. First, it is a skill that you have to nurture and refine. Second, there are many obstacles, including many societal factors, working against your path to employing those skills. For too many people, their skills require going against the grain, going against people's expectations. There are times when your pursuit does not lead to the greatest wealth.

For that pursuit, I would have offered the cautionary tale of the Indonesian monkey trap. I would have asked them if they knew how they caught monkeys in the jungles of Indonesia. I would have explained how the natives create a hollow coconut, stake it to the ground, and then fill it with rice or peanuts. I would have described how the monkey will squeeze a hand through the small opening, clench the goodies, and then be unable to pull the wider, larger fist back out through the opening. Trapped, the monkey just sits there, pulling and pulling without success. The natives return and capture that monkey. I would have explained how many of us are like those monkeys. Too often, we allow ourselves to be trapped, holding on to the wrong goodies. Some of those treats look tasty, but they can be poisons. The good opinion of others can trap you. A financial reward can trap you. A lifestyle can trap you. How do you escape from those traps? It takes more than just an act of letting go and breaking free. It takes more than a refocus on finding your gift, developing your gift, and sharing your gift; it takes a change in your thinking and your assumptions about what leads to your happiness.

That's where Ali Hafed went wrong. He failed to realize that happiness comes from your friends, not from your possessions. Your friends can test your tolerance. Your friends can make offensive remarks. Your friends can become jealous of your skills and your path. But friendship and love are still the most important components of anyone's life. When you scale a mountain, there's no joy in being alone at the top. You need companionship. You need friends and family. You need your gift; you need to share your gift; but you also need the people you love (and who love you) to be around that gift. Those people are the true goodies of life. Look around you, at your roommates, your fellow students, and your family. Take those people on your journey. Friendships—not a handful of diamonds—are the real reward for a life well lived. As stated by Emily Dickinson: "My friends are my estate." If you have learned nothing from of college, know this. Develop your gift. Share your gift. Follow your passion and purpose. And develop great, lifelong friendships. Accomplish all of that, and your life will be more than outstanding. It will be incredible.

Now, aren't you glad I did not have a chance to address your class?
Babbo

PART TWO

Letters to My Younger Daughter, Austen

FRESHMAN YEAR

8/22/08 Finally, College Has Started!

Dear Austen,

    As a starting point, I want you to know I realize these e-mails will be perused with a fair degree of skepticism. After all, you had to sit next to me for those daily drives to high school, one-hour round trip, for four straight years, so you already know my many perspectives on life. But your hesitancy will be my challenge. Can I overcome it? We shall see. You may be surprised how much I am changing. Of course, you would be first to disclose how these letters are written more for my soul's salvation than yours. Still, because I am so desperate to save my own soul, I am going to push forward, sending you these periodic e-mails, hoping to offer some unexpected insights. More importantly, I am hoping these e-mails keep us a bit more connected, especially since, with your absence, Mom and I are living in a tomb. We are not quite yet corpses, but can you sense our feeling of loss? Our sense of emptiness? Over these next four years, we want to feel as connected to you and your daily life (and Skyler's last two years of college) as possible. So, my e-mails will be a nonstop part of that letter writing effort. Ridiculous? Yes. But that is *me*!

    There is another facet to my e-mails that needs to be addressed. Some people would prefer to forget a recent setback. Some people would rather put that incident behind them, quickly forgotten. Not me. I tend to perseverate, which is why many of these e-mails will be written late at night. I get into bed, but I cannot fall asleep, as my brain is racing. I head downstairs to the computer to compose a letter to clear my own thoughts. In that process you may find me repetitive. You already know the facts, but I may repeat them once again. If you want, glance over those parts. They are written to fulfill a need in me, not a need in you. But they help me clarify the landscape of the problem, and they often help me better understand the solution. So, peruse my e-mails at your usual breakneck speed, pausing only when you hit a new point. Again, try to ignore my repetitive nature. It is not a mental illness. It is just an idiosyncrasy. Just ask Mom to list my many idiosyncrasies. Her list will be longer than any of my e-mails. Patience. That is all that I can ask. And if I do not clear your thinking, perhaps I will clear the fog within my own mind. Fingers crossed for both of us.

I have to start with a confession and an apology. I expected your move into USC to be far easier than Skyler's transition into NYU. Wrong. Skyler's initial move was done under pouring rain; your move was accomplished under a bright sun and ninety-degree heat. The problem was not the weather; it was the unexpected quality, or should I say the lack of quality, of your USC roommate. We both know how USC has a strong reputation, well deserved, for having good students who will become your friends for life. It was your poor luck and my poor judgment that got you into this predicament. As a Presidential scholar, you had the chance to stay in the dorm for Presidential scholars or select a regular, random dorm. Remember how you were hesitant, leaning toward a dorm with the regular students? But I encouraged the selection of the dorm for the Presidential scholars. Even though it was the smallest dorm on campus with just three floors, and even though it was the only dorm, I think, that did not offer air conditioning, I still thought it would be a good fit. Was I an idiot? You could make a good case for that conclusion.

My thinking? You would have a roommate who might be as studious and hardworking as you, making it an easier transition. I never thought you would have a paranoid roommate who would blanket the bedroom's door with Post-its that read, "Always lock the door whenever you leave." A closed, locked door to a room that was ninety-five degrees? On a campus known for its openness and friendliness? In a dorm filled with students who would be the least likely to break any rules? I could not imagine a safer place. However, from the first moment I met the girl, I felt your roommate was mentally unstable. There was no warmth in her handshake, no smile on her stone face, and there was an odd affect in our interaction. She reminded me of those patients on the inpatient psychiatric unit, already heavily dosed with antipsychotics. They could be smart. They could be talented. But something was missing, not likely to be repaired anytime soon. Do you remember my first comment on your roommate? I waited over twenty minutes before expressing my discomfort. How about you? Were you feeling uncomfortable in the first five minutes?

With such a roommate, I want to congratulate you on surviving that first meeting and the first several days. Yes, you have a small room with the bathroom far down the hall. That's acceptable. But a roommate who seems averse to opening the door for a cooling breeze, a roommate who seems to swallow up the entire room by placing her stuff everywhere, and a roommate who makes no attempt to be friendly or considerate? That was not acceptable. Worse, her behavior seems to border on paranoid, even locking you out of the bedroom in the middle of that first night when you headed to the bathroom but forget to lock the bedroom door? And then, as I understand it, she refused to let you back into the room when you returned from the bathroom, even with your repeated knocks on the bedroom door? To force you into awakening the hall monitor to reenter your own dorm room? Christ. You have suffered through a lot of trauma this past year, you have persevered through more life-threatening moments than most kids will ever face. And you are now presented with another emotional challenge? Wasn't almost dying in the Medical ICU enough? Wasn't having your teeth wired shut for eight weeks, eating only through a straw along your gums, and losing seventeen pounds—when you needed more weight, not less weight—more than enough? Wasn't going through three months of physical rehabilitation to reopen your jaws more than enough?

Before you become overwhelmed by the current challenge, I want to repeat the obvious. We are proud of your high-school record, proud of your acceptance into USC's Thornton School of Music, and proud of your merit-based Presidential scholarship, which has saved me half of your four-year tuition. We think you are amazing, just as we think Skyler is terrific. We have two great daughters, and I am not hesitant to broadcast that opinion. In fact, I am going to write an e-mail that will *never* be sent. How stupid is that? Again, it's like the above repetitive descriptions. They clear my soul. And, to further soothe my soul, this is the e-mail I would have loved to have written to USC, or at least to Gary Glaze, one of the judges for your USC vocal audition, telling him what I thought of you. I know you are going to view this letter as another sign of my insanity. But since the letter will never be mailed, you can't say I have totally lost it. At least not to the extent of your roommate. It's a father wanting to share his perspective of his daughter, especially since she has suffered through a long slate of undeserved misfortune. Dare to read it? Your choice! But here goes…

Dear Mr. Gary Glaze and the Thornton School of Music,

It's been several days since Austen finished her vocal audition for the USC Thornton School of Music. By the time you read this e-mail, I figure the assessments will have been made and a group of outstanding students will have been selected to the music program. Still, I thought I would take the long-shot chance and submit an e-mail with a father's perspective on Austen Courter, just in case she was still being considered for acceptance. If this e-mail is inappropriate or unacceptable, just hit delete. Since you have now met Austen through her recent vocal audition and short interview, my observations might bring a smile to your face.

With my elder daughter, Skyler, her high school requested a parent's perspective letter in the senior year, and that parent's perspective letter was mailed to the student's counselor, thus helping the counselor write her letter of recommendation. For Austen, at the Orange County High School of the Arts, there was never any request for parental feedback or parental perspective from her main counselor, so I never submitted a word in her support. They based their recommendation only on the superficial: her talent and her grades. You can relax. I am not one of those intrusive, hovering parents. As I sit here tonight, feeling there is nothing left to lose, I thought I would submit my perspective on Austen, just like I would have submitted it to the high-school counselor, if asked.

For my opening, I want to offer a disclaimer. I have no music talent, so this e-mail has nothing to do with her musical ability. It's more personal. However, I will attest that my observations are accurate and truthful. I graduated from Williams College in Williamstown, Massachusetts, and I am a physician, receiving my training in facilities ranging from New York to Los Angeles, including three years at the USC/LA County Medical Center. If nothing else, as a physician, I have learned the value of evaluating the whole person, not just the presenting, or most visible, features of a person such as his or her GPA or number of awards, academic or artistic. So, in that spirit, I am offering a description of the "whole person" of Austen and her personal qualities, which transcend the classroom and the stage.

If you want someone who is supportive to others, that person would be Austen. I will give you one example. When your wife held her masters class at OCHSA in the fall, the head of the program, Robin Follman, had five students who were scheduled to sing with Austen, listed as the back-up sixth singer, the last one if time permitted. Austen was placed at the bottom of the list because she was still receiving physical therapy on her jaw, trying to further open her jaw after surgery, and because she had just restarted vocal lessons after four months with no singing. On the day of your wife's visit, in the afternoon opera rehearsals, one student did not know her slate or the words to her song. Robin was furious. The girl was given a rebuke to correct those unacceptable mistakes, or she would be dropped from the evening master's class. For Austen, any setback to this student would have been to her advantage. She would have had the chance to move up the list, and she would have had the chance to sing for your wife, increasing her chances of admission to USC. Once that class ended, Austen went up to the girl and told her she would help her learn her lines after school, well before the evening master's class. Austen worked with the girl for several hours, first helping her learn the proper slate, and then helping her learn to sing the song a little better. The girl sang the song over and over again while Austen played the piano, helping her with tone and phrasing. Austen helped change a poor performance into a good performance. The result? At the evening master's class, the girl did fine, benefitting from Austen's tutelage, while Austen never received a chance to sing. That helpful, not selfish, behavior is typical of Austen.

If you want someone who is focused, hardworking, and self-disciplined, that person would be Austen. With our older daughter, Skyler, who took piano lessons from age five to age thirteen, we had to constantly remind her to practice. With Austen, who started piano lessons at age three years and nine months, and who is still taking weekly piano lessons, we have never had to remind her to practice. Well, maybe a half-dozen times in fifteen years. Try awakening, as a parent, at 6:00 a.m. to the sounds of your young daughter on the piano, already practicing. The same discipline applies to her school assignments. Skyler would often study until 2:00 or 3:00 a.m. before a big test. Austen could count the number of nights she has studied past 10:00 p.m. on one hand. She works at a steady pace, and she has never been forced to cram. With the opera conservatory program at OCHSA, that pattern was especially evident. If something was assigned for the spring, she had it memorized during the fall. Honestly, she is the most disciplined and best-prepared student you'll ever have in your program.

If you want someone who will learn quickly, that would be Austen. At OCHSA, Austen only had one chronic complaint. She was always confounded by how long it took others to learn their music. When my wife was at USC/LA County nursing school, the assistant dean gathered the new students on the first day of classes. He had everyone stand and say his or her first name and last name. Then for the next hour he proceeded to offer his assessment of what these young nursing students would need to master to become good nurses. Near the end of his lecture, he wanted to underscore the importance of memory. To highlight how much effort must be expended on developing this skill, he randomly pointed to my wife and asked her to go around the room, repeating as many names as she could remember from their initial introductions. Clearly, he was expecting her to remember but a couple of names. My wife named everyone's first name and last name, over forty students, without a single error. The assistant dean was so taken aback that he became almost speechless, abruptly dismissing the group. Austen has my wife's memory. That memory has helped simplify any academic challenge, but it has been, and will be, equally valuable in learning her music studies and any performances.

If you want someone who is a musician to her core, that person would be Austen. When we head to a movie and then return home, she will often go straight to the piano, replaying parts of the score by ear and by memory. At the piano, she has been composing songs since she was five years old. Her first song, "Wishing on a Rainbow," seemed melodic and beautiful. Right now, as I write these words, she has twenty-four recent original compositions (twenty-four sheets of lyrics and music) on the piano. They cover a wide range of her songs from pop to Broadway to classical tunes. I am not in a position to speak to their quality. But more importantly, I wanted to make one point. Any time there is a family setback, my dad's death or her older sister totaling our car, Austen goes right to the piano to play or compose. The same impulse was paramount when we brought Austen home from the Medical ICU after her jaw surgeries. Weak from a seventeen-pound weight loss and barely able to walk without support, she hobbled right to the piano and starting playing some of her own original songs. Music is her passion, and music seems to give her solace. I am certain that description does not qualify for Webster's definition of a musician, but it qualifies for mine.

Lastly, if you want someone who can handle obstacles and setbacks, that person would be Austen. She was born with strabismus (severely crossed eyes), and she had four eye surgeries from age eighteen months to six years. During the time of her eye surgeries and for several years after, she wore eye patches every other day for over eight years. As a child, she learned to live with physical setbacks, and she learned to live with stares, teasing, and bullying—well before bullying became a topic of conversation. When her eyes were successfully corrected (you would not notice anything at this point), she progressed from one challenge to the next. She started a ten-year course of braces. Actually, it was four courses of braces over ten years. She even had surgery during that period with the dental surgeon inserting screws in her maxillary bone to help draw back the lower teeth. Unfortunately, that approach did not prevent the need for further surgery to both her upper and lower jaws.

In June 2007, she had major jaw surgery; from June to August 2007, she had her teeth wired shut; and from September to December 2007, she had physical therapy to help open her mouth so she would be able to sing. Those experiences were not pleasant, but she triumphed with her usual stoic perseverance. If you need an example of how she handles the worst of setbacks, there was one day in the Medical ICU, after a second surgery for an abscess, where she was struggling to breathe through the constant bloody exudates and equally struggling through episodes of vomiting (try vomiting through wired teeth). The ICU nurse asked her if the staff could be put on any Disney movie on the TV, right above her ICU bed, to offer a diversion from her nausea and physical difficulties. In response, since she could not speak, she scribbled a note to the nurse, "Do you have the movie, **The Exorcist?**" The nurse did not laugh, but we did. Austen's humor, and her perseverance, always remained intact through that ordeal, even when she became toxic and started hallucinating from the strong combination of three antibiotics.

One final point. For the USC audition, Austen had probably received fewer singing lessons and less coaching in the past year than any of your applicants. Robin, Austen's *excellent coach, was available during the months when Austen's teeth were still wired shut, when she could not even open her mouth. Unfortunately, when Austen could finally start to practice after her stint in rehabilitation, Robin was unavailable, as she was performing professionally back east. Lastly, Robin was also not available for the first half of January, as she was performing out of the country, and Robin was not available for this past week, as she had a terminal illness in the family. We have only respect for her coach, but Austen was repeatedly short changed with almost no singing lessons for the past six months, the crucial period leading up to her college audition. But she practiced on her own for the last two months with no complaints about the lack of any guidance. If you want someone who will not complain, who will sing without offering any excuses, and who will find her own path toward preparation and success, that would be Austen.*

As you can see, like any father, I could write for pages and pages. But, thank God, I won't. This will be the one and only e-mail of this type. As someone who has played sports in high school and college, I will finish with a sports analogy. If Austen were on a college sports team, she might not be the first person selected for a scholarship. However, she would be the person who does the little things—on the field and off—that make the entire team better. I will close with the viewpoint that she will be one of those students who will make the program—and the other kids in the program—better. She will do that with leadership, by helping others when they struggle, and by example. In my experience in sports, that person is sometimes much harder to find than the apparent star, and that person is often much more valuable to the team.

Thanks for allowing me to share.
Bill Courter

Are you pleased I did not mail that letter? It still says what I would want to say today, if given the chance. We think you are fabulous, and we think they are lucky to have you in their program. I hope we can help you through this initial nightmare with your roommate, and I hope we can help you through these next four collegiate years. That contribution would keep us alive in this tomb of a home. This home misses Skyler and her lovable energy and enthusiasm, and this home misses you and your delightful humor and wondrous music. The above comments are huge understatements, as we love everything about each of you. You two make the Courter family. Over these next four years, we want our family to become better, even stronger. We miss you. We wish you the best. One last point. In a strange way, I think this negative experience with this roommate can make you stronger and make your college life even better. Isn't your favorite quote the Robert Frost line, "The best way out is always through"? Well, that is all that we can do. We can just work our way through this challenge.

Still, I realize, the quicker the solution, the better.

Dad

8/24/08 Another Parental Apology?

Dear Austen,

When Skyler was born, we brought her back to the hospital on the third day. That was, I am certain, a record for a healthy baby to return for emergency services. Poor girl was stuck with needles to draw blood, and we were directed to obtain a breast pump for Mom, as she was struggling producing milk. The problem was us, not Skyler. Now, on your fourth day at USC, we have dragged you back home for the first weekend. I wanted to apologize if my interference created more problems for you. Good intentions do not always lead to good results. But I want to share our bias. We felt you needed a safe break from the bizarre behavior of your roommate. We felt you needed a further break from the ninety-five degree temperature in your stuffy, always closed-door bedroom. We felt you needed a break from the three hours of interrupted sleep where you have had to carry your bedroom door keys to the down-the-hallway bathroom to make certain you could get back into your own sweaty, stuffy bedroom.

I know this is a nightmare. You are away from home, stuck with a paranoid roommate, and unable to extricate yourself from an untenable living situation. To be honest, I do not trust her. Paranoid people can snap at any time. I am not saying it is the girl's fault. Maybe she was sexually molested at a younger age. Maybe she has become hypersensitive and hypervigilant, suffering from posttraumatic stress disorder. Who knows? It is wrong for me to judge, as she may have triumphed over her own horrendous setbacks. Nevertheless, after this weekend, let's reevaluate our options. Let's see how the USC Thornton School of Music lives up to its tremendous reputation. Let's see if you have some exciting classes. Let's see if you have some inspiring teachers. Let's see if you meet interesting students—the typical USC students—who might become lifelong friends. As I now say to Skyler, it does not matter to me how you do in your classes. It does not matter to me whether you are the best or the worst student. I just want you to be happy with yourself, your personal development, and your path. That would be enough to sustain me. For you, that may require escaping from your roommate and the current prison of a bedroom. That's one of the challenges I want to discuss with you, especially the question of where you would like to live.

However, before we get to your options, here's a saying that will help you to not take things personally: A snake's bite doesn't kill you; it's the poison within the bite that can be lethal. That poison is hers, not yours. It's too easy to accept that poison, thinking it's yours. It's too easy to become the prey and let her be the predator. When away from her, try to forget her. Try to let go of her antics. Try to find some area of peace within you. Try to find some area of self-appreciation and self-love. Somehow, try to manufacture some inner vaccine against this person. Use her as a test. Over these next four years you need to become independent of the good opinion of others just as you need to become independent of the bad opinion—and horrific behavior—of others. If you can learn to rise above those things, you will find greater peace and a stronger sense of self. Of course, until then, let's get rid of this bitch. Did I just say that? See, I need to work on reducing my own judging and negativity. Those behaviors tend to clog the soul, which seems to have been trashed enough over this first week. Let's save the learning until later.

Fair enough?

Dad

08/27/08 OK, So How Do We Survive?

Dear Austen,

    It sounds as if your roommate is not getting any better. Has she been posting more and more notes on the walls to remind you to lock the door? Did she really lock you out once again, in the middle of the night, when you dared to go to the bathroom without your keys, leaving the door, God forbid, unlocked for five minutes? Is she not willing to talk to you or discuss the matter? Here are my thoughts. First, these first few days of college are like the ten days in the hospital's Medical ICU. This, too, shall pass. Second, I think we should cross our fingers and pray for your move to a new dorm. I will talk to administration today and ask for a room change. Let's discuss other options during this weekend, if you do not get that dorm change. Remember, until this issue is settled, you can come home every weekend to escape that roommate and the heat. Our happiness depends on your happiness. That is what happens to any caring parent. Worse, the mood of any parent is never any higher than the lowest mood of any of his or her children. We are feeling depressed and angry. We are a family. We are forever linked. Let's work together. Let's find a way out of this prison. Let's find a way to reject this poison. I look forward to seeing you on Friday. Until then, preferably stay away from your crazy roommate. Hide in the library, if necessary. Or perhaps study in the cafeteria where you can at least try some emotional eating.

    As Skyler will tell you, after hundreds of e-mails, I am nonstop in giving advice, even when I claim there will be no more advice. Right now we are miserable because you are miserable. We find ourselves constantly worrying, waking up for long stretches of the night, because you have received such misfortune. You do not deserve such bad luck. You are too good, too special, and too dear to our hearts. We are still optimistic that things will work out in the long run. In a school with two thousand students in the freshman class, and with USC's well-deserved reputation for creating a family feeling, there has to be a ton of good, social roommates. How about a girl who will not lock you out of your own bedroom in the middle of the night? How about a girl who will leave the bedroom door open for a breeze? How about a girl who will communicate without Post-its? Or how about a girl who will care for your well-being as much as she cares for her own? Until you find such a new roommate, bury this negative paranoid student in the nearest trash bin of your mind. You have my permission. I promise. If necessary, I will post the bail.

To get past the first hurdle, keep us apprised of how it goes with administration. After I spoke to them, they wanted to speak to you. But there is good news. With the right paperwork (I've already written a letter), they sounded receptive to a move to a new dorm. In my conversation, I was told it cannot occur until after the first two weeks unless the move is medically based. I think I convinced them, as a physician, of the medical urgency via your surgery, your ongoing rehabilitation, and your risk for upper respiratory infections, which would more likely occur in closed, dusty, hot quarters. After you receive a call, if administration agrees with our request, please let them know we would like to move you on Friday, and we will be there to help. Around 2:00 p.m.? Again, if administration agrees, you might want to ask if we can find a bin like we had on the first moving day. That initial move, well organized by USC, took only half the day. My hope for this next move? We could get your stuff transferred on Friday and head home for a weekend of relaxation before your new start in the new dorm. For the short weekend, we can take some decompression outings. A movie perhaps? Some good talks and good meals? In between, we can give you space to complete your homework. We will make it a relaxed but productive weekend.

Let's make this weekend a turning point for all of us.
Dad

8/29/08 Another Freshman Year Challenge?

Dear Austen,

From our last conversation I think the negative situation with your roommate has carried over into your initial assessment of yourself and your new classes. Moods are like that. They follow you everywhere. Do you really see yourself as having received insufficient music education at the Orange County High School of the Arts? Do you think you had too many singing performances and not enough teaching of music theory or aural skills? Do you see yourself as way behind your vocal peers? Even if true, I would not worry. You have always risen to the top. With your work ethic, after four years at USC, you will be ready to move into a career in music. You will find a spot that gives you satisfaction and joy. The Thornton School of Music is a top-ten music program. Any college program *that* good will not be easy. I want to tell you what I told Skyler. Allow yourself to focus on more than grades. Do not stress about your scholarship and any grade requirement. I couldn't care less if you keep the scholarship. I would have traded the full scholarship for a half-decent roommate. Focus on finding some good friends and improving your mood. Some parents seem to want to raise kids who are rich. I just want to raise kids who are happy. OK, so we have *not* gotten off to the best of starts for college.

I hear you have another challenge. All the other students in your vocal-related classes talk about opera as their chosen career, while you want to be more of a musician, not just a singer. After being isolated with a paranoid roommate, are you finding yourself isolated, and a bit different, from your fellow voice majors? And since clubs and social activities have not started, are you finding yourself isolated from the student body? Once again, it seems as if you are forced to walk your own path, distinct from your peers. We have one area of agreement. I have never visualized you, despite your beautiful voice, as developing a career as an opera singer. I can't see you going through life traveling the world and singing to 11:00 p.m. You may have the ability, but that lifestyle does not fit you or your natural style. You like to be at home. You like to get a decent, early-to-bed sleep. Truthfully, I can see you as a professional songwriter, not a professional singer. Or as a music teacher. You were always so good at helping other students learn their assignments, starting from grade school and lasting through high school. You even used to love playing teacher when you were a child. As for the possibilities of pursuing a songwriting career, I have always thought you were a wonderful composer, even as a child. In your current program, is there a way for you to follow those passions? You know me. I am a believer in following your natural gifts and your passions, not someone else's dictums. The choice is yours, not theirs. When have you sounded the most excited since your arrival at USC? For me, it is an easy answer. It was that night, right after your first songwriting class, when you called us to state you finally felt "at home"! That tells you something. Just persevere until you can clarify your class options, much like Skyler did in her first semester at NYU.

As I wrote the above paragraph, guess what? You sent the lyrics to your new song for your songwriting class. How long did it take you to write? The usual twenty to thirty minutes? I loved it. I thought the lyrics were heartfelt, original, and fresh. I thought your title, *Unravel*, fit the tone of these first few days of college. The lyrics ("Please tell me I'm not wrong… for choosing something out of line…for wanting something that's mine… for not always feeling fine") could not have described your plight any better. I am very proud of you for having the courage to play your song and share those feelings with your entire class of songwriters. It's so much easier to share an uplifting song than to share a setback. But expressing those feelings, instead of keeping them bottled inside, is crucial for feeling better. By the way, one of the highlights of my life, if I were standing in front of God and had to admit it, would be the privilege of listening to you as you compose your original songs. I consider that one of the unexpected honors of my parenthood. I admire you so much. I love you so much. Hang in there until the initial college dust settles.

I believe the view will be markedly different.

Dad

9/01/08 Finally, a New Dorm?

Dear Austen,

I awoke thinking about your approved move to the new dorm. Congratulations on escaping from your roommate. Getting out of a psychiatric unit is often not that easy. Embrace your new setting. Fluor Tower has to be much better than Marks Hall, and your current group of roommates seem far superior to your first roommate. For me, there has been an additional positive note. I have spoken to you more in the last two weeks, on issues of emotional substance, than all those days when I drove you to high school. Back then we just listened to pop music for the sixty-minute round trip while I offered a periodic opinion. Let's keep up our ongoing conversations about your challenges and your feelings—the good and the bad. As you recover from the creature from hell, I want to make one offer, which we could never extend to Skyler. If you ever need a break over this first semester, you are welcome to come home on any weekend, even if just for one night. Consider it your safe haven. It's something many college freshmen could use. Just remember Skyler's smile when she came home on that surprise weekend after her first six weeks at NYU. For you, we can't surprise Mom. However, we can still create a relaxing weekend for the three of us. That sounds pretty good to me.

In the meantime, as things slowly begin to stabilize, I hope you can find balance in the coming weeks. Friends are a great starting point, and it sounds as if you might be able to develop some friendships with your new roommates and with several of your vocal classmates. You know my perspective. As you meet more and more fellow students, don't change who you are. You are too special. So what if you are one of the few students who does not drink alcohol? So what if you are one of the few students who turns down marijuana at the dorm's party? You could offer an excuse. You are a singer and you cannot drink or smoke because of potential damage to your vocal cords. But I know you. You will not offer any excuse. You will probably just say no to alcohol and drugs without offering an explanation. I respect you for that commitment to your values. But on the flip side, if someone else drinks and uses drugs (hey, Skyler drinks, but I do not think she uses drugs), just tolerate them and refrain from judgment. As stated, judgment kills the soul, regardless of whether it's self-criticism or criticism of others. Plus, the soul is the foundation of your music. Oh well, like most parents, I need to curtail my suggestions. After all, I have found myself in that same college predicament, and I was not as successful. I inhaled. I criticized. In closing, I am proud of you for surviving the initial setbacks of your college experience and for sticking to your high standards.

As for the coming days? College life will get better.

Dad

9/26/08 Forget Grades in College? You Beat Me To It!

Dear Austen,

Now that you have settled into a routine and regained your balance, I was going to address grades with you, much in the style that I addressed grades with Skyler. However, in our recent phone call, you beat me to it. I loved your comment about how you were not going to focus on grades, and how you were *not* even going to look up your grades online for any of your classes. Not this year. Not any year. Instead, you were going to focus solely on learning. That approach, so rare in our society's competitive educational environment, sounds refreshing. May I add a perspective for learning? Learn to love the plateau. In any learning situation, you may learn some knowledge in a linear manner, class after class, but you gain skills in a pattern of waves and troughs, not in any straight-line progression. The same perspective applies to any type of self-improvement. There are times you make progress. There are times you backslide. Be patient with yourself. Embrace the slow development. Embrace the plateaus. They come with all pursuits, but especially with something like singing or songwriting. Appreciate the pace of your progress, even if it varies more than you would like. For me, I love the concept of "the speed of going slow." I am not certain what that phrase really means. But from my perspective, going slow is more than acceptable.

I applaud your change in focus. Your perspective fits my view of the educational purpose of college. For me, the game has changed. High school forces you to be good in every course. In life, you can't be good in everything. No one, not even a genius, is good at everything. You just want to be good in something that matters to you, and that is reflective of your gift. Therefore, there is no need to focus on grades. I think college students are far better served by narrowing their focus to learning the areas that are associated with their passions. I know I am late to this viewpoint, but I have learned from my talks with Skyler. You know me. I am a great believer in having specific goals. But grades should not be the goal. The goal should be broader and bigger. For you, perhaps it's the goal of becoming a better musician? Or do you maybe want to aim at something more specific? If you are going to focus on becoming a better musician, do you want to improve in all areas? Or do you want to work especially hard to develop specific skills? The skills of teaching must be different from the skills of performing. I do not know the keys for your field. So, guess what? I am going to leave you alone as you focus on learning what you want to know, not just what the teacher wants you to know.

I will leave you with this thought, which matches your perspective on grades. Did it really matter what John Mayer received in music theory class? Did it really matter what Imogen Heap achieved in aural skills class? No. What matters is that you learn what you want to learn. What matters over time is how you find, develop, refine, and then share your gift in the future. In that framework, what counts is not how good you are today; what counts is how good you will be tomorrow. What matters even more is how much you are enjoying the process as you learn these skills. I think one of the dividends of shifting your focus from grades to learning is that it also shifts your focus toward yourself, not others. One of the things I admire about musicians and artists is that they really do not have to compete with one another. Any competition with others is a personal flaw, reflective of their character, not their craft. People should just focus on their own personal development and growth. They should focus on being themselves with their own style. Ah, if I had only understood this truth when I was younger, I would have been a far better person, a far better friend, and even a better student. Who knew it would take me so long to learn this secret? But it is never too late for a parent, right?

With that confession, let me share an observation. Of all the classes that I took in high school and college, the one course I needed most was the one course that was never taught. I needed a "Textbook of Life" course, or some course that addressed the habits of the most successful and happy people. My suggestions in my e-mails to you and Skyler were unknown to me during those crucial years. I was never taught any of this material. I picked it up slowly through my own independent reading. I picked it up slowly by watching those people who did well and those people who seemed to hit so many setbacks. Over time, I realized what was missing in so many of those people. Over time, I realized what was missing in me.

It was not intelligence. It was not lack of effort. I was, and have always been, a grind, both as a student and as a worker. However, I was often off target, focused on the wrong things, learning the wrong things. I went for the superficial—the grades and the income—not for the personal growth, which would have made such a difference in the quality of my life. Maybe that is another reason why I am sharing so much. I do not want you to make the same mistakes.

So, good luck with your new approach. I am not a Woody Allen fanatic, but I have always appreciated how he eschewed award shows because he was opposed to artistic competition. Be yourself, young woman, be yourself. As I repeatedly say to Skyler, and it applies equally well to you: be safe; be good; be you. Especially the last part—be you! That is all anyone can ask or want. As long as you make progress toward that goal, there will be happiness in the pursuit. From my experience, happiness comes from getting better at something you love. Too many students are anxious and depressed because they are not following their passions. They are not getting better at something they love. Instead, they are getting better at something that does not qualify as a real passion. They are listening to their parents or their peers, telling them which courses will lead to the best future. If anyone thinks he knows what's best for you, he is wrong. Following others' suggestions often leads to stagnation and emotional deadness. Thank God you have already mapped out an approach to move away from that common mistake. You, young lady, are heading toward happiness, not superficial success.

You are making some smart decisions.

Dad

10/02/08 Career Choices? So Soon?

Dear Austen,

    You have reached close to the halfway point for your first semester at USC and several things stand out to me. Of course, I am repeating them for my benefit. First, you got off to a rough start because of your paranoid roommate, a situation that you were able to overcome. Second, you learned you were way behind some of your classmates in your level of formal music education. At OCHSA, you were constantly performing in personal homes, museums, conventions, and even in embassy celebrations. You were constantly performing in gala festivities and in the seasons' final performing arts performances. Those events were supposed to be for the seniors, but you seemed to perform every year from ninth through twelfth grade. Great experiences, but were they teaching you aural skills? Expanding your knowledge of music theory? No, but once again, you have survived this first semester, slowly catching up to your peers both academically and socially. Better yet, you seem to be hitting your stride thanks to your usual hard work, your disciplined approach, and your natural talent.

    At this halfway point, I think you should congratulate yourself and acknowledge your intelligence and talent—at least acknowledging it to yourself. No one needs to boast, but you need to appreciate yourself and respect all of your successful efforts. How can I tell you are doing well? By your stories of how you are helping other students with their assignments. Typical you. Mom and I congratulate you on your ability to shift your focus from yourself to others, and we congratulate you on your personal growth in all areas. If I understood our telephone chat, you will be singing another one of your original songs this week to the songwriting class. It must be a dramatic switch from singing a classical opera song for thousands in high school to singing your own personal, original pop song for your fellow college students. I suspect the latter is much more stressful. I have developed the habit, whenever I listen to a college musical performance, to ask the performer if he or she also composes music. I have been shocked at how so many of your fellow musicians can perform so well but cannot create. Composing songs, versus just performing songs, has to be much harder than people realize. You have our respect.

Your upcoming performance this week raises three questions. How much do you want to compose? How much do you want to sing your own songs? How much do you want to have others sing your songs? It also raises the question of which you prefer—writing songs or teaching others? Even over this first half of the first semester, Mom and I have realized how much time you spend helping other students, just like you did in high school. Even on subjects where you feel you were undereducated in high school. Which of those options do you prefer? Over the next four years, it will be interesting to watch you assess your own gifts and your own passions. As always, we encourage you to dream and follow your heart. Time after time you seem to face an unanticipated obstacle or hurdle, and time after time you manage to blow right through that challenge to a new height. The music gods seem to come to your rescue. My message tonight? Realize how far you have come in just the first half of this semester. Believe in yourself and your future. Maintain your own vision. Don't listen to naysayers. Find a place where you can feel you are contributing, giving to others.

Those are actions we should all follow.

Dad

10/05/08 How Do I Become a Better Parent?

Dear Austen,

    There are times when I ask myself, especially late at night when I am tired and climbing into bed, what can I do to be a better parent? I have tried to encourage you and Skyler to dream big. I have tried to encourage you to go after those dreams, regardless of society's expectations. I have tried to encourage a belief in yourself with reduced negative self-talk. I hate any negative self-talk. The world already puts you down. Why join its forces and put yourself down, too? I believe in judging yourself with kindness, not too harshly. I believe in *not* comparing yourself to others. Winning or succeeding should be secondary to the journey. At the same time, I try to preach how you should never lower your own standards. Never accept someone else's standards. Why do I keep mentioning these perspectives? Because at my age there are times when I feel as if I am struggling with some of these same issues. I work much too hard. I focus on my income far too much. I get frustrated when I have limited time for my own passions. If I am struggling with these issues at my age, then these challenges must constitute a lifelong battle. After eighteen years of living with me, don't hesitate to give me some coaching on how I can better help you through these years of college, through the challenges, and through the transition into adulthood.

    Want to know another lifelong battle? Well, not lifelong, but just these past five years. It's all those Saturday-morning visits to my parents' house and my current visits to my mom's house since my dad's death. I have tried to vent to Skyler, as you have enough on your plate. However, I must report that each visit is the same. It is like opening up a faucet with no ability to shut off the flow of water, although the flow is words, not water. Those words are negative, not positive. One complaint after another. One criticism after another. Does she ask about Skyler and you? Does she ever offer any assistance? No. When I leave after each visit, I am always relieved, finally feeling free from her self-preoccupation. She is a person who has never asked how she could be a better parent. That thought has probably never entered her mind. Maybe that's equally true for most parents of college students. How many of them have asked themselves what they could do to be of greater service to the ones they love?

Maybe that should be an assignment for all freshmen as they enter college. When they hit college, there should be a questionnaire entitled "How can your parents be better parents?" That questionnaire should be mailed back to each parent. It would not have to be specific or individualized. The college could collate the answers to the questionnaire and provide copies of the responses to all parents with students in the freshman year. It's way too late for my mother, as she is too self-obsessed to ever change, but it's not too late for the majority of parents. Even if most parents never ask, I think many would admit to needing some advice and some pointers. Most of us are ready for any suggestions. We just don't have the answers. Do you?

Just follow Skyler's lead for feedback. I promise I will listen.

Dad

10/29/08 A Father Alert: Wisdom Attacks?

Dear Austen,

    I do not have Mom's endearing love attacks, but I do love you dearly, and I think of you all the time. Better yet, I do get wisdom attacks, which I hope will slowly seep into your consciousness, as I think they are keys to life. So, here are two wisdom attacks. I know my sports metaphors do not strike much of a chord with you. But just think about it. The football player with the most touchdown passes in history is the same player with the most interceptions. The baseball player with the most home runs in history is the same player with the most strikeouts. What is the common denominator? Successful people are not afraid to fail. They know failure is part of the learning process. The more you are scared of failure, the less you will learn and the less you will succeed. That girl in your vocal classes who has a meltdown with each mistake? I do not care if she is the most talented person you have ever met. Or if she comes from a famous family with multiple Academy Awards. With that attitude, she will not be able to maintain her level of happiness, regardless of her level of success. Happiness, even more than success, depends on attitude, not aptitude. Be kind to yourself. Tolerate mistakes. Learn from them. Grow with them. That is how you become better at what you do, and that is how you become a better person. Which is more important? Becoming a better musician? Or becoming a better person? For happiness, you need to become a better person. Success? Let it follow, not lead, your pursuit of happiness.

    I know it's early in your college career, and I know we have already discussed it. But how do you choose your future career path? I think the answer lies outside of the classroom more than it lies within the classroom. When you are outside of class and not working on a specific academic assignment, to where does your mind drift? What things do you think about? Or dream about? Are those daydreams reflective of your chosen field? Whom do you admire the most? Are those people reflective of your field? Who would you most like to be? Is that person in your field? If you can answer yes to those questions, then that is the field that draws you forward. Is it what you are studying? If not, change your classes and major. My opinion, which I have shared with Skyler, is that if you let it, the path will choose you. How can you facilitate that development? By talking to people you respect, sharing your own observations about yourself, letting them know where your dreams seem to lie, and then asking for their advice and counsel. You are at one of the best music schools in the world. You are surrounded by talented musicians, varied backgrounds, and different perspectives. I would not pass up the chance to absorb those perspectives. Their views may not match your own. You may not even agree with their opinions. But those discussions with cohorts and friends, as opposed to a classroom lecture, may help clarify your own vision of your future. Too many students attend class after class but fail to ask the right questions. The questions that extend beyond the assigned material. They fail to ask for guidance. I would not pass up any opportunities for outside interactions. Life is there for the taking. You just have to take those first steps outside, not inside, the college classroom.

Enough wisdom attacks for one day?

Dad

11/02/08 No Wild Parties? No Drunken Blackouts?

Dear Austen,

    I just want to say how proud I am of you and how you make so many sacrifices for your goals. You have not gone the way of so many freshmen, drinking themselves into a stupor on a weekly basis. I do not think many of your peers would have given up a set of weekend parties to attend classes nonstop for a Saturday and Sunday. We were impressed you attended a music industry conference, separate from USC. That takes discipline to add work to an already heavy schedule. From my perspective, it does not matter if the weekend conference takes time away from study or reduces a grade. It only matters if the conference helps you clarify future options in the music world. What matters is you put forth the effort, looking at the larger picture, outside the classroom and beyond the college. Tell me, do any of your classmates make an effort to attend outside events? Or are they too focused on their classes? Or too focused on their parties? In my opinion, those two groups of students fall short of reaching their potential. The real winner is someone like you who maintains a focus on the larger long-term picture. As I constantly repeat, nothing is more important than clarifying your gift, your passions, and your future career path. I applaud your efforts outside of the classroom.

    My only wish? That you accept an occasional reward. You deserve a new keyboard, which we would like to buy for you, for all of your hard work in high school, for your Presidential scholarship, and for all of your continued efforts in college—and, to be truthful, for persevering over some pretty strong setbacks in childhood, at OCHSA, and at the start of this freshman year. You tend to underestimate yourself and the value of your efforts. The world will never value you more than you value yourself. Besides, I enjoy being able to give something to you, especially when it may help you along your music path. I am excited about your soon-to-arrive guitar. You deserve both the guitar and the keyboard. Although they are rare gifts for someone in the opera program. As I understand it, many of your cohorts can sing at the professional level, but they cannot play the piano or the guitar with any proficiency. So strange to me. Please accept the gifts and make the most of the presents by improving your skills. Isn't that really the key—learning new skills and expanding your professional toolbox? Again, I think too many students rush from class to class, completing the regular assignments, without making an effort outside of the classroom to develop additional, but valuable, insight and skills.

I know finances are important to everyone. Maybe it's a reflection of our difficult and challenging economic times. If you talk to Skyler, she may share an example. The father of one of her friends declared bankruptcy. Her friend may not be able to afford the tuition. She may or may not have to drop out with just one semester of college left. For her, it may mean a sudden change in the course of her life. Sad. But here is the point. Life can change in a heartbeat. While you have the opportunity, make the most of it. That is one of the many reasons I am so proud of you. Repeatedly, you make the most of your situation, persevering against the odds. So, more than accepting the new guitar and new keyboard, please accept our pride in you and our respect for you. We think you are something really special and growing more special with each year.

Keep focusing on what truly counts. Value, not price.
Dad

11/19/08 Time to Blow Up Your Balloon?

Dear Austen,

 I know it bothers you when you are overlooked by your suite mates for a planned activity. Some of it is bound to occur when you forsake a weekend party to attend an off-campus, non-USC music industry conference. It falls into the category of a sacrifice, which many students do not want to make. I feel sorry for your subsequent distance from your suite mates. Still, we have to admit there is another issue at hand. I have gone through much of my life, like you, pretty quiet and rather shy. I recall how, in college, the soccer coach once described me, when highlighting my contribution at the end of the season, as "the quiet and silent force" on the team. He meant it as a compliment, but it reflected a shortcoming in my character. There is a downside for people like you and me for being so quiet and shy. Mom is the same. We three are like small balloons with little visibility. Skyler is just the opposite. Her balloon is blown up to the maximum capacity, so everyone seems to know her. Our personal challenge? How much do we want to blow up our balloon, and how much are we willing to share in order to become more visible? To be socially successful, I think you have to blow up that balloon.

 When I think back to your experience at OCHSA, I ask myself how many of those high-school students knew the extent of your interests and talent. Did any of them hear your original songs? Not one. I remember once how one high-school student played his own new song over and over again to impress his classmates. You offered positive encouragement, but you never said a word about your own original songs. Let me ask you this: How many of your suite mates know you are more than an opera singer? How many of them know you play the piano, rock the guitar, and have written dozens of original songs? Probably none. How much of yourself you share is a challenge to everyone. For some, it results in bragging. So how do you share more of yourself without bragging, especially in the freshman year of college when fellow students are trying to get to know you? Maybe that's why so many freshmen get drunk? They can drop their inhibitions and share more of themselves? That makes it especially difficult for someone who does not drink. Still, haven't you observed that you do not need liquid courage for witty commentary? How about utilizing some of your liquid courage to share more of yourself? Good luck in expanding your balloon. It just makes friendships so much easier to establish. And God knows how much we need that friendship.

For Mom and me, we feel very lucky to have you as our daughter, and we feel very blessed to know such a wonderful, talented, smart person. We hope some of the students get to know you half as well as we do. I was lucky finding Mom. I was lucky because quiet, shy people are the most difficult to know, the easiest to overlook, and the hardest to find. It's the diamond-in-the-rough metaphor. But that diamond can be there for a long, long time. Again, I am sorry you are overlooked for some planned outings and left on your own. Just realize that some of it is a choice, and some of it is the skill set. I think you, as a child with four eye surgeries and daily eye patches, developed a style of being as invisible as possible. That pattern spared you some, but not all, bullying as a child, but it does not work as well as an adult, especially when you are trying to connect with others. Especially when friendship is so crucial for happiness. For someone so special, you deserve to develop great friends. I hope you find a couple lifelong friends through your USC journey.

Do you remember how I met your Mom? As a medical intern, I was signing the death certificate of one of my patients. OK, I admit it, as a medical intern, a number of my patients died. It happens, OK? Exhausted, I joked to the petite Medical ICU nurse, "You know, next to the corpse, you look pretty good." At that hour, around 3:00 a.m., she was equally tired, probably could not see me that well in the dim light, and she accepted my impulsive invitation for a date. Would either one of us have acted the same if it had been 3:00 p.m. versus 3:00 a.m.? Probably not. We would have been more controlled and more inhibited. So, we all need a little luck with our timing. For us, our life course changed in those five minutes while I was completing the death certificate. I never dated another woman. Your life course could change at any time. I am not just referring to a romance. I am referring to any interaction that leads to a new opportunity. Good luck in keeping your eyes open. Good luck in expanding the balloon. Good luck in taking advantage of those unanticipated moments. Those unexpected friendships that grow into something so much more. May some of those moments come your way.

Another challenge for college, yes?

Dad

11/30/08 Thanksgiving Slumber?

Dear Austen,

Thanks for making our Thanksgiving such a great respite. It was wonderful to have you and Skyler back home. Sorry for my mom's criticisms during the Thanksgiving meal: how the turkey should have been moister, how the gravy should have been thicker, and how you two should have been fined for every table manner transgression, such as resting your forearm on the tablecloth. I could add more of her comments to the list, but why bother? Besides, unlike my mother, I believe that criticism backfires. I believe it is like a virus in a computer. Nothing gets better. Things only grow worse. So Christmas should be a blast for the four of us, with only a short visit to my mother's house to open a couple of presents. In the meantime, I will hold any further comments except one final confession. I can spend an hour with almost anyone, even the devil. But a full day with my mother? That is a challenge. If you locked me in a room alone with my mother for eternity, and I had to listen to all of that negative chatter and all of her focus on the superficial, it would be enough to make me consider suicide. Of course, she might feel the same about me and my constant focus on the importance of character and personal growth. Regardless, you deserve credit for withstanding the usual onslaught and saying nothing in return. Unless, of course, you were deep in slumber?

Now, do you know what I much prefer to discuss with you? At this point, you have made it through most of the first semester, which should be the hardest one. At this point you have made it through the hardest transition. Good luck with your remaining classes. Good luck at the next meeting with your adviser and with clarification of your classes for next semester. I would keep trying to take the courses that match your passion, not the required courses. On the other hand, I have one question: Is there any chance you will want to attend graduate school? If there is any chance, ask the counselor for any suggestions for the best academic approach toward your passion. Sometimes, to find your passion you may have to explore courses that seem off target from the prescribed path. Whatever you decide for future courses, we support it. Make the decision that feels right to you. What counts, as strange as it sounds, is not your ability to make the right decision; it's your ability to make the decision right for you. Apparently, studies show that 75 percent of all decisions are wrong, but successful people manage to make those mistakes work for them. Good luck in making your decisions lead to the right pathway for your happiness. While you are at it, rest those forearms on the table and just munch away, deep in thought. We think the posture suits you just fine!

You will receive no criticisms from us.

Dad

12/08/08 A Transfer of Majors? Taking Action?

Dear Austen,

    I just wanted to congratulate you on your decision to transfer from bachelor of music to bachelor of arts in music. When I look at college students, how many students stick with their initial plans or their initial majors? I think the students who are the happiest are the ones who change course. For me, that means they are exploring new options, new passions, and new career paths. From my perspective, I see you as happiest when you are playing music, not just singing some opera piece. I remember the joy you experienced in the recording studio when you had to submit a series of songs for your acceptance at the performing arts high school. I also see you as happiest when you are helping others. I remember your satisfaction, even during this first semester, when you helped other students pass a difficult music exam. Pay attention to your own sources of happiness, and try to not let other forces distract you from these sources. On that note, I know how much you like your opera singing coach, Gary Glaze, so I applaud you for addressing the change directly with him and seeking his opinion. Your change of plans could have been received with disapproval and disappointment. I smile at your courage. I also smile at his response. The best professors? They are the ones who support your vision, not their own vision. Professors and parents are not so different. Thanks for sharing the news, and thanks for sharing Gary Glaze's e-mail response to your official notification of changing your major and adding a minor.

Dear Austen,

    Thanks for talking to me now about this. I did not know you were planning on a minor in songwriting. That is an exciting endeavor. Even though you are moving to the BA in music, you will be able to continue studying singing with me. Just this year our Dean has encouraged the major teachers to teach the most promising singers in our BA program—of which you are one! I would, of course, expect that you will be able to attend the Vocal Forums on Friday. We all realize that our BM in vocal performance allows very little room for other courses, but it is a standard voice format that all other universities also follow: Song Lit, Vocal Ped, Diction, Foreign Languages, Stage Training, etc.

It is to prepare people for a career in performance. I think you have the talent to pursue that kind of career track, so we will figure out a way to keep you up to speed in these areas as much as time allows. You have a wonderful vocal talent, and I would not like you to think of it as a secondary area. I look forward to continuing our work together. You have made such outstanding progress in just one semester.

All best wishes for a Happy Holiday!
Gary

Again, thanks for sharing your changes of majors and the department's reaction. It's one of those time-honored college challenges that happens to so many college students. To change majors while still receiving full support—that is quite an accomplishment.

I can't wait for the next semester. It will be so different.
Dad

1/13/09 Kudos to Your Own Academic Style

Dear Austen,

First, I want to thank you for making our Christmas so special and so enjoyable. I loved having you home, and I loved hearing tonight about your return today to USC. As I understood our conversation, on your return to this second semester, your counselor congratulated you on your grades, and you interrupted her, explaining you would prefer to *not* know your grades. She acquiesced, replying that you were doing fine, while addressing the options for new courses. I thought it was a cool interaction, and I thought it was great that you could still take most of the same classes, plus continue to take songwriting and any other music classes for all eight semesters. You only miss those additional language courses and those courses in stage training, but since you have already taken Spanish, Italian, and French in high school, and since you have already been in so many stage productions, how much are you missing? More importantly, it looks as if you are free to follow your passions, focusing on learning what you want to learn. You have developed your own academic style. I wish more students followed your lead. Too many of them are so grade focused, believing their grades will determine the quality of their careers. They do not know how much they are off target.

Second, we want to thank you for sharing so much about your first semester and the start of your second semester. I suspect a lot of students do not share much with their parents, especially the amount of alcohol and drug use. I laughed at your comment that you could probably purchase any drug I might want within fifteen minutes. Were you surprised I turned down the offer? But I was more impressed with your ability to go against the grain, not drinking alcohol, not smoking marijuana, and not using any drugs. I also loved your willingness to help your roommates, including driving one roommate to the emergency room when that person was hung over from partying and dizzy from some drug. It's one thing to go on your own path; it's another to be tolerant of others. Helping others seems to be wired into your DNA, but it carries a downside: it interrupts so much of your valuable time. Still, we are proud of how you are maturing in college, even after one semester, and we are proud of how you are fighting for your individuality, going against the peer pressure. I think that bodes well for your future. For me, conformity leads to competence. Individuality leads to brilliance. In you, I see future brilliance, even if it comes with a price of some initial personal isolation and a lack of camaraderie with some of your drug-crazed suite mates.

Best of luck for sticking to your own style.
Dad

1/25/09 Your Second Semester? Already?

Dear Austen,

For your first semester, I want to thank you for coming home on some weekends. For us, it was a special treat, one we could never enjoy with Skyler. For this second semester, stay on campus on the weekends when there is something that attracts your interest, like a USC football game (it was great to have student season tickets, yes?), a musical performance, or some theatrical performance by one of the upperclassmen. But, if there is nothing but parties and drinking, then come home on some periodic Saturdays for some of Mom's cooking, perhaps a movie, and a good night's sleep in your own bed. For us, there has been an additional benefit. It has been fun to sit in the family room, listening to you write a song for your songwriting class, camped at the living room piano or curled with your guitar on the living room sofa. I am surprised how quickly you create some melody and how quickly you scribble lyrics on the sheet of paper beside the piano or the guitar. When I was younger and listening to a new Lennon and McCartney song, I would wonder how they came up with the melody and lyrics. With you at home some periodic weekends, I have seen how the process works. For us, USC has worked out just great. For parents, when your son or daughter selects a local college, those weekends are unexpected treats.

At this point, let's just improvise a week at a time. Still, I noticed on the calendar that we are approaching a three-day weekend in mid-February. I'm curious. How many of your suite mates go home for the long holiday weekend? How many stay each and every weekend like Skyler did at NYU? For us, three-day weekends are great. On some regular weekend, you might arrive home, unpack, have a night or two with us, repack, and then drive back to school on Sunday. A three-day weekend allows for three nights, especially if you can slip away from school a little early on Friday, perhaps after your afternoon vocal forum. Is the time coming up for your own singing performance? I congratulate you for jumping back and forth between singing in your classical operatic voice for classical lessons and vocal forums, and then singing in your pop voice for songwriting classes.

That cannot be an easy vocal transition. But what do I know? Like most students, you have moved well beyond our areas of expertise. I can help you if a roommate gets sick, but I can't help you with any of your academics. I have heard that scientific knowledge doubles every few years. I do not know if that is true, but your knowledge in music exceeded mine before you were a freshman in high school, let alone a freshman in college. All parents hit their own academic limits. I guess you are on your own. Welcome to adulthood.

However, there is always our support in the rearview mirror.
Dad

3/01/09 Waking Up with a Couple in the Next Bed?

Dear Austen,

    We were delighted to have lunch with you. That is the other difference between your attending USC and Skyler attending NYU. With you, we get those periodic weekend visits at home, like our three-day February weekend, but we also get the chance to drive up to Los Angeles on a Saturday to take you out to lunch at some local restaurant. Those interactions give us a much clearer picture of your daily life at USC. With Skyler, despite our good communication, we were often left guessing at her daily activities. With you, we have a much clearer picture of your activities. It's educational for us when you discuss some of the classes and the homework, explaining how your music classes expand your musical knowledge. It's also educational, although a different type of education, when you share some of the wild nights of your roommates. I suspect USC is no different than any other college. Do I like the visual image of your roommate bringing a boy back to her bed while you are sleeping in the other bed? Do I like the visual image of your waking up to see the two of them cuddled in the next bed? No. But it makes me think back to my college years. I never had to go through that experience, but college was the first time I saw people drunk and stoned. There is not much you can do. Clean up the mess? Get out of the room early, so you can avoid the pleasantries? Personally, I think you have taken the right approach. You seem to be ignoring their behavior and focusing just on your behavior.

    Hurray for March and your upcoming ten days for spring break. That's one of the surprises of college: your college school year seems much shorter than your high-school year, and your college breaks—Christmas and spring—seem much longer than your high-school breaks. No complaints. We will enjoy having you home. If you want to plan some activities with classmates, go right ahead. If you want time with us, I will take a few days off from work. How about a morning at Disneyland? What if we get to Disneyland just as it opens, catch a half-dozen rides before the crowds, and eat lunch on Downtown Disney before heading home (which leaves me time for exercise). Which reminds me that I wanted to applaud your visits to the gym. Now that's something new since high school. Whenever we arrive at USC and head to your dorm, we survey hundreds of bikes parked around the massive, high-tech gym. Maybe for every bad behavior, some of those students are developing a good behavior. Regular exercise at the gym is a great habit to develop for life. Good luck with your own transition to regular exercise. During spring break, you can use our treadmill or perhaps walk around the lake. I don't remember that level of activity during high school.

Three cheers for some new college habits.
Dad

03/04/09 Honor Roll? Who Cares?

Dear Austen,

    Thank you for forwarding the USC letter inviting you to attend your induction into their honor-roll society. I know you well enough to know you will not plan to attend. I guess administration must feel compelled to reward all students with a high GPA. Which makes me pause and reflect. Wow, have I changed between high school and college, both for Skyler and now for you. Both of you are obviously doing well academically, but I have learned from each of you the benefits of moving away from a narrow focus on grades. For Skyler, it has been a shift in focus to more extracurricular activities, learning outside the classroom. For you, it has been more of a shift in focus to learning all aspects of music and improving your craft, pushing aside any particular focus on any one course. I wonder how many students make those shifts versus how many remain preoccupied with just their classes and their grades. I also wonder how many parents make that shift. Or do some parents still push grades all the way through college? There are many studies comparing the level of happiness in one country versus another country. The United States does not do very well in those comparisons. As a collective group, we are not nearly as happy as citizens of other countries, and we seem to work longer hours for most of our lives. Is that a reflection of our prolonged focus on grades? Or our extended focus on competition, inside and outside the classroom? Or is it a reflection of our societal desire for more possessions? I am proud you two girls have broken free of those financial concerns. I am proud you two girls have discovered a better path.

    I am also proud of both of you for making the sacrifices that come when you select a different path. You are taking a different route with your voice and songwriting than all of your fellow voice majors. In your classical voice classes, there is not another songwriter, and in your songwriting classes, there is not another classically trained singer. Personally, I think you are really cool, but what I think is irrelevant. I can applaud your sticking to your own academic path; I can applaud your sticking to your personal choice to stay away from alcohol, drugs, and the "hookup" scene;

and I can applaud your keeping your own high values, not lowering your standards just to date someone. But that does not change the subsequent isolation. You do not harp on your isolation, but I know you must be left behind in the dorm room on Saturday nights when everyone else is getting wasted. That cannot be much fun. Can I offer you any hope for a better life? For more enjoyable Saturday nights in your future?

I could use the example of Mom and me. We are scheduled to attend an upcoming ocean memorial and subsequent reception for a friend who has died. To be honest, Mom and I will feel as though we do not belong with that crowd. Our paths have crossed through the years with many of the people who will attend, but we have never partied with those people. Why? Because we felt so different from them. They wanted to drink and party. We preferred to be by ourselves on a date night for a quiet dinner or movie. My reflection at this age? It may not be easy being different, but it is the right course, and the right long-term course, if that fits your character. As I have shared, you just need some luck at some point. You need some close friendships. You need to find someone who likes your different style. You need to find someone with the same preferences. Stick to being different. Do not change. You will attract the right person just like Mom attracted me, and, thank God, I attracted Mom. It may not happen as quickly as all of those hookups, but it is well worth the wait. The relationship is infinitely better, more fulfilling. So, suffer through some boring Saturday nights. Your future will be much, much better.

That's a promise.
Dad

3/29/15 Dreaming about Summer?

Dear Austen,

As you head to the home stretch, I wanted to address our upcoming summer with our family trip to Europe, arranged by Skyler. What are you going to do for those six or eight weeks before we fly to Madrid? When I think of my own summers in college, my best choice was to dedicate one summer to writing. That partially completed novella helped me create my own independent writing course at Williams. For Skyler, I think one of her best summers—although I know she would strongly disagree—occurred when she wrote her own novel, *Knightfall*. I offer that opinion not because it sold many copies, but because it further developed her writing skills. The better you write, the clearer you think. Or so I was taught. For you, I would encourage you to avoid the pull of money and a nonskilled job for that initial month of summer. Too many people go down the wrong path with the pursuit of extra money. I recommend you devote the first free month, the last part of May and all of June, to enriching your music skills. What specific skills? It does not matter. The goal is personal improvement, not extra cash. For this summer you have something that you will not always have—free time. Use it wisely. Invest in yourself. Invest in developing your skills. Trust me; it will be the best investment you could make. Then, while feeling good about yourself, you can celebrate July with the family trip through Europe.

I also have another suggestion. I know, I know. I am like the pain-medication-addicted father who reaches for another pill, promising it will be his last. No, this suggestion will not be my last. Do you know the story of the Chinese bamboo tree? Even when it is well tended by the farmer, in the first year, there is no growth. In the second year, there is no growth. In the third year, there is no growth. In the fourth year, there is no growth. In the fifth year, there is, again, no growth. But during the sixth year, there is a short period where the tree grows eighty feet in just six weeks. Now, I am not saying that all of my suggestions will take six years. However, I am repeating my admonition to remain patient and steady, sailing against the breeze. I once read a study on how quickly people give up on new endeavors. The question was simple: When you try something new, how many times do you allow yourself to fail before you give up? Do you know the most common answer? Well, prepare yourself for the worst. The answer for most people was *one* failure. That borders on the absurd. That question also applies to how quickly some people give up a new style. Or how quickly some people succumb to everyone else's bad habits. For you, you have lasted through many Saturday nights. Persevere through the rest of the year and see if anything changes at some point in the future.

Until you hit that point, let's enjoy a great summer.
Dad

4/07/09 The Key for Course Selections?

Dear Austen,
    You have worked so hard for so long, I think it is time to focus on really selecting courses that would give you the most pleasure. I also think it is time you be rewarded for your hard high-school work and high AP scores. If you have set yourself up to avoid the science courses, embrace the freedom. If you have worked your way out of a third semester of a language, that is fantastic. Instead of those courses, I love the idea of your taking some classes that are aligned with your interests. Like guitar? Or drumming? That would be fun yet challenging. You would just get better and better at those music skills. A semester (or two) of additional elective music courses would complement your piano expertise, your singing, and your songwriting. Go for it! Even if the classes do not satisfy any requirements. Some of those requirements could be done later. I like Skyler's approach of saving her Spanish requirement for the summer of her junior year. That will turn out to be a great decision for her, allowing her to live for six weeks in Madrid, and it will turn out to be a great decision for us, giving us a starting point for our upcoming summer vacation in Europe. Again, play it as it comes, leaving room for spontaneous decisions. Go for your own fun choices. Follow your heart. If you do, you will simply become a better and better musician. Now that is pretty cool.
    I would also add a dose of reality. So many students feel they have to take the right course to get into the right graduate program or get the best job. I disagree. In truth, most of what you learn in college is not going to translate into what you need to know to do your job. Look at me. I wasted so much of my education on premed courses from chemistry to biology to physics. Did those courses help me in medical school? Maybe a little. But did the material in those courses impact my ability to work as a physician? Not at all. What I learned in medical school, my internship, and my residency was the medical information that I needed to work as a physician. That is how most jobs work. They train you when they hire you because so many jobs require a specific set of skills. Even as a physician, that is the dictum. See one. Do one. Teach one. Hence, don't waste your time on

those so-called required courses. Take the courses that awaken your intellect or at least get your emotional juices flowing. When I think of all of the great courses I missed in college…well, it makes me sick. Back then, I received the wrong advice. Years from now, if you ever look back on these e-mails, I hope you find the right advice. If not, you have my permission to shoot me on sight. Or course, I will probably be dead by then.

Cremation usually does not leave much of a target.

Dad

5/14/09 A Freshman-Year Gift?

Dear Austen,

    I want to congratulate you on an extremely successful year at USC, persevering academically and socially. You faced a number of tough challenges, from difficult classes to difficult roommates, and you still managed to triumph. I am very proud of you. I want to reward your excellence with some summer treats. For this Saturday I would love to take you to the Guitar Center and see if there is something you would like to have to expand your current recording capabilities. A better microphone with a good stand? A new computer better for laying down music tracks? I, of course, have zero expertise and knowledge, so it would be completely your choice. I also want to support any singing lessons or guitar lessons if you want to take any lessons over the summer. Maybe before or after our European trip? Lastly, since you are planning to continue classical voice work with Gary Glaze, let me know if you needed anything for that endeavor. Whatever you need for self-improvement, you have a green light.

    I know how hesitant you are to spend money, but I have to repeat my viewpoint. There are no better investments than education and personal development. I would like to contribute to any areas that would improve your continued education and expand your development. If there is something I have missed or forgotten, please bring it to my attention. We, of course, are expecting you to relax and chill over the summer. Still, after our trip to Europe, you might want to refocus on your personal growth. Think of athletes. Over the summer they do not stop lifting weights or stop running sprints. They continue to work on improving their physical abilities. The same applies to your musical abilities. For me, the same applies to all students. If they have some special skills or areas of passion, I would keep improving those facets all year long, week after week. The better you become, the easier it becomes, and the better you become, the more fun it becomes. A little effort goes a long way.

    So, keep on trucking.
Dad

SOPHOMORE YEAR

8/22/09 Thanks for the Summer

Dear Austen,

    I want to thank you for a great four months of summer. You were a delight to have at home. You were a delight on our European trip, and I am certain those two young Greek boys found you a delight when you locked yourself in the Santorini hotel bathroom with only your towel. Now, I could recount how they had to unhinge the door so you could slip out, barely covered, or how they offered to stay longer to fully fix the bathroom door, but I will spare you the details. I am certain they are well embedded into your memory. By the way, I was impressed with your stamina in Europe. You survived twelve planes, multiple trains, and numerous taxi rides without ever losing a step. For us, your quick mind, your funny, often sarcastic banter, and your random, but on-target observations were a crucial part of our daily laughs. Our summer would not have been half the fun without you. Our family would not be the same without you. That is why, on this first night of your return to USC, I am already looking forward to next summer. We can't recreate our European trip, but maybe we can have fun during our trip to New York to attend Skyler's graduation. I am sure it will be another once-in-a-lifetime experience. That is why I miss you so much tonight. The hole in the heart never gets smaller, but somehow, as they say, you have to make your heart bigger so the hole *seems* to be growing smaller. When I place my head on the pillow, I am going to try to balance my sense of loss with my optimism for you and a great sophomore year.

I am sorry none of your roommates were available tonight for your first night at USC. They scattered just as we arrived to move your possessions into the suite. I was not surprised, just disappointed, as I was hoping this year would be better than last year, with roommates who were more available. I was sorry your best friend from freshman year will not be returning to USC because of her family's financial issues. I know you are going to miss her company, as she was level headed, not a party girl, yet lots of fun. I also realize how it forced you, at the last minute, to switch dorm-room assignments. My other disappointment was your bedroom situation. It was not what we expected. Three, not two, girls—all in one bedroom? I guess my advice will remain unchanged. Focus on what gets you through each day, decompress when you need to, and stick to your own habits and your own routine. Keep us posted on how you do over this first week. It has to be better than the first week of your freshman year. If you could get through last year, you can get through any year. For me, each college year got better and better. Think of the good things coming your way: new classes, new materials to learn, new classmates, new friends, and your own growth as a musician. Nothing is more important than the latter. Except perhaps finding a few friends. Embrace the sophomore year.

Thanks again for a great summer.

Dad

8/30/09 Reflection from First Weekend at Home

Dear Austen,

    I want to thank you for coming home this weekend. It was a delight to pick you up on Friday, and enjoyable to have you home for the two nights. I appreciated hearing about all your courses, and I appreciated your heavy workload. I also appreciated, especially when we dropped you off at your apartment, your hard challenge of readjusting without your best friend from last year. It's difficult to lose your best friend, but it must be equally hard to live in a two-bedroom suite with students whom you do not know that well. I wish I had an easy answer for you, but burying yourself in your work only gets you so far. I know what I hope for you for this year. I hope you are able to find someone, or several people, who can become those good lifelong friends. It can't happen overnight, but it will happen. You found a great friend last year. Maybe this year you will find several good friends. Like Mom and me, you don't need a ton of friends, just a couple. I do not pray very often, but I will pray that several friendships develop over this year. Until then, and even after then, please use home as a place to decompress, especially if you are struggling for a good night's sleep with three noisy, staying-up-late sophomore roommates. I realize that statement is hyperbole, as you stay most weekends at USC, but we are ready for you on any weekend. As for this coming weekend, we already have tickets for the Saturday football game at USC. See you before the game. Until then, good luck with your own goals for your sophomore year.

    Next summer seems a long way away, yes?

    Dad

9/27/09 Ready for Some Good Habits?

Dear Austen,

    The older I get, the faster the time flies, and the older I get, the harder it is to offer any suggestions. Would Skyler love that confession! Yet, here I go again. For me, it is amazing you are already heading toward a week of examinations. It seems like we just moved you into your suite in the later part of August, and it seems like you were just home on that first weekend. From our conversations, it sounds as if you have enjoyed your new classes, have met some new friends, and have adjusted to three girls in a room, at least as best as can be expected. I still sense how much you miss your best friend from last year, and I still sense the loneliness that comes from that loss. So I thought I would send along my "emotional thermostat" recommendations. These suggestions are just a group of habits I wish all students would develop. I think they would improve their moods and upgrade their performances. For you, I pass them along as some "food" for your consideration for the sophomore challenge.

    Did you know the quality of your life is reflective of the quality of your thinking? Your internal thinking, the thoughts inside your head, set the foundation for your external world. Why? Because you live life from the inside out. What you think about is what you become. Or as they say, "As you think, so shall you be." My first recommendation? Try to gear your thinking toward what you want to happen, not toward what you do *not* want to happen. How do you create a space in your thinking for more positive thoughts? You make an effort to delete your negative thoughts. Why is this so important? Because 90 percent of people's daily thoughts are negative, not positive. My suggestion to delete negative thoughts and focus on what you want does not mean avoiding problems or some painful emotions. It means focusing on the possible solutions, not just the problems. Constantly think about favorable outcomes to your challenges. The more you think about a positive outcome, the greater the odds it will come true. That is a fact, not a myth. Dream more. Worry less. And stay positive. That's my first suggestion for your current sophomore year.

Did you know that the quality of your life is also reflective of the quality of your external dialogue, your conversations with others? Most students use only three thousand words on a regular basis. Worse, many students, on a daily basis, use a basic core of five hundred words. The worst part? Most students use three times more negative words than positive words. The key for improving your vocabulary isn't adding more impressive words—save that trick for your college papers. The real key is increasing your percentage of positive words. A more positive vocabulary improves your attitude, raising your emotional thermostat. How can you do it? By becoming more aware of the number of positive words and negative words that filter into your conversations. By taking control of your thinking and your conversations, you can shape your attitude, and your attitude can shape your daily emotional mood. Your internal dialogue and external dialogue (your total number of positive words versus negative words in a day) can work as a powerful force on improving the quality of your mood. I do have one warning: if you place a group of students in a confined space for a year, which they do in every dorm and every suite, those students develop similar vocabularies, both in the actual words and in the number of positive versus negative words. That is one of the reasons you need to be around students who are positive, not negative. Students who support you, not put you down. Listen to the different vocabularies that fill your dorm room. Are they always complaining? Putting someone down? It might be best to purchase some earplugs.

Are you aware of this analogy for your emotional thermostat? If an orange is cut open by a knife and squeezed, what comes out? Orange juice. If an orange is hammered on the kitchen counter, what comes out? Orange juice. If an orange is run over in the driveway by a truck, what comes out? Orange juice. The external trigger is irrelevant. What matters is what's inside that orange. That's what I learned from Wayne Dyer. The same truth applies to all of us. Your emotions are your emotions, regardless of the external triggers. What comes out of you, in any situation, is a reflection of your own orange juice and your own emotions. How can we improve our orange juice and raise our emotional thermostat? We each need to take more responsibility for our emotional status, and we need to make an attempt to raise our emotional platform. Of course, who wants to be run over by a truck? Day after day? Which is why you may have to avoid certain students. Especially those students who are self-centered, overly critical, and judgmental. And while avoiding them, even if they judge you, try your best to not judge them. A little less judgment and a little more tolerance make it easier to stay focused on your path. This is not an easy habit, but it will make your sophomore year easier if you can master that approach.

Can you withstand one more suggestion? This recommendation is something that you already do. How many of your fellow students get up, scarf down some fast food type of breakfast, and scurry off to their first class? Or how many students rush all day long and stay active late into the night, right to the point when they climb into bed? How many students fail to use the first hour and the last hour of each day to full advantage? Many studies have shown that the first hour and the last hour of the day, the first hour when you are awake and the last hour right before you go to sleep, are the most important hours of the day. The first step is to allow yourself sufficient time at the start of each day to give your mind some positive mental nutrition. For some students, that translates to some early exercise or perhaps some light, but positive reading. The second step, at the end of the day, allows each student time to decompress from the day's activities, giving each student a chance to restabilize the mood. How do you maximize these two periods? I know how you already do it. In the morning, you take time to create your "To Do" list, focusing on creating time for some positive outcomes. At night, you take time to read for fun in your bed. I commend you for these habits. You cannot control the events of the day, but you can control the first hour and the last hour of each day. At least if your roommates don't chatter late into the night. So, how are you doing on these core habits?

Or am I just driving you crazy?

Dad

10/26/09 Want to Relive Our Shared Weekend from Hell?

Dear Austen,

    OK, so when did my life start to go south? Could I mention from birth? That would be premature. From marriage? That would get me killed before nightfall, kicked to death by a wife with pins in her feet. Yes, that is a reference to Mom and her upcoming foot surgery. Hey, maybe it began when you two girls left for college? The truth? This weekend at the Westin Bonaventure—what a day from hell. I realize you know all the details. I also know you prefer not to relive the details. Still, I need to vent. I need to get this poison out of my system. For me, that process comes through writing. When I finish this e-mail, I will feel much better, a little like coming out of a confessional. Except, for me, I lied more in the confessional booth than I did in real life. I had to have something to confess, right? Did I ever tell you how much my sister claimed she hated me? She said I did everything right and she did everything wrong. She said that was why our parents always favored me, not her. Actually, with my mother's unexpected pregnancy and the derailment of my father's life plans, don't you think his relationship with my sister must have been twisted well before I was born? Me? I came along five years later. But hey, after this weekend, we all know something of a shared nightmare.

    Does my memory match yours? First, after checking into our two hotel rooms, we discovered you were sick with a temperature of 102 degrees. That occurred *after* moving into the hotel, not before. Thus, the USC Health Clinic was not an option. After checking with the hotel front desk, and after they directed us to a local physician, we were able to set up an appointment at 10:30 a.m. Fortunately, you only had strep throat, not something worse. An antibiotic to the rescue. What about our plans for the USC 5:00 p.m. football game? Was I going to toss aside our expensive tickets? Do you remember, as you slept on and off, how Mom and I watched you through the day, rechecking your temperature, debating whether to go to the first half of the game, undecided whether we should leave you in the hotel for another nap or bring you along? Good parents, right?

By 4:00 p.m., did you feel any better? You looked a bit better. Your temperature was closer to normal. The three of us, with you dragging a bit, set out for the football game, heading into the wall of traffic. But the traffic turned out to be a blessing because it held us up, and we never made it to the parking lot. Around 4:30 p.m., while we were still en route, our neighbors called to let us know their daughter, who had been taking care of Paris, had just found Paris drowned in our pool. The poor girl, just twelve years old, had jumped into the pool, carried our dog up the steps to the concrete, and started CPR. But Paris was dead. It was a terrifying incident to her, a shock to her parents, and a sad horror to the three of us. Remember Mom's tears? The three of us returned to our hotel rooms. Gone was Paris. Gone was the football game. Gone was the good weekend. Thank God for the nice neighbors who drove their van to our house, loaded Paris, and took her to an animal care center. After telephone calls between us and their staff, while you were curled on your hotel bed, we had Paris cremated. During the coming Thanksgiving break, the four of us can bury her ashes by the tree beside the kitchen door, close to where she used to love to sleep. We can pay our respects to Paris, grateful she was our dog, and hope we never have any more weekends like this past weekend. There, I feel a little better already. For me, writing is like therapy. It gets the venom out of my system. And you? Reading my drivel is probably not particularly therapeutic!

Now how about today, Monday? Mom and I got up at 5:00 a.m. By 6:00 a.m. I had Mom at the podiatry surgeon's office. I waited while she was having her surgery, reading your recent essay on the Armenian genocide and its horrible, devastating impact on Armenian women. Lovely topic. Rather timely for this weekend. Mom survived and the surgery went fine. I, of course, wanted to take her to Disneyland so we could use the wheelchair entrances to the rides. Ice packs every twenty minutes to her foot? We could just do Splash Mountain every thirty minutes as that water is freezing. Or take a few rides on the plunging Tower of Terror. That would drain the blood and reduce the swelling in her foot. No go! Home we came, right after the surgery. Since 10:30 a.m., I have been rotating ice packs on her feet, responding to her requests, and pretending to be the nurse. Really, I do not know how nurses do their jobs. It is so much easier to be a physician and simply write the orders. Someone else does the work. In any case, I am taking a twenty-minute break, writing this e-mail to keep you up to date on the condition of dear Mom. Tomorrow I will be returning to work, as Mom should be self-sufficient within twenty-four hours. Which brings up another point. Work keeps calling, asking me to handle various items, and I keep telling them I will be back to the office tomorrow morning. Whoops. My twenty minutes is up. It's back to my nursing skills. I told Mom to swim a few laps in the cold pool water. That would ease any swelling. With Paris's drowning, that joke fell flat. I miss Paris, much more than expected. So does Mom. The house seems empty without her. I remember how she loved curling under your piano, listening to you practice. Those memories lift our spirits. I hope your grief is easing a little.

Which reminds me, I may need to reread my e-mail on good habits.
Dad

11/11/09 What, the Student Is Teaching the Parent?

Dear Austen,

On my dad's birthday, I want to express my admiration for you. If he were still around, my dad would have been very proud of you. Every time we turn around you are doing well in some course. You either receive some positive remark from one of your teachers or some uplifting banter from one of your fellow students. I appreciated your story from your music theory course where you were submitting new compositions based on suggestions from the prior lecture. Your classmates liked your composition, and one student blurted out that you should get extra credit. I laughed at the teacher's response: "Austen? Extra credit? She doesn't *need* extra credit." I especially liked your stories of all of those students you are helping with these difficult music courses. You seem to be mastering all of the material and then helping those who do not have your level of ability or talent. I am not certain of the appropriate word, but you are remarkable. It is as simple as that. You should never forget how much you have helped others. You should never forget how much you give of yourself and your time. In many ways you have become, and maybe you always were, a teacher—a very good teacher at that. All of your pupils seem to do well with your help. Is it a sign of your future? Who knows where your future will lead. Your gift is yours, not mine.

I also want to applaud your participation in this year's USC's Gospel Choir. One of the few white girls in a choir of black students? Saying prayers with the group before your singing practices and performances? It is not something we would have expected, but it is something we support. You can gain so much education by interacting with people from a different world. We appreciated your story about how various members of the gospel choir share their struggles before each practice. The black girl who asked for prayers for her younger brother who was shot that weekend? Another girl who asked for prayers because one of her girlfriends was raped? That sure beats the complaints of a student who received a "B" on some exam. That is one of the great things about USC: its diversity. Ironically, you and Skyler selected the two universities with the most culturally and ethnically diverse student bodies. We are glad we raised young adults who are tolerant of other races, tolerant of other beliefs. That's another wonderful characteristic for a future teacher. Unless, of course, you become a singer and songwriter. Actually, it's a wonderful characteristic for anyone.

Do I need to bother offering a snapshot of the flip side of that equation? You just wrote the paper on the Armenian genocide and researched the Holocaust. There is not anything worse I can offer. But I can share one more story about my mother. Not long after my dad's death, on one of those Saturdays where I drove to her house and tried to offer help, I asked if she could share some of the best times with my dad. I clarified how I would love to know about his best days, when he was happiest, as he was not one to share much from the past. For her response, she explained she did not know his best day, but she knew the worst day of his life. It was the day I married your mother. Now, my father was not prejudiced. He treated your mom with respect and kindness. I mean…who does not like your mom? Only one person I know—my mother. Instead of acknowledging the sentiment as her own, she projected the sentiment onto my father, knowing he was not around to refute her assertion. I did not attempt to ask why my wedding was the worst day of his life. I did not have to say a word. My mother rattled off her disappointments. I married someone who was not wealthy. I had married someone with an ethnic background different from my own. I could go on and on, but you get my point. We are proud to have two daughters who are about as far from my mother as the north and south poles are from each other. By the way, my mother audibly gasped in horror when I told her you were in a black gospel choir. I have to admit it. I enjoyed that moment.

If only you could educate her as you have educated us.

Dad

11/30/09 Are My Outbursts Better When You Are Asleep?

Dear Austen,

You and Skyler are sleeping upstairs, so it may seem a bit odd that I am writing while you are still home. But today was the day we buried Paris, and I am still grappling with my emotions. So for me it is back to the tradition of letter writing. Therapeutic, yes. But I need to follow my own advice on better habits. I need to focus on the positives of this Thanksgiving. Skyler was home for ten days of the break. Don't ask me how. That's how college seems to work. Sometimes you have classes spread through the week. Other times they are bunched together on just a couple of days. It made for a great family reunion. In one way we were lucky. My mother seemed more quiet than usual, so her criticisms were far fewer than normal. Maybe it was the burying of Paris's ashes while my dad's ashes still sit on my computer desk. Maybe she had not yet recovered from my disclosure of your participation in the USC Gospel Choir. She has not accepted any of our invitations to attend one of your performances. She never will. Can you imagine her reaction when one of the audience members stands and screams out, which can happen right in the middle of a spiritual song, "You tell them, sister! Praise be to the Lord." If I ever want to give my mother a heart attack, I could just bring her to one of your choir concerts. She would not feel comfortable being surrounded by black people, and she would not feel comfortable with their abrupt, heart-driven proclamations during the show. This raises some interesting questions: Why do I tolerate my mother? Why do I go Saturday after Saturday and listen to all of her complaints and criticisms? Why not just walk away and leave her alone in her own misery?

Are you ready for the worst part? At some point in our lives we are going to have to ask her to live with us. She will reach an age where she cannot handle taking care of herself and the house. Many parents who are my age are depositing their own parents into retirement homes. For me, that is the last resort, and only if she has failed at living with the family. Don't get me wrong. If my mother is gnarly now, imagine her as her ailments grow worse? Or as her disposition gets worse, not better? Do I respect her values? No. Do I like her or respect her opinions? No. But since she gave birth to me, I feel a sense of responsibility to provide assistance, and at some point, that assistance will include an invitation to sell her house and move into our house. It's like the old days in our country when families of several generations lived together. Maybe they did not have such disparate views of the world. Maybe they did not have such a difference in tolerance and prejudice. Maybe those families offered a better version of unconditional love. Maybe those families just did not have my mother. Regardless, an invitation will have to come at some point. It is the decent thing to do. It is the loving thing to do. Until then, let's enjoy one another and our time together. I love it best when it is the four of us—with nothing but our love. You agree?

Thanks for allowing me to vent.
Dad

12/03/09 Care to Discuss Balance in Life?

Dear Austen,

The older I become, the more I repeat myself. That means I am either becoming wiser or more organic. But I want to take a moment to repeat the advice from one of your mom's childhood friends. In his most recent letter to us, after a friend's death in Japan, he wrote, "Let me tell you: do not put off those things you want to do for another day because that day may never come. Do not reserve your fine china and crystal for only the special occasions that are too few and far between or that favorite perfume you apply only on special occasions while the bottle remains full. If you have favorite outfits in your closet that you wear only on special occasions, simply abandon that frame of mind and wear them while you are shopping at the market. Those nice pieces of jewelry that only adorn your body during special occasions should be worn on a daily basis, if you so desire. In short, make every day a special occasion because too soon there will no more days for us or for those whom we love. Pass that concept on to your precious daughters and follow-up with reminders because youth has little concept of its own mortality."

Now, how do I apply that perspective to your college years? Simply put, I would enjoy the days of college as much as possible, regardless of any repetitive routine. In fact, I would try to break up that routine. That does not mean skipping class, or shortchanging efforts to learn the material. It means developing a habit (habits are the keys to success, right?) of maximizing your life by embracing something new and different. Attend more concerts, on and off campus. See more movies. Enjoy more dinners. Take "mental health Saturdays" with zero work. I know! Have you applied to be a volunteer at the Grammy show? Spread your musical activities beyond the classroom to capture those experiences, which you may not be able to reproduce later in life. Your participation in gospel choir is the perfect example. Where else would you have that chance? Go for those experiences like Skyler went for London and Madrid. Do not waste these college years on just the assigned homework. Focus on the more interesting parts of life, making the most of each week. That is easy to say, but hard to do. Hear the words of Mom's friends in the back of your mind, and attempt to treat each day in college as a special day.

Speaking of something "special," I heard from Mom that two boys recently wrote you love songs? And you turned them both down for dates? In fact, you wrote your own love song, asking for more than just another love song, asking for someone to really get to know the *real* you. Did they know your favorite book? Your favorite actor? I applaud your approach, and I am certain I will love your new song. It's nice to have someone enjoy you for what's on the outside, but it is more important, for the relationship to last, to have someone enjoy you for what is on the inside. That was one advantage for Mom and me. Since we worked together in the hospital, I was able to see how she handled crises, and she was able to see how I performed under pressure. She was an outstanding nurse, one of the best. We got to know each other better and better, and we got to like each other more and more. Physical attraction is one thing. Emotional balance between two people is equally crucial. Here's hoping some young man does more than write you a love song. Here's hoping some man takes the time to get to know you—and love you. As always, not today. Not tomorrow. Just some day in the future. You deserve it.

Now, go for something special.
Dad

1/11/10 Post-Christmas Parental Blues

Dear Austen,

If you think you are the only who wakes up in the middle of the night or early in the morning with a jolt of the blues, you are mistaken. See the time of this e-mail, starting around 4:45 a.m. on Monday. When Skyler left for New York, I felt depressed, and when we dropped you off at USC, I felt depressed. When I woke up this morning around 4:40 a.m., I felt depressed. I woke up thinking about how much you will be missed during these next few years of college. Do not worry. Once I get myself going, once I get myself busy working at the office, I always feel better. Not great, but better. Feeling great occurs when I am on vacation with the four of us. But each of us has to push forward with life and make the most of our lives. You do it by overcoming setbacks and doing well in your pursuits. Besides, what is the alternative? We need to embrace life and make the most of it, and we need to make the most of our skills and opportunities. Life is a wonderful miracle. When you consider the myriad of eggs and sperm and the millions of genetic options, we are each the product of miracles. We should make the most of our wonderful blessing. So, how do I get over my own blues?

Believe it or not, I have been trying to meditate on a regular basis. I have preached my group of habits, but this habit is a tough one for me to sustain. For me, meditation is more than a chance to relax; it is a chance to connect with God. I did not mention religion. I believe in the benefit of a spiritual connection. I am not a great advocate of all of our religions and their conflicts. I like Gandhi's quote: "In heaven there is no religion; there is only God." There is an added benefit for me. A connection with God reminds me how we enter life with nothing and leave life with nothing, and how our focus should be on giving, not receiving. A sustained sense of happiness comes from something you contribute to the world, not something you get from the world. So, when you or Skyler leave for another semester of college, I turn to meditation. I also turn my focus away from myself and my sense of loss, and I try to focus on what I can possibly give to the world. Maybe that is why I write these e-mails. First, it gives me a sense of connection. Second, it allows me to feel as if I am giving something of value. Third, it offers my own self-therapy. Do I recommend writing more e-mails to you? No. Do I recommend meditation for you? Perhaps, but I am not convinced. Whenever you have a setback, or a surge of the blues, you seem to find your renewal through music. That is your lifeline. For my own sanity, I will stick to writing these e-mails. And if you suffer the blues, while I spring back to a good mood as I write these notes, so be it, right?

Hey, I feel better already. You?
Dad

1/28/10 Clothes? Or No Clothes?

Dear Austen,

    In all of our e-mails and in all of our conversations, have we ever discussed your clothes? Or makeup? Strange question, yes? Well, let me offer an explanation for another moment of madness—or perhaps another moment of insight. Over this past weekend, I was clearing out some old possessions in the garage and came across my mother's diaries from high school into college. I gathered the diaries, piled them beside the computer, and began to peruse some of the entries. The diaries, I presume, were written to provide her with a memory of her transition through high school and college. During these journal notes, did she write about her courses? Did she address any academic challenges? Let me give you a series of her entries, and then I will make a point. Repeatedly, she wrote about the season's fashions and her purchases of clothes: her wine-colored suede dress, her blue lace dress, her gypsy blouse, her apricot satin skirt, her black silk gabardine Lyrolean jumper, her blue-patterned satin weave, her white, large-brimmed felt hat, her gold bracelet, her green but gold-framed watch, her alligator bag, her white linen sandal wedges, her brown-and-white spectator pumps, her blue coat with the white collar, etc., etc. Her focus on her appearance matched her college slogan, highlighted in her diary, "Always be a fashion plate."

    You know me. I can critique my mother. But let's forgo any judgment of her. Do you think she was representative of women of that era? Back then, right before World War II, there were not many opportunities for a career for women. Back then, the key for women was not their academic success but their appeal to young men. Back then, the purpose, as I best understand it from my mother, was to get married by the time you left college. Now think of your situation. Your focus is not on your attire. Your focus is not on attracting a guy. For women today, the average age range for marriage is twenty-eight to thirty-three. Your focus is your career. You enter college and leave college with a different expectation than women did seven decades ago. In your era, you may need to support yourself. You can't depend on some man. That's why I have been such a stickler on finding your gift, following your passion, and creating your path. Do you think my mom's father wrote to her about managing her fashion and purchasing the best clothes? Do you think he harbored any illusions that my mother might have to work for a living? Forget how my mother trapped my father. Forget her lack of character and lack of tolerance. Maybe she never put forth the effort to improve those areas because she never saw much of a need for those characteristics. Ah, how women have evolved over these past three generations. Mom was a Medical ICU nurse. Skyler will work in films. You will make your mark in music. What a different, and better, world for women. It makes me so happy to have two girls rather than two boys. But, hey, now that I think about it, the world may have changed as drastically for the men as for the women. Different challenges for different genders? Different challenges for different generations? I would like to read a father's letters to his college-aged sons and see what differences I find. Thanks for any perspective on these issues.

Thanks, too, for never mentioning your clothes.
Dad

2/08/10 Ready for Some More Old Memories?

Dear Austen,

  After finding my mom's old diaries, I kept searching and found some of my old diaries from your grade-school years. Tonight I focused my reading on your first several weeks of first grade. Do you remember your response to your first day of first grade? You liked your teacher and the other kids, but you were disappointed there was no assigned homework. How many first graders have that response? Of course, by then, you had become used to homework through your participation in Kumon, the private Japanese program for reading and mathematics. With those programs, which we started well before first grade, you completed daily homework assignments and weekly tests. Mom used to sit with you for the homework, and you and Skyler seemed to enjoy it. So, your desire to seek extra work was already ingrained, well before you got to first grade. Was it part of your DNA? No, it was probably programmed by us. Despite my changing view on grades, I am still glad we placed you in that early Kumon program, as it gave you a head start with math and then with English, and it developed—right from the get-go—the habit of learning. Hey, did we do something right? I do not know. But it sure beats fostering an early focus on your attire!

  There were other interesting parts of the description of your first weeks of first grade. There was the announcement of a talent show. Your friends were apparently upset when you announced you would play the piano and sing some song. I think they wanted some group effort like dancing. None of them could play the piano, and none of them had your voice. So, even at that young age, you wanted to perform. You talked about the fun of performing. What happened over the years? You enjoyed performing in grade school. I remember the brochures announcing the talent show and highlighting your name. You had a reputation for your performances. I think your desire to perform changed in high school. In the performing arts environment, they forced you to perform too much. As a charter arts school, it needed fund-raising, and they sent you everywhere to raise money. At some point, you must have become a little burned out from all of your weekend performances. You must have felt like one of their pawns. But even in high school, you still seemed to love practicing and learning music. That has not changed over the years. Again, that component must have become ingrained. It must have become part of your personal style. God, it is fun reading old diaries. I encourage you to keep a journal when your own kids are growing up. It really is educational.

By the way, do you remember what you did in the weeks after you announced you would be playing the piano and singing in the talent show? You acquiesced to your new first grade friends, eventually joining them in a fun dance routine. The key, however, is that you put a high priority on not just helping your friends with their dance; you placed a high priority, without even thinking about it, on the value of those initial friendships. Those friendships lasted all through your grade-school years. Several years later, when you had your first sleepover, those same girls stayed the night. At an early age, you could stand on your own, but at an early age, you also elected to stand with others. For me, that was a win-win combination. True for the first grade, the third grade, and your sleepover. True, even, for college. You lost a close friend at the end of your freshman year of college, and it stung, but wasn't it great having her as a friend for that year? Maybe you are at that point again. Do you want to stand alone, squeezed into a room with three beds, or do you want to research other options where you can stand with someone you much prefer? The key is always to take action. With friendships, that level of action becomes even more crucial as you grow older. Too many of us let those friendships slide.

Is it time for some more action?

Dad

2/18/10 What? Another Room Change?

Dear Austen,

    I am reluctant to admit it, but at Williams College I never had a roommate. Oh, I shared a suite, but I always had my own bedroom within the suite. Once I became an upperclassman and received a high lottery number, I was lucky to have a single room each of my final three years. I pity you in your predicament with five individuals in a two-bedroom suite where you have to share your bedroom as a threesome. Remember when Skyler offered the viewpoint that it would take two or three months before everyone was comfortable with one another's habits and schedules? Well, she did not have any awareness that one of your roommates would be the filthiest roommate I have ever encountered. Whoops, there goes my criticism and judgment. I have to watch that tendency. But I hate visiting on the weekends. If I have to use your bathroom, it is impossible to step through the debris—hers, not yours—littering the floor. You deserve kudos for your ability to survive in such a pigsty. The other roommate? Whenever we arrive, she sits in the corner, repeatedly trying to write the same song for her band. No music courses. No music talent. Just part of a band. What's taken her months to compose, you could have finished—and finished far better—in fifteen minutes. If I were you, I would have killed one of your roommates by now. Thank God you have some friends through your classes. Thank God USC has a lot of great students, good people. In a bowl of apples, you got the wormy ones.

    Can I push aside those frustrations? What a lucky break! I was shocked when I heard that Jennifer, your roommate from last year in Fluor Tower, asked if you would move into a single-bedroom unit with her in the same complex. I did not know she was tired of her own roommate. Wants something better for the remainder of the sophomore year? I, for one, would leap at the chance to switch rooms. Jennifer seems like a nice girl, and she is certainly a friendly girl. When we visit your current suite, your other roommate never says a word. Not hello. Not how are you? Instead, she just pinches off the incense, grabs her belongings, and leaves. Personally, I think she is stoned half the time. I am probably mistaken. Judging too much once again. That's something I should not be doing. But it would be nice to be with someone who is gregarious, friendly, and fun. Fingers crossed that you and Jennifer can make the room switch, and fingers crossed that you can have the last two last months of your sophomore year living with someone you like. And to think this predicament would never have happened if your best friend from last year had not been forced to switch colleges at the last minute, derailing the chance for the two of you to live together. That would have been fun. What's another setback? Just something to propel you toward a new adventure.

Best wishes for some better luck.

Dad

3/06/10 Ah, a Successful Room Change!

Dear Austen,

My e-mails have not been as frequent over the past month, but it has been very interesting and fun to watch you adapt to Jennifer and the room switch. Similar to freshman year, you have exchanged some bad luck for some good luck. You sound so much happier and less stressed. I know she likes to drink. I understand she also likes to party, but I also can see you have a better, more personal connection with her than with the previous roommates. Yes, you have to take care of her from time to time, secondary to her wild ways. In terms of that predicament, I thought your most recent song, titled "Devil's Child," captured your situation. I loved the lines "shards of glass on my kitchen floor...well-known cops banging at my door...you know I am not a saint...I like it when guys smile...now I'm doomed to eternal fate...all because I'm the devil's child." Ah, if most parents really knew what happens in those dorm rooms or apartments for college students. In your case, they are not reflective of your life, but they are reflective of the life around you. You tolerate far more than I could. You always come to their aid. You improve your friends' lives without acknowledging it. So, as always, you have my respect for the person you have become.

I wish I could say I was half as nice as you when I was in college, but that was not the case. At Williams College, our house was renowned for throwing a wine party each year, inviting all the teachers. It was rather cool drinking wine and eating cheese with the professors, getting a little bit drunk. Such fun. Some of the students would sometimes smoke marijuana before the occasion, just to loosen themselves up for the annual night. I remember one student, a bit like your roommate, who liked to party a bit more than the others. On one night, he snorted some cocaine just as the first teachers were arriving. As he started down the steps, I paused by his side, whispering, "You know, doesn't it seem as if they are all looking at you? How weird is that?" Well, he became acutely paranoid and disappeared back up the stairs, never to return to the party. Pretty mean? I think I did him a favor. I think it would have been apparent he was a bit drugged with more than wine, and I think he would have found himself in trouble trying to explain his altered mental status. Still, I cannot pretend to have your thoughtful nature. I was not the devil, but I was no saint. Until I met your mother, of course.

Congratulations on the move to a new room.
Dad

4/05/10 Some Things Never Change?

Dear Austen,

    When I have a quiet night, I will periodically pull out one of my old diaries, now that I have found the entire group from my college and medical school days to your grade-school days. Tonight I came across an entry from when you were in the second grade, and Skyler was in the fourth grade. There was a description of an interaction between some of the students in your second grade class. I do not know if the story came from you or perhaps from Mom, as she volunteered at the school during those years. In the midst of a class assignment, one second-grader asked another second-grader if he knew the answer to the assigned question, and the little boy responded no. That second-grader then went to a second and third student in his row and asked each one if he or she knew the answer to the assigned question. Each said no, but the last second-grader was less cooperative than the first two second-graders because he blurted out, "If you want the correct answer, go to Austen!" So, by the second grade, you were already known for knowing the correct answers and being willing to help others. They may not have liked the fact that you knew the answers, but they seemed to depend on it. You helped your classmates back then. You help your classmates, and your roommate, now.

    The same observation seems to hold true for Skyler. In those diary entries, you were in the second grade, and Skyler was in the fourth grade. The fourth-grade teacher must have asked the students to write down something they would want the teacher to know about them. Some boys wrote down how they loved soccer, swimming, or playing baseball. Some girls wrote down how they liked dancing, singing, or playing the piano. Skyler? She wrote down, "I am stubborn." The teacher was surprised at her character-revealing answer, so different from all the other answers, so she asked the class, "Is Skyler stubborn?" Finally, one student lifted his hand and answered, "Skyler is not stubborn. She is *very* stubborn!" The class and the teacher apparently laughed, but her personality was already set, much like yours. But we would not change anything about you. Both characteristics are equally helpful. Skyler's stubbornness was needed to battle me and our initial fights over high-school grades and the choice of the best college. Your willingness to help and your ability to learn the correct answers have carried you quite a distance. So for each of you, your well-established characteristics have paid dividends.

But the above examples present challenges for the parent. More importantly, they present limitations. How much can parents do to impact their children's transition through college, their transformation from adolescence to adulthood? You can take my approach and write an endless stream of letters (e-mails), packed with well-intended advice. But perhaps it is preferable to get out of the way, letting the characteristics of the student determine a future course. After all these e-mails, I think there are some actions that are crucial for every parent. I think we have to offer consistent love and support, regardless of whether the college student veers from our preferred path and regardless of how many setbacks the college student may experience. I also think we should be asking more questions, not offering more answers. What do you really want? Do you think that course will bring you money or happiness? Do you see the difference between those two end points? How much are you willing to do to achieve your goal? Are you willing to go further in school? Are you willing to make the sacrifices? Do you need more help from us? Do you need less interference from us? In short, our best role as parents is to help clarify the student's vision and path, not redirect the student's vision or change the life direction. Lastly, our underlying role is to try to become better parents and future lifelong best friends. Sound simple?

For me, it has been anything but simple.

Dad

4/15/10 Do Some Parents Really Change?

Dear Austen,

You are feeling better with an improved roommate and a renewed friendship, even though you are often the caretaker. Can you see the differences in yourself? You are eating right, exercising right, and feeling physically healthy. Do you remember your early preoccupation with illnesses? Yes, you had those early surgeries and the constant eye patching. But do you remember, at age five, coming downstairs for breakfast and announcing that, as you slept, your spleen had ruptured and your scapula had broken? Do you remember keeping lists of your daily symptoms? I just glanced at one of your old diaries, and you wrote your list of physical symptoms for the school day: headache, itchy scalp, sore neck, vertigo, possible brain damage, nostril problems, mucus, hurt hip, and extreme tiredness. Years later, when we were vacationing in Maui and derailed by a day of rain, do you remember how the four of us huddled together and wrote down a list of possible activities for the rainy day? Skyler wrote, "Swim to Lanai," and Mom wrote, "List all of Austen's illnesses." You were quite a quirky kid with multiple real illnesses, but an equal number of fictitious ones. However, please note that it is all of those idiosyncrasies that make you so special.

For some of those idiosyncrasies, I share the blame. Or take the credit. Back in those days, I acted as a husband and father, not as a physician. I focused on providing some fun, not preventing disease. On the weekends I wanted to give Mom a break from cooking. Do you remember the breakfast menu from McDonalds with the eggs, bacon, and nuggets? Do you remember the stops after Saturday soccer matches at one of the fast-food restaurants, grabbing hamburgers and fries with a soda? Do you remember Sunday mornings and how I always used to drive to the donut store to grab muffins and coffee for Mom and myself, plus varied donuts for you and Skyler? Do you remember our tradition of Sunday nights? Always ordering pizza and settling down to watch a television movie? It was my fault. I did not think of nutrition and health. Worse, I did not realize until later how you were allergic to gluten, dairy, and so many other foods. I think it is safe to say, for the first decade of your life, your father was poisoning you each and every day—it was a miracle you survived.

Look at us now. I am well versed, finally, in health and nutrition. You? On health and nutrition, you are better educated than me. Of course, some of this stems from your habit of researching all of your illnesses on the Internet. Still, you purchase healthy foods. You avoid gluten and dairy products. You avoid sugar, salt, and processed foods. When was the last time you even drank a soda? Maybe the change from how you ate as a child to how you eat as a sophomore is emblematic of your personal development. If I have any additional advice to a parent, it would be to pay closer attention to your children's health, from the early years all the way through college. That suggestion applies to more than their diet; it applies to their entire list of activities. Pay attention to their living situations in college. Listen to their dreams and concerns. Stay in close communication, even if you have to initiate the sharing. In fact, during these college years, I think it is the perfect time to share more of yourself with your children. Maybe some of the stories that the parent has withheld from sharing up to that point. The more your child knows you and your many mistakes, and the more authentic you are, the better for them. Trust me. It will bring you closer. How much do other parents share? I do not know. As for me, I hope my sharing has helped inspire just a little of your personal growth. You are moving toward the halfway point of your college career, and already I have witnessed such tremendous personal growth. I salute you.

Just be glad I am no longer purchasing your food.
Dad

5/01/10 Sophomore Year? Over So Fast?

Dear Austen,

 Once again I cannot express my amazement at how you handle these difficult music classes and difficult general classes, just soaring through them with such ease. I appreciated your sharing the story of your recent music history test. In art history, the teacher would flash a painting or sculpture and you would have to identify the artist, the date, and offer a description of the style. For music history, as I understand it, you have to remember the composer, the date it was composed, and date and place of its premiere, plus the original conductor and lead singers at that premiere performance. Sometimes, on those exams, there is even a question about who first played some of the minor roles. Compared to art history, music history seems to require an exponential jump in memory. I would have been terrible, but you? I thought it was amusing that your teacher, a bit disgruntled, elected to hand back one test personally so he could see who received a one hundred on the test, something that had not happened in his previous classes. I applaud your success on that test, but I wonder why you kept your 100 percent grade to yourself, never mentioning the grade to any of your classmates. I can visualize you, when asked whether you received the perfect score, playing dumb with a shrug, "Who me? You kidding?" But I still have to ask: Can we readdress this style? Expand the balloon?

 For now, good luck with your upcoming finals. I know you will not bother to check online for the grades. I know you will be far more interested in quickly packing, heading home, and catching our flight, just hours after your last final, to New York for Skyler's NYU graduation. It should be a fun week for all of us. I expect we will see Skyler for brief periods, as she will have several graduation parties for her double majors and additional parties with her various groups of friends. There is some good news: Skyler is going to stay behind in Manhattan to take advantage of the last full month of her rented apartment, so you are welcome to join her for several weeks in New York after the graduation. During our initial stay, we have reservations at our favorite hotel, The Giraffe, but once we head home after graduation, you can stay for as long as you want. Perhaps you can explore New York like we explored Venice, Florence, or Rome. Perhaps you can get yourself locked in another bathroom with only your towel. In any case, have some fun, as you deserve it for how you have handled your sophomore year, especially the loss of your best friend, the forced last-minute room change at the start of the year, and the second room change in the second semester. Well done.

Now on to Skyler's graduation?

Dad

JUNIOR YEAR

8/22/10 Your Junior Year? Already?

Dear Austen,

    I worry at the beginning of each of your college years. First, you have to return to a college campus, which is loaded with alcohol and drugs. USC is no different from NYU or any other college campus. Second, you have to return to an environment where so much focus is placed on a high-income major and future wealth. For this year I know you are living with three business majors, including a close friend from high school. Good, strong, young women. But they like to brag about their future jobs and potential wealth, and they have a tendency to denigrate your music major and the possibility of your becoming a music teacher with a lower salary. For them, that's too little money and too little prestige. That is not my viewpoint. I think a person's contribution to the world is more important than his or her income or lifestyle. I am proud of you for developing the same perspective, but it cannot feel good when you are the target of their banter. I wonder if they have any appreciation of the real value of teachers. I wonder if they are aware that in Finland, you have to rank in the top ten percent of your academic class to be a teacher. Or how those teachers in Finland earn some of the highest salaries for any teachers in the world. Or how Finland's high quality of education improves the quality of its citizens' lives and the country's global competitiveness. Your friends may know the price of a meal, but do they appreciate the true value of things?

Sometimes I worry if I have done you a disservice. Would you have felt any more comfortable with a different major and the potential of a higher income? Would you have felt more comfortable if you were aware of your grades? Knowing you, you would still not have said a word in your defense. But, if you have been more grade focused, would it have made you feel more grounded and more secure? Clearly, you get feedback from your professors through their various in-class comments, and you can't escape the periodic tests or papers that are returned directly to your lap, but since you don't look up your grades, you stay in the dark, not having the complete picture. On the one hand I love your perspective of focusing on learning, not grades. On the other hand I wonder if I am setting you further apart from your peers. I think that must be a challenge for all parents. How much should we, as parents, bow to the pressure of our children's selecting the right major and establishing a future high income? How much should we fight against society's demand for superficial rewards as opposed to giving, contributing, and helping others? How much should we cave to the pressure of "winning" versus just enjoying your craft? In our country, finances seem overrated and happiness seems underrated. Worse, many parents still see them as one and the same. They don't realize that higher income does not equate to greater happiness. It makes me wonder what the right balance is.

As for your situation, I wish I could do more to help you. It's easy for me to know how well you have mastered each class, but I also know how no one else knows. Then I listen to your wonderful original songs, and I wish your roommates would have the chance to listen to them. That is not your style. That is not size of your balloon. You are different. I see you as special, extremely special. I see you as someone who can make a difference in this world. I see many of the other students lacking some of your qualities, not worthy of their attempts to bring you down. But there is nothing I can do to solve the problem. You alone must decide how much to share. You alone must decide whether to stick to your silent path. Do I have suggestions? Not really. I encourage you to press forward, chasing your passions that give you the most pleasure. I encourage you to become independent of the opinion of others. That is not easy. I just read the *LA Times* article on the Afghanistan Taliban's treatment of a young couple who fell in love and decided to elope without any parental consent. Instead of a life of romance and passion, they were apprehended as they eloped and, without any trial, taken into a field and stoned to death. The Taliban do not show any mercy to those who do not follow the prescribed path. I loved your song "One for the Women's Team." Clearly, more than others, you feel a resonance with those women who have suffered from society's pressure. I only hope you follow your gift wherever it leads, ignoring those stones and enjoying the personal rewards of your separate journey.

I have another recommendation. You know me and my list of suggested habits. One of the habits is the benefit of long-term thinking. Too many people think short-term, not long-term. Too many of your wealth-driven peers will end up in jobs they hate. Or at the least, they will end up in jobs that do not give them a high level of personal reward. They should focus, on a lifelong basis, on what matters and what gives them the highest level of happiness. That type of thinking might cause them to deviate from their current, superficial pursuits. In addition, long-term thinking might help them better deal with obstacles. There is the old saying that obstacles are useful because they instruct, not obstruct. Norman Vincent Peale offered his view of obstacles: "A smooth sea never made a skilled navigator." And of course, "When God delivers a gift, he wraps it as a problem." Long-term thinking allows the person to be less affected by the opinions of others, less affected by setbacks. Why is this so important? Because success, of any type, typically takes three times longer than anticipated. To be successful and happy, you need to map out your long-term goals, stay focused on them, and tolerate the slow progress toward those goals. During your journey, you will need that perspective to persevere through the peaks and valleys of everyday life. Sometimes college seems like a series of mountains. Here's hoping you can persevere through the rugged terrain and emerge with some solid, comfortable footing.

Here's hoping you can have a great junior year.

Dad

8/28/10 Happiness and Wealth? Not the Same?

Dear Austen,

    I am impressed with your classes, your teachers, and your schedule for the fall of your junior year. I also want to offer my support for your application for the Thornton Outreach teaching program. I think that classroom experience, helping another teacher in a local school, is an excellent opportunity to see how much you enjoy teaching. I think it would offer a good counterpoint for your songwriting. As I understand it, you will be writing and performing songs outside of class this year, both by yourself and with a band, plus both in a café situation and a club situation. Junior year in college is often a time when the student clarifies what she really wants. From my perspective, you have an upcoming fork in the road. Do you want to be a music teacher? Do you want to be a professional songwriter or part of a band? Obviously, I think you would be successful in any endeavor, but the key is not what I think. The key is what *you* want. In that regard, we have already discussed the need to go against the current, the need to go against the societal push for wealth, and the need to focus on happiness.

    By the way, I just read an article on happiness. When happiness is compared to income, happiness is a bell-shaped curve. Higher income, at some point, leads to lower happiness. The article explained how the decreased happiness at higher incomes often comes from constant stress, the time away from the family, and the time lost from other hobbies or passions. The article did not offer anything different from the tabloids. What do they tell us? They describe the high level of divorces among the wealthy. They recount the long list of famous people with drug and alcohol problems. Heck, they highlight the drug and alcohol problems in the children of wealthy families. The families may have money and fame, but they seem to have lost something far more important. Their basic values? Their shared love? Their time together? Their shared family happiness? I thought it was a good reminder to keep focusing on what pleases you the most. That's the key issue. Nothing is more important.

As an aside, you always seem reluctant to spend any of my money. Remember how much money you saved me with your Presidential scholarship? That money belongs more to you than to me. From our conversation, I understand that this year's songwriting will be lessons with one teacher—that keyboard singer/songwriter from Pink—and you will be working on increasing your number of songs and expanding the arrangement of those songs with different instruments. Did I hear that correctly in our last telephone chat? When you submit your songs, you have to layer them with vocals, a piano track, a guitar track, drums, and other instruments? All played or created by you? Here's a key question: Do you want us to purchase any additional music equipment, or upgrade any current equipment, for your songwriting class? Although I am opposed to focusing on money, and although I am opposed to the spending patterns of the wealthy, I am not opposed to spending money when that money is an investment in you or your education. You know my opinion. One of the secrets to success? It's investing in yourself. Just read the stories of successful people. Try Henry Ford. Do not shortchange yourself by limiting purchases of necessary equipment that could upgrade your skills for success and happiness. Do many people spend their money on the wrong things, not investing in themselves and their future? We both know the answer to that question.

Just give this type of investment some thought.
Dad

9/19/10 Your Sharing? So Much Appreciated!

Dear Austen,

 Thanks for joining us for the weekend and thanks for sharing two of your new songs. I was impressed with both songs, and I was very impressed with your songwriting teacher. I thought she gave very specific and effective advice, and I thought she made the songs even better. I really like the structure of your songwriting course in that you get time with a group but also get individual time with her. I also thought of another hidden benefit: there are not many people who know of your upcoming fork in the road. Will you become a songwriter or a music teacher? Your songwriting teacher has done both. She played in a band that had multiple hits, wrote a number of good songs, and she is now a teacher because she has a young child and wants to spend time with her son. I think everyone needs some mentoring for future plans. I do not know her well enough to know if she could fulfill that role, but it would be nice if your relationship blossoms into that level of closeness. As I understood it, you could stick with her through both your junior year and senior years, receiving good training and good advice. In the meantime, enjoy this unique class. Who would have guessed, back when you were in high-school opera shows, that you would be writing pop songs and singing them in different venues? That is one of the great benefits of college, as so many students go in different, unexpected directions, and it's one of the fun parts for the parents, watching this growth. For all parents, there are surprises. To me, that is worth the cost of college.

 I also want to comment on the synchronicity in your classes. I think that is also pretty cool. Too many students take classes that have no connection. If I heard you on the last phone call, you are writing an article on improving performance in one class while performing in another class, yes? I do not know if those performances are good for your nerves, but I found your recent topic very interesting. I never knew Johnny Cash would sing one of his songs one hundred times before recording it. In those repetitions, would he focus on phrasing and artistic elements? Would he write and rewrite the lyrics? Your areas of study, and even Skyler's areas of study, are so different than mine. Reluctantly, I took one science class after another. You two? Because of your high-school advanced placement courses and tests, you do not even have to take any science or math courses. Such good fortune for your interests. Enjoy the Thornton School of Music. You seem to be learning so many interesting components, from music theory to aural skills, music history to composition, songwriting to computer recording, playing numerous instruments to performing. You have made such massive progress. Two years ago you felt musically behind your freshman classmates. How about now? Your progress is more than small steps; it is big steps heading toward a bright future. Again, forget the naysayers and make the most of the USC experience. You are becoming an excellent musician through your own path.

Pretty friggin' amazing!
Dad

10/01/10 The Gospel Choir Story? An Unexpected Surprise.

Dear Austen,

    I want to thank you for the gospel choir story. Again, if I heard it clearly from Mom, did the head of the choir ask the students whether they were coming to the choir from a religious or a spiritual perspective? Were half of the students claiming they were religious, and the other half of students asserting they were spiritual but not religious? That reminded me of our country's current statistics. More and more people are growing up without a direct connection to religion. On the surface, you would think that trend could lead to increased bad behaviors, but studies show the opposite. Do you know that the people who are most religious tend to be less accepting of other religions? Or the people who are most religious tend to less accepting of scientific facts such as global warming or toxins in our foods? People who are less religious are more likely to treat others as they would wish to be treated. People who are less religious tend to be less judgmental. Now, I know those findings are just the result of some studies. How about you? Do you see any difference in behavior between those students who have come to the gospel choir from a religious perspective and those from a spiritual perspective?

    You and Skyler are quite an opposite pair. Skyler will fly to Rome to see the Pope. If you ask her, she will say, especially after four years of Catholic high school, that she and God are "tight." You? You would certainly not fly to attend any mass. Skyler is religious. You are spiritual. However, I do not see any difference in the way you two think about the world or in the way you two treat others. Maybe those studies are not correct? Maybe other factors are involved? For you, I support continued participation in the gospel choir and continued spirituality. As I have shared, people like you and me who are quiet and shy seem to benefit from spirituality through an increased sense of connection to God—and a subsequent increased connection with others. We need that sense of connection to help lift our moods. Skyler is so outgoing she does not seem to need the same degree of spirituality. Maybe for her, religion is the answer. With all of the world's chaos, we need more tolerance, regardless of how we achieve it. Thank your head of the choir for raising that point, and thank you for sharing the story with Mom. If you ever get a chance to ask him his opinion on the two avenues to his choir, and how they lead to any different behaviors, please let me know his response. I need a little education myself. Well, let's be honest. I could benefit from a *lot* of education!

Just another parent trying to learn,
Dad

10/19/10 Refusing to Learn Your Grades?

Dear Austen,

    I want to congratulate you on your recent counselor meeting. I want to pass along my respect for once again passing up the chance to learn of your grades or your GPA. More importantly, I want to congratulate you on bypassing her suggestion of how you could have graduated early, not waiting for another year and next summer. I presume they pass along that suggestion to all students who have sufficient credits. The counselors are well aware of the financial struggle for so many parents. However, even with the financial challenge, and even with the high number of student loans, I support your staying for all four years of college. Yes, there are times when you are overloaded with assignments. Yes, there are times when things go wrong, both inside and outside the classroom. Yes, there are plenty of down moments in college. I remember them well myself. Times that seemed totally wasted. But college is also a special time that will never be repeated. Another semester with Gary Glaze? Another semester with an individual songwriting coach? When would you ever have that opportunity again? From my perspective, once you get through this next semester with your final required course, you will have tremendous flexibility for your senior year, especially for your second semester of that year. I would utilize that flexibility to take those courses you would most like to study. There may be some hidden gems for music classes. There may be some areas that strike your fancy, something that would not be easy to study away from school. Keep doing just what you are currently doing, focusing on maximizing your education. And saying no to an update on your grades.

    Did you know Skyler could have graduated in three years at NYU? Several of her friends graduated at that early date. For her, I think it was a reflection of her number of advanced placement credits. For those high-school students who take the AP program, it gives them a better chance for being accepted at the college of their choice, but it also gives them a better chance for graduating from college in three years. Don't think of how much money I would have saved. Think of how much Skyler would have missed. She was able to add that summer session in Madrid. That allowed all of us, as a family, to take a once-in-our-lifetime trip through much of Europe. Think of the interesting courses she was able to take in her senior year. Better yet, think how she was able to live in an apartment with her same roommates from the freshman dorm. Those experiences create deeper friendships. From my perspective—and I know I am lucky because I am a physician and I can work harder to cover the cost—I still believe it is worth every penny. I still support my own dad's conviction that his best investment was in my education. Again, I am glad you decided not to shortchange yourself. You did not even have to ask, nor did Skyler, about continuing your education. That makes me proud of both of you girls. Or, at this point, should I say women? You already knew my bias toward learning as much as possible.

Either way, I toast both of you.

Dad

11/10/10 Groupons? New Adventures?

Dear Austen,

    In our recent telephone call did you say that you used a Groupon and received treatment from an acupuncturist about twenty minutes away from school? That action echoes my perspective of using college for new experiences. It was your first time with an acupuncturist, right? What did you think? Did you know how I recently developed a trigger thumb, where my thumb would not bend? I stopped by our urgent care where the physician gave me six shots of cortisone into my thumb (with more pain than I would have liked), placed me in a soft hand cast, and ordered me back in a week. I returned with zero improvement. The physician tried another course of shots with continuation of the soft hand cast. I followed all of the instructions and returned, once again, in another week, with no improvement. The physician offered me a referral to a surgeon who could operate on my tendon. Did I go to the surgeon? Of course not. Since when do I follow a physician's advice? Instead, I went to a local acupuncturist, received four treatments over four weeks, and regained complete mobility of my thumb with no need for any surgery. Were you as fortunate? From our conversation, it sounded as if your complaints were completely remitted with no further discomfort.

    How does acupuncture work? Who knows? The acupuncturist explained how he viewed my body as having barriers along certain healing paths. His task was to open those channels through the correct positioning of needles to allow healing energy to flow into my thumb. In each treatment, I could feel the sensation of something healthy, a palpable healing force, as it surged into my thumb. Did you have the same sensation? In Chinese medicine, the lowest class of medicine is the treatment of an illness. In our country, that is 90 percent of our health-care system. In Chinese medicine, the next higher level of care is the prevention of illnesses. In our country, that preventive component is probably 10 percent of our health care. In Chinese medicine, the highest form of medicine offers the goal of helping the patient achieve maximum health. Regular acupuncture. Healthy eating. Daily herbs. Different types of exercise routines. In our country, we don't offer those health-care services. Here's my recommended substitute: use college to maximize your health. You are improving your level of knowledge through all of your courses. Why not spend an equal amount of time and energy on improving your level of health? Now that's a good way to complete your education, setting you up for the real world. You need to keep studying your narrow food choices, and you need to keep hitting the gym. Sound reasonable?

For you, life can be especially challenging. You can't eat gluten or dairy products. You are allergic to a significant number of foods. It is easy to view those dietary restrictions as negative. I view them as positive. There are too many foods in our country that are loaded with contaminants, chemicals, antibiotics, GMOs, and other toxins that cause inflammation. Your restrictions already eliminate many of those problematic foods. Here is what I suggest. Chinese medicine offers the perspective: "from within to without." That means that any physical symptoms, whether a rash or some discomfort, must be treated and healed from the inside, not from the outside. You have already heard my perspectives on the mind-body connection. Just expand the umbrella. Improve your thinking. Upgrade your conversations. Eat healthy foods and exercise regularly. Open those channels for healing. Let college be a time of your life where you establish great health—physical and mental. For these last two years of college, use the time to upgrade not just your mind, but also your body. I wish more students worked on their health as much as they work on their grades, and I wish more students would try different approaches to their health, whether a change in diet or a drive to an acupuncturist. That is one of the many things I like about USC. There are a lot of active, healthy students. Glad you are becoming one of them.

So, keep exploring. Outside the classroom?

Dad

12/06/10 Grammy Invitation?

Dear Austen,

    First, we received your Grammy invitation today at home, and we are going to bring it up Wednesday to USC. We want to applaud you for being chosen once again, as a volunteer, to participate in the preparation for the Grammy show. Do you get to help escort the musicians on the day before for the show? Do you get to watch them rehearse on that day of the show? Do you also get a chance to get to know them a little? I have so many questions. Are some of them approachable? Are others pretty self-absorbed? Do they seem as if they are enjoying the rehearsal? Or do they seem as if they view it as work, not as fun? After all, it is their career. I would love to know how many went to music school and how many went to a performing arts high school. I know several pop musicians who went to a music college. But I suspect it's the composers, the conductors, and the other instrumental musicians who perfected their craft in the college setting. When I think about it, it makes me realize how many more options there are for today's college students. In my era, it was a straight line for most of us. When you finished college and made a career choice, that was often your career for life. Today, experts claim most students will have multiple careers, not just multiple jobs. The only constant is the endless change in the workplace. You have my empathy for having so many choices, now and in the future. All those choices make life harder, not easier. Still, that's another reason to applaud your focus on learning. It looks as if you are going to have to make learning a cornerstone for every future job and every career.

    That's not a bad cornerstone.
    Dad

12/15/10 Another Semester? Getting Better and Better?

Dear Austen,

The more I text, the less I write or e-mail. That fact probably brings a smile to your face. I want to use this e-mail to congratulate you on completing another successful semester. I will not even ask about the difficulty of the final exams. That would have been automatic four years ago, but not now. Instead, I want to express my appreciation for how you have been able to synthesize the material from your music courses into an overlapping and broader understanding of your entire music field. Your third semester of music history and your just-finished course on music in films seems to have cemented your understanding of recent music history. So, congratulations on learning so much about your field and mastering a deeper understanding of the music industry. That, after all, is the purpose of college. The goal is not to do well in any specific course; the goal is to develop a broad understanding of the field of your choice. When Skyler finished NYU, she had a grasp of the film industry and its relationship to the world. When you graduate, you will have a grasp of the life of a musician and all of the different options for sharing your love of music. Do the other students take the same approach? Do your business-major roommates talk about their increasing understanding of the various business options? Or do they only discuss their possible jobs? I hope for the former, as they need to develop a better understanding of all of their choices.

Along those lines, I also want to repeat my congratulations on your becoming a better musician. I am not the best judge of this field, but I have been repeatedly amazed by all of your original songs, from those five to seven guitar songs you wrote during the summer to the numerous songs you composed during the course of the semester. But I was most impressed by your acoustic set of your own songs in the café around midsemester, and I was blown away with your full band performance at the recent evening show. I was impressed not just by the quality of your musicianship, but I was impressed by how you seemed to take the lead of the band. It was pleasing to see how much you seemed to be enjoying yourself with the full band. That must be quite an experience. As someone who has attended his fair share of concerts, I have always wondered what it felt like to be on the stage with all eyes focused on you. I will never know the answer to that question, but it's nice to realize that *you* know how that feels. It is also nice to know that you have become a professional, no longer an amateur. At this point, for the first time in my life, I can see why some students leave college early. They are ready for the next level. That applies to an athlete; it also applies to a musician or artist. I still support your going through four years of college. But like with so many other things, I am learning. I am gaining a better appreciation of the options. For me, I am just thankful to be able to witness your progress. In so many college fields, the parents never get to see the progress of their child. What's there to see on someone's written final exam? When Skyler dove in her senior diving meet or when you performed your set of songs onstage, those two performances were something we will never forget. Again, I wish more parents had the opportunity to witness their child's growth.

What can I say? Thanks for the memories!

Dad

1/10/11 Do You Feel Any Parental Pressure?

Dear Austen,

As always, it was great to have you home for the Christmas vacation. You and Skyler were fabulous! At our recent Steak House celebration, I felt as if the three of us (Mom, you, and I) were treating Skyler, Eric, and Brandon to dinner, so I offered a toast to each of them. But I want to save my toast to you for this e-mail. I realize I am limited in my texts, but does that also mean I am limited in my e-mails? I will assume the answer is yes, and I will try my best to make the most of my e-mails. I am very proud of you and how you have grown in college. For 2011, I wish you the very best for continuing to follow your heart, creating your own path. Do you feel any pressure from me for selecting a specific path? I hope not. One day at a time, one class at a time, and one semester at a time. Truly, I do not know which path will lead to your greatest happiness. I may love your songs, but I love your happiness more. Keep doing what you are doing. I wish I had been as focused and independent as you are when I was your age. I did not have your internal strength to go my own course. If I had had that strength, I would not have gone to medical school. I would have kept writing. But no complaints. Medical school led me to Mom. She's been the love of my life, and she gave me Skyler and you, my two biggest achievements. Stick to your heart. Stick to your dreams. You have my 100 percent support, no matter how you do or what you decide to do. In my eyes, you will always be fabulous. I could not be a luckier father.

It was also a delight to move you back into your apartment. I love USC. I think your schedule for this semester looks great. I have your index card, which I always place on my work desk, right before me. It is always fun to follow your daily schedule: three classes today, with two of them music and culture, plus one English class. It sounds great. Good luck with your new classes and good luck with your new solo room as your prior roommate heads overseas to another campus. This will be your first time living by yourself in your own room. You can let us know how that feels. That's a choice many students have to make. Live alone? Or live with some roommates? I can imagine it will be a big adjustment, with some isolation at night. Facebook with your friends? See more of your suite mates or other students at the apartment complex? Come home more on the weekends? I hope one or all of these options help limit any isolation you might feel in a single room. If not, concentrate on the good features. No interruptions, fewer disturbances while trying to sleep, more free time to watch something on your computer. Keep slipping in those morning trips to the gym. You are looking healthy and fit. We love you. And we love your calls. They are always the highlight of my day.

Sleep well. Without any parental pressure!

Dad

1/24/10 Your Songwriting? Your Singing?

Dear Austen,

   Thanks for tonight's call, especially because you were exhausted. It sounded as if your songwriting coach was planning to have you focus on three different areas of songwriting, including pop songs (in a lower voice), classical songs (in your higher voice), and some other song type, which I did not clearly hear. Was it "comical" songs? Or songs with a quirky, humorous component? Ala Alanis Morissette? I know your coach has loved some of your quirky songs, like "Another Love Song," because of its comical flavor. Of course, since that's your style at home, it might as well be included in some of your songs. But different genres? I have no idea how hard it is for a songwriter to switch genres. In any case, good luck in pursuing all three areas. I bet this semester will be the time of your biggest growth as a songwriter, and I bet it helps clarify your direction, especially with your continued work in the local classroom. I think your teacher is nice for repeating her compliment, claiming you are much like her. Look how well she has succeeded. She toured with top bands and she teaches at USC. That is impressive. You are so very lucky to be at USC at the Thornton School of Music with your own individual songwriting coach and own individual vocal coach. What school can beat that? So enjoy yourself this year. For once, the future can wait. Just enjoy each day.

   As for Gary Glaze, it sounded as if you were not quite as excited as he was about your option to sing opera in some of the upcoming school productions. Mom said to fake it and give it your best shot. Me? I do not see you as one who ever fakes it. You always try your best. I like that approach. When you try your best, that's when you are most alive. And when you do anything, your extra effort shows. Do I have any advice for you and your two performance options? More opera performances? More pop singing? If you want to reduce the pressure with Gary Glaze, just say no. Let him know you are going to enjoy the courses you have, you are going to make a decision about your future next year, and you will either select teaching music or writing songs, not a career in opera. That decision will not require any further opera performances. He might feel as if he has spent three years developing your talent for nothing, but you can ease his disappointment by explaining how you plan to give vocal lessons, and how his coaching has helped you to define your own teaching approach. Anyway, you cannot please everyone, as we have repeatedly seen, so you might as well please yourself. For me, that approach is crucial for maximizing your enjoyment this semester. Let this semester help you gain further clarity on your vision of your future. Let this semester lift you above the chaos of so many options—even if you have to disappoint one of your mentors.

Dad

2/04/11 No Awareness of Grades? But Phi Beta Kappa?

Dear Austen,

    I was shocked when you forwarded me the e-mail from the Phi Beta Kappa society notifying you of your selection to their society, and then I was further shocked when you asked me if you should even bother to join? As much as you have bypassed grades, Phi Beta Kappa is the top honor society in the United States. It selects only the very best students. If you received the offer to join as a junior, that means you must be in the top 1 percent of your class. If nothing else, the recognition validates your approach to college. You followed your heart and your passions. You focused on learning, not grades. There is a hidden lesson in your success. I learned the first part of the lesson from Skyler and her commitment to her vision of her future—as opposed to my vision of her future—and I learned the second part of the lesson from you and your commitment to learning your craft, not just competing for grades. The lesson is simple: if you enjoy the journey, and if you make the most of the journey, you do not have to worry about rewards. You will find happiness and success, and you will reach your destination. I am reminded of those studies of how many people are in the wrong job or the wrong career. If they took Skyler's and your approach to college, and then continued the same approach toward their careers, that type of mistake would never occur. Parents should love and support their kids, regardless of what path they select or what grades they obtain. Parents should get out of the way. Of course, I am just as guilty as any other parent. Maybe both of you succeeded in spite of me? If true, that is good news for all parents.

    As to Phi Beta Kappa, that is your decision.
Dad

2/10/11 A Parental Gift? Willing to Accept It?

Dear Austen,

In appreciation of all of the hard work and your Phi Beta Kappa achievement, Mom and I want to give you a gift. Since you have never focused on any financial reward (or really any external reward), and since you repeatedly encourage us not to buy you anything, we want to give you something along a different line. You will find below our written comments from your baby book. Yep, comments about how we felt when you were born. We were going to save them for later, but now seems to be a good occasion. Hope you enjoy.

Dear Austen,

I couldn't understand why I was so tired all the time. I stopped nursing Skyler and expected to have more energy. Then when I tried on a bathing suit and found that I had gained a little weight, I knew something was going on! Sure enough, I took a pregnancy test, and the results came back positive! Another blood test at the doctor's office confirmed the results! We were shocked. We were thrilled but scared—scared at the prospect of having two children so close together in age. After the initial shock wore off, we began to get progressively excited and make plans for this wonderful addition. You gave me no trouble at all during the pregnancy—no morning sickness, no edema, twenty-three pound weight gain. Except for lower back pain toward the end, I felt great, and I remained in good health. Then when the big day came, Dad and I were ready for you! Seeing your black hair, pulling you by your little fists and torso, and placing you on my tummy made me teary eyed! What an incredible feeling! Thanks to you! It was such a gratifying experience! The moment it happened, we bonded for life! I wish I could relive that moment just to see your face! I love you!!!!

Love, Mom

1/22/90

Dear Austen,

    With your sister Skyler, it was high technology: test tube, CryoFreeze, thawing, and then pregnancy. With you, it was the old-fashioned way. I skipped working one morning, stayed home until 1:00 p.m., and then two weeks later we experienced total shock. What was once difficult had suddenly become easy. Ah, the unpredictability of life. It's what makes life so delightful. We announced our pregnancy at our gourmet dinner club, describing a "slight and small interruption in our attendance," and everyone laughed. But no one was more pleased than the two of us. Did we want a second child? Absolutely! As much as we wanted Skyler, that's how much we wanted you! With Skyler, we cracked the barrier of infertility, but with you, we had moved full circle from a couple alone to a couple with a complete family. Two girls? No, I was not hoping for a boy. So, I was pleased with the pregnancy, relieved at the amniocentesis (no genetic problems), and delighted with your birth. Although I must confess it was a shock, a wonderful shock, when you emerged with Mom's black hair, Mom's eyes, and Mom's complexion. Lucky you. You were beautiful, and you were the perfect counterpoint to Skyler, who had my features. And you got better looking by the week! Your face lengthened, your color blossomed, and your hair grew even darker. By January, you were more beautiful than ever, drawing praise from everyone except, of course, Skyler, who is still taking a while to adapt to your arrival. My hopes? That we become great friends, not just father and daughter, and that I can be supportive and appreciative of your life journey. And that the Courter family can be a great family. It would not have happened without you, as you have really completed the family, adding the final ingredient! Austen, I love you. Welcome to our world!
    Love, Dad
    1/22/90

Those baby letters beat a new car, right?
    Dad

3/01/11 Another Father Confessional?

Dear Austen,

    You and I are a lot more alike than you realize. Of course, I would say that after you were accepted into Phi Beta Kappa. No, I never came close to that level of academic achievement. Getting into medical school is one thing. Getting into Phi Beta Kappa is a different level of achievement. But my comparison of the two of us does not relate to academic success; it relates to our personalities. You were accepted into Phi Beta Kappa, and yet you have told no one? Just like you did when you received a 100 percent on your music history examination? That is a remarkable level of modesty, but I am not going to address modesty. Instead, I want to readdress the topic of sharing. As I have previously observed, you and I are similar in that we tend to keep things to ourselves, and consequently we tend to have only a small group of friends. I am not saying we are lacking something. I am just saying we might want to reevaluate our style and our level of sharing. At my age, I may be too old to change. At your age, you have plenty of time. You just need to ask yourself how much you want to change.

    When you were growing up, you had a lot of setbacks because of your health issues. I had a lot of setbacks, but they were social, not physical. We moved every few years, so I was forced to say good-bye to friend after friend. How much did I hate moving? I reached the point, as a middle school kid, where I would rush home after school just to hide the For Sale sign in our front yard. Bit by bit, I think I learned to go my solitary route without sharing too much. At the lowest point, during one of my family's moves, my best friend did not know I was moving until that day. For us, as baseball teammates, there was no good-bye. There was also no final handshake. That style, once it solidified, led to less emotional pain, but it also led to fewer friends. In the long run, I was lucky. I met Mom, and I now have Mom, Skyler, and you. Without the three of you, my life wouldn't be one-tenth as enjoyable or satisfying. Why? Because the key to life is sharing, and the key to happiness is friendship.

    Your election into Phi Beta Kappa was great. I hope it made you feel proud. You are the only Phi Beta Kappa in the family. My mother was a straight-A student who skipped one grade. Her brother was another straight-A student who skipped two grades, starting college at the age of sixteen. But look at my mother. As smart as she is, she still is not representative of how to live life. What does that tell us? There is more to life than brains, there is more to life than competition and grades, and there is much more to life than her style of judgment and criticism. In retrospect, if I had to do it all over again, I would have put more effort into friendships. I would have been more vocal, less silent. I would have been more open, with greater sharing and giving. Now, why am I sharing this confessional? It goes back to our earlier discussion of the balloon. It goes back to our earlier discussion of sharing. There is part of me that wishes you would share more of yourself with your peers. From my standpoint, it would not be bragging; it would just be sharing. And in life, the more sharing, the greater your number of friends. Life may feel complicated, but it is really quite simple.

For you, what do I want? I could fill this entire e-mail with pages and pages of praise. But that praise is insignificant. I just want you to be happy. You know how much I want you to create a path that gives you satisfaction and joy. At the same time, I want you to be as fortunate as I was with love and marriage. You are already well on your way to professional success. We both know you will be successful. However, no journey is satisfying unless it can be shared. I want to offer you another challenge. I want you to see, over time, if you can expand your level of sharing. If you need a model, think of Skyler, not of me. If you can expand how much you share—both the good and the bad—that sharing will attract someone special into your life. But you have to put it out there. I do not want you to change who you are; I am suggesting your life might be even better if you could share more of exactly *who* you are. Start small, but try sharing more. Then see what (or who) you can attract into your life.

Sound simple? For me, it has been a lifelong challenge.

Dad

4/09/11 Want to Know My Secret Birthday Wish?

Dear Austen,

    If these e-mails seem to be focusing more on me than on you, then it is perhaps a reflection of my growing age and emerging dementia. After all, what do old people like to talk about? Their memories from their earlier years and, of course, their ailments. As for me, I am still thinking about my earlier e-mail to you with the recommendation for both of us to share more of ourselves. What brought out those thoughts? First, there was a stack of presents, arranged on the breakfast table by dear, sweet Mom, for my birthday. Some of the presents came from Mom, and some of the presents came from the two of you. Second, there was her observation of how it is getting harder and harder to buy me a birthday gift. But what is the best present you can give to someone? In my mind I ran through a list of possible presents, and then I realized I could top all of those gifts with something far richer, far more satisfying, and far longer lasting. Can you guess what it is?

    Let me give you a clue. You know how I like to cite studies. I recently read that on a daily basis, the average spouse spends four to twenty minutes, one-on-one, with his or her mate, and the average parent spends two to twenty minutes, one-on-one, with each of his or her children. Those are pretty pathetic statistics. So I am going to encourage you, when the time comes, to spend more time with your family. I am going to suggest something even more important. Something you can't wrap in any box. The best gift each of us can give to our loved ones is to become a better person. So that is what I am going to try to do. That's what you should try to do. Become a better person. For me, that translates into being more available. It also translates into sharing more. How about you? How do you attract the best people, or the right man, into your life? It is not by applying more makeup. It is not by buying some fancy shoes. It is by becoming a better person. Frankly, I already think you are a wonderful person. But more sharing? Could you be even better?

    However, becoming a better person takes more than increased availability and increased sharing. It requires all the things my mother is not doing, and it requires so many of the things you are already doing. You are helping fellow college students with their work. You are helping young grade-school students as a teacher's aide. You are even helping people you do not know. I just listened to your new song about how you talked to the homeless man on the street, how he shared his predicament, and how he asked you to pray for his soul. Of course, the policeman gave you a ticket, your first ticket in your life, for jaywalking toward the homeless man. What is giving without some sacrifice? But, as I heard the story, you still promised to pray for the man's soul. Despite that policeman, that's what we all need to do. We need to focus on being more tolerant, less judgmental. We need to focus on giving, not receiving. We need to focus on sharing, not hiding. If we can do all of that, we will become better people. That will make you richer in the true sense of the word, and it will make those around you live a richer life. You don't want gold in your pocket; you want gold in your soul. That is my birthday wish for the both of us.

Let's see how much better we can be.

Dad

5/1/11 Ah, the Award Ceremonies and Recital

Dear Austen,

    I want to thank you for the two spring award ceremonies. The Phi Beta Kappa was, I suppose, voluntary, but the school's Pi Kappa Lambda's dinner seemed mandatory. We were glad we attended both of them with you. At the Phi Beta Kappa ceremony, I was surprised by the predominance of women. Where were the men? Do they not study in college? Really, for every one guy, there were six girls receiving the award. Same for the Pi Kappa Lambda dinner, although there seemed to be a few more men. Maybe we should be paying women more than men? Just saying! Congratulations for receiving the artistic and academic award for the best junior at the Thornton School of Music. As always, I was proud of you. But I have more questions for you: Do you think academic success is a reflection of a student's clarity of what he or she wants to do? Do those students who are certain about their future profession do better in class? In your situation, you are still debating whether to become a teacher or a songwriter. That debate does not seem to be holding you back from learning. My initial theory is probably wrong. If people select a profession too quickly, they often seem to make a mistake. The same holds true for jobs. Most people seem to jump into whatever opening is available. That could be a job, a career, or a relationship. I like your approach. Maintain high standards and make certain it's exactly what you want.

    Mom and I also enjoyed your junior-year recital. We were not aware of the required degree of preparation. Is it true what we heard from your colleagues, that you had to rent a small auditorium on campus, post announcements of your recital, and pay an accompanist, at least for the section of the performance devoted to your classical songs? Then you had to print those brochures, listing your songs, the composers, and the history of each of the songs? I enjoyed reading about your classical song choices, but I especially enjoyed your inclusion of several of your own original pop songs. I thought you sang beautifully, and I think the audience loved your performance. I watched your classical vocal coach, Gary Glaze, and he was smiling throughout the entire performance, even when you played the piano and sang one of your original pop songs, and then played the guitar and sang another one of your original pop songs. He seemed to enjoy your classical voice and your pop voice. My only wish? I wish more of the parents knew how much work goes into the Thornton School of Music program. It is not easy. Then again, if I were exposed to the other programs, maybe they are not easy either. As a parent, I wish I could have been exposed to some of those programs. Regardless, congratulations on a well-done series of spring events. They were wonderful treats for us.

Now, on to your final papers and final junior-year exams.

Dad

5/13/11 What, an Example of Your Work?

Dear Austen,

Years from now, you will forget the quality of your work, including the quality of your singing, the quality of all of your original songs, and the quality of your essays in so many of your classes. We already have many of your songs on CDs. I also know some of your performances are on the Internet. But how about all of those essays? I thought it was only fair to include a couple of paragraphs from one of your recent essays. It is the essay entitled *Laurie Anderson: A "Homeland" Musical Iconoclast*. Since it is a long essay, double-digit in pages, I decided to include the opening paragraph and the concluding paragraph in this e-mail. Will you save any of my e-mails? If you do, you might find a hidden gem in one of them. That would be this essay. I hope you enjoy this e-mail and the below essay, or at least remember it.

Appealing to a broad audience, while maintaining artistic integrity, has been a constant challenge for musicians. Many artists stray from their artistic goals, succumbing to the lure of financial reward. This conflict is most visible in the popular music genre, with critics arguing that popular music often offers nothing new artistically because of the demand for a financial profit. In fact, Theodor Adorno, one of the leading critics in popular music studies, contends that popular music "will lead back to the same familiar experience, and nothing fundamentally novel will be introduced" (1). One artist stands in defiance to the assertion that popular music remains recycled bubblegum fluff. Her name: Laurie Anderson. One of the most iconic artists to emerge from the select subcategory of "performance artists," Anderson creates innovative musical landscapes that serve as foundations for her social and political lyrics. Her use of multiple (and personally created) instruments and her varied methods of presenting her voice create original works of electronic pop that redefine the genre while still satisfying a larger audience. Laurie Anderson's unique style is most recently showcased in her critically acclaimed 2010 album, Homeland, *which utilizes diverse sounds but remains unified as a solid musical entity.*

Through Homeland, *Laurie Anderson has once again created controversy by repeatedly offering contentious topics of debate, including the role of experts, the market crash, the fragile economics of average Americans, the invasion and destruction of Afghanistan and Iraq, the use of machines, the expansion of technology, and the constant rush of change toward a new world order. Anderson doesn't offer solutions; instead, she poses questions, asking the audience to join in the debate. With her atypical topics and her original sounds, Anderson is one of the most unique musicians in the categorization of popular music. She continues to defy the norms of the genre with her unusual mix of instruments, her fresh sounds, and her thought-provoking lyrics. Her songs are far more varied—musically and lyrically—than those by other popular musicians, ranging from dreamy tunes to sarcastic laments to international wonders. By confronting today's social and political issues, by mixing these issues with original musical backdrops, and by establishing a special relationship with her audience, Anderson has established herself as a cultural force. After five decades, she remains one of the most innovative musicians in today's musical landscape. Her music is still a vital ingredient for a society that needs to change and adapt to a new world era. From the high quality of her most recent album,* Homeland, *there is no doubt that she will remain a musical iconoclast, utilizing her music to help people make meaningful assessments of their lives and the world.*

One last thought. When I read Skyler's senior-year thesis on horror films, I was surprised how films reflect our world, and when I read your papers on musicians, I am equally surprised how their work also reflects the world. For a parent, it is comforting to know you are receiving a rich education; it's even more comforting to know you are receiving an education that not only addresses more than your specific major but also the forces within our chaotic word. You are both going to need that knowledge to be able to adjust to our new world and its growing chaos of challenges. As previously stated, the world is so much more complex than when I was your age.

I am glad you are so prepared.

Dad

SENIOR YEAR

8/17/11 Your Last Undergraduate Year? Too Fast?

Dear Austen,

You just left for your one-hour trip to USC, your red, banged-up Honda Accord loaded with groceries, suitcase, and other items, as you make your final trek to your apartment before starting your senior year at USC. Well, I miss you already. It was great to have you home for a good part of the summer. Your teaching at St. John's worked out great for us because we were able to see more of you. I will admit I have not been looking forward to this day. Part of me would love to have you stay home forever. Of course, that is not a possibility. Instead, I am going to concentrate on the positive features of the start of your senior year. I remember my senior year of college as being a great year. The first semester may be rough, but the second semester gives you a chance to relax. Since you have done so well learning the material, I would continue your current style. From my perspective, I am hoping your senior year provides you with time for friends, time for fun, and time to clarify your options for your future.

Mom and I support your application to the Masters of Arts in Teaching program. We think you would be a fabulous teacher. In your senior year, I hope you can find even more time for some volunteer teaching experiences at that local school. We love your stories of the kids and how funny they can be. That must be a wonderful feeling to have them rush up to you for a big hug, and it must be a satisfying feeling to know you are expanding their confidence and improving their character. But I have one warning. The senior year passes by in a blur. Take time to smell the roses. Take time to enjoy the USC experience. The same philosophy holds true for us. Mom and I would like to make more of an effort to attend music events and any other school events, including football games, during your senior year. We can always extend an invitation to Skyler since she is back in Los Angeles and working in the film industry. It will be fun to have the four of us together, attending a weekend activity. I, for one, vote for a new habit: a monthly dinner for the four of us, just so we can stay in touch. Besides, for us, you two can be such a fun pair.

Which brings me to another point. Last night I came across an entry from my 1994 journal where I noted how Skyler had run into my computer room yelling "Austen said a bad word. Austen said a bad word. Austen said a bad word!" So, what was that bad word? You said, "I can't!" Apparently, that was the time, when Skyler was seven years old and you were five years old, when I was trying my hardest to train you both to say "I can," not "I can't." No, I wasn't the smartest of fathers, but it must have worked because both of you seem to carry forward the "I can" philosophy. Thanks for tolerating me through those early childhood years. Thanks, too, for tolerating me and all these e-mails through college. And now how about a tribute to the "I can" attitude? A tribute with a continued focus on all the great possibilities for all of us, as you finish your USC education and head into your career. Here's a raised glass of wine, as Mom and I are drinking chardonnay with dinner, to your future success and that continued confident attitude that needs to precede any type of success.

Feel free to rock it with the "I can" attitude.

Dad

8/28/11 Racing to the Finish Line?

Dear Austen,

    I want to congratulate you on finishing the first week of your senior year. Not only did you not get senioritis, you embraced your classes and your new schedule. I was hoping you might go easy on yourself in your senior year, but I know you too well. Of course, you would opt for another heavy load of classes. But seven classes? Is that not a bit too heavy a load? I applaud your positive attitude toward learning as much as you can, but there are limits. Nevertheless, I understand your sentiment. One year from now your cohorts will be working at a job, probably 8:00 a.m. to 5:00 p.m., with classes long since forgotten. Classes are a gift. Just make certain you are taking the courses that interest you, the courses that will not be available one year from now. Part of me understands. As I have shared before, when I graduated from Williams College, if I had been given a magic wand ala Harry Potter, I would have liked to reaccept the acceptance letter from Stanford, go back in time, and start all over as a Stanford freshman. There were so many subjects I would have loved to have learned, as I had no chance to educate myself in those areas with my premed load of classes. Yes, I have spent years listening to educational programs on my drive to work, but that is still only one hour of education per day. For me, that was never enough. So many of your classes cannot be duplicated by an audio program. Will you ever have the chance for vocal coaching, songwriting coaching, and drumming coaching? Who knows? Make the most of it. As other seniors daydream of the real world, focus on what is piled on your plate.

    Thanks, too, for calling last night. Mom and I appreciated the update, especially with your current schedule. It's one thing to take eighteen units, another thing to have your two-unit classes assign as much homework as your four-unit classes, and another to have to find so much practice time for singing, drumming, and songwriting—plus needing time to mix all of the instruments for your songs. My advice is the same as always. With your decision to apply to the master's program, this could be your final year of songwriting, so enjoy it as much as you can, even with the overload. It is a rare opportunity. If you feel the need for a break, how about we come up and take you to lunch? We could go to that Italian restaurant, order a tasty, gluten-free, veggie pizza, swing by Whole Foods, and return you to your dorm, grocery shopping done. Were you doing that as a freshman? No, you were eating from the college food plan at the cafeteria. Now, you are cooking many of your meals. Life is changing. Like your fellow seniors, you are growing up, getting ready to face the real world. Until then, we will see you at the coming football game, if you can take a couple of hours off from your studying. This year, we get to bring along Skyler, and you know she will demand some type of tailgating, even if it is just a picnic for the four of us. I know you don't drink, but do you mind if we polish off at least one bottle of wine before the game?

Better get back to your homework.

Dad

9/18/11 Need A Short Break? How About More Memories?

Dear Austen,

    With your heavy workload, I thought I would rummage through the garage, find my diaries of some of our prior vacations, and send a few memories your way. Maybe you can think of them as your head hits the pillow, pushing aside thoughts of your class assignments. It'd better be good, right? How about the trip to Maui when you were ten years old and we stayed at the Grand Wailea Resort? Do you remember how we had booked two rooms for five nights, but they botched our reservations? Since the hotel was booked solid, they had to place the four of us in the only unoccupied room, the Grande Suite, which would have cost $10,000 per night. Obviously, we did not pay a penny above the cost of our two regular ocean-view rooms. Oprah had stayed in the Grand Suite. Michael Jordan had stayed there. Multiple actors and musicians had stayed there. Do you remember the suite? It had a living room, a family room, a dining room, a grand piano, three porches, three bathrooms, two Jacuzzis, one sauna, three television sets, one fax machine and ten phones, plus two bedrooms, one for us and one for you and Skyler, with the two rooms being one hundred steps apart (I counted).

    Do you remember our routine for those five days of paradise? After our buffet breakfast, where you would often eat miso soup and rice (how many ten-year-olds eat that combination for breakfast?), you and Skyler would play some games on the television. Then we would head down to the 2,000-foot-long activity pool with nine pools on six levels. We would start at the top pool, take the first two small slides, then try the Amazon Gorge, and then attempt the raging waters. If we survived, we would recover at the sandy lagoon, and then wait in line for the two massive slides or use their water elevator. By noon, we would be water logged. We would eat at the Volcano Bar beside the pool, head upstairs to relax, and then head out on some shopping excursion. Do you remember the day when Skyler threw up while she was heading down to the pool? Right into the nearby bushes. She recovered and participated in all of the day's activities. Do you remember the hotel luau where you discovered welts on your arms, apparently from something you had eaten that you were allergic to? I had to return to the room to get you Benadryl and cream. They worked, but you stumbled around the luau like a drunken ten-year-old, almost resting your face in the food, because of the sedative effect of the medication. It is nice to have a physician for a father, right? Ready to ruin any special night.

Do you remember our routine of taking a last swim before leaving the hotel? We would swim through all the slides, dive in the most turbulent waters, and search for hidden treasures. Do you remember some of the objects we found? A gold bracelet? A shiny, polished blue rock? A lost room key? Do you remember how we would pack them up, bring them home, and display them in our typeset drawer as our reminders of the vacation? Want to know a secret? Before those scavenger dives, I would slip into some of the hotel's shops and purchase many of those items. The gold bracelet. The blue rock. I never said a word, letting you think they were our secret treasures. Yes, we found some of the pieces without any assistance from me. But the other pieces were carried in my swim trunks and dropped as you two prepared to dive and search. I may be making a mistake revealing that secret. Sort of like revealing that parents are actually Santa Claus. However, there is a point. Magic can be created by chance, but also through your own effort. As you struggle through this tough schedule, create some magic of your own. Give yourself some time to remember our great vacations where we had unexpected luck. Or perhaps just remember the best moments at USC. You have to give your mind and body some intermittent rest. Many of your classmates accomplish that needed break with a rowdy night of drinking. There are healthier and safer ways to create the same effects. Go for it.

Try whatever works for you. Like some fun memories?
Dad

10/02/11 Senior Year? More Difficult Than Expected?

Dear Austen,

    Your senior year, with your packed schedule, sounds a lot like the first two years of my medical school experience. No wonder you have disappeared into your work. In the first two years of medical school, I lived in a dorm situation. However, almost every weekend, most of the students were gone from the dorm. As I have stated before, if I could have taken a pill on Friday night and awoken on Monday morning, I would have paid gold for that medication. Each weekend, I was essentially alone. I studied alone. I ate alone. And if I went out, which I did on occasion to see a movie, I went alone. Really boring, which is absurd since I was living in New York. How did I survive? I just focused on my academic work. I studied every Saturday morning, Saturday afternoon, Sunday morning, Sunday afternoon, and Sunday night. Somehow, I got into the top 5 percent, which allowed me to take my final two years of medical school anywhere, so I selected Los Angeles and the USC County Medical Center. Those final two years of medical school were a delight, so different from my first two years. Maybe you will experience that same differential between the first semester of your senior year and your second semester.

    After medical school, I slid directly into USC's medical internship. I was no longer alone; I had a great co-intern. It got better, so much better, within my first two months in medicine, when I met your mom. My life score changed from 3/10 to 10/10. All of a sudden I went from being mostly alone to being with someone who was really, really fun. It made every weekend better. It made my life better. So, my advice for you? For this semester, put on blinders. Try to pay limited attention to distractions. My earlier advice for freedom and fun? Toss it aside. Focus on what you want to learn. Right now your friends are having fun with the least possible amount of work. Your time will come, just as my time finally came. In some ways, this hard work now will just make it sweeter. Do you know the analogy of the well? The longer it takes to pump water from a well, the cooler and better tasting the water. Just have faith that better days are ahead. At this point, you are halfway through an overloaded semester. You just need to survive until the second half. Do it as you have always done it: by just learning all of the material.

When you finish this semester, let's celebrate. I will plan on taking several weeks off from work for Christmas. We can head to Disneyland on several mornings. We can visit the San Diego Zoo. Let's play the other days as the urge strikes. Maybe you will feel a desire to head to the mountains for some snow? I am certain we can find something fun for the entire family. And don't forget Maui. Once you graduate, I would love to head back to Maui, back to the Grand Wailea and back to a condo in Kapalua. We can dive for some hidden treasure. We can try that zip line. We can eat another delicious dinner at Mama's Fish House. Good times will be coming. I know you have to focus day to day, but know there is a light at the end of the tunnel. Know that the hard work will end—at least this specific type of hard work. To be honest, you will be engaged in some kind of hard work all your life, and it will pay off. For now, you have learned a ton of material this semester, and you have mastered it. See you on Saturday for lunch?

Just don't bring your books.
Dad

11/11/11 Negatives? They Can Become Positives!

Dear Austen,

    I was a little bummed this morning when I discovered your left front tire had a leak, and I was further bummed when we were not able to get anyone to fix it, as you were stuck in back-to-back-to-back classes. But that negative setback turned into something positive, as I enjoyed driving up to USC, fixing your tire, and then driving you home for a rare weekend. It reminded me of the good old days of the first semester of your freshman year when Mom would pick you up some Fridays, and I would drive you back on Sundays. Our conversations have certainly shifted. Back then I was curious about your courses and how you were handling your approach to learning. Now I know how well you are doing, and I do not worry about your academic approach. Instead, we discuss graduate school options and your many, varied career goals. However, despite our enjoyable conversation, I must be honest. One of the best parts of my driving excursions is still the solo drive home. For one hour I get to listen to uninterrupted original Austen Courter songs, now replete with instrumentation. Not a bad song in the bunch. For me, it is like dying and going to heaven. I miss you when I drop you off at the dorm, but once I get back inside the car and start driving home, I get to hear your voice. Instantly, I still feel connected. Where would I be without your songs?

    Hey, I just arrived back home and Mom wants me to express our thanks for your weekend visit. The house seemed fuller and more complete with you around, even though you studied each day. If you attend graduate school, that will be one of the rewards for us. It will be like having another year at USC with you being able to come home some weekends. For us, it is another blessing to have you so close. Of course for you, right now it's all work. In retrospect, I think you will look back and view your first semester of your freshman year and your first semester of your senior year as the most difficult semesters. I wonder if that is true for the other students? It is not true for your roommates. Their tough year appeared to be their junior year. In your case, next semester should be your easiest semester. Good luck over these coming weeks with your series of finals. I am just sorry when I realize how much you study. Has it been like that all four years? Have you worked much harder than you have acknowledged? Did you not want us to worry? Over this last weekend, when we saw your stack of essays, we were shocked. I thought my college years were hard, but yours were more difficult because of your high load of classes. Each and every semester.

You have my respect. But I question your sanity.

Dad

12/12/11 You Survived the Semester?

Dear Austen,

Congratulations on finishing your fifth final exam this morning. As someone who never took more than four subjects and four final exams per semester, I have no comprehension for what it must feel like to have to take seven final examinations. You have your sixth and seventh final exams tomorrow. Then finally, you have freedom—a well-deserved Christmas break. You have lived up to your Phi Beta Kappa moniker. Congratulations on forgoing any study tonight, not even trying to cram, so you could participate in your students' musical concert at their local school. They were lucky to have you. Again, you were great to volunteer when you could have been preparing for your back-to-back final exams. I hope their show did not run too late so you could get to bed at an early hour. Like me, I know you do not study past 10:00 p.m. What's the use of staying up late and cramming? That is not learning. That is passing an exam. Right now, since it's just after 10:00 p.m., I hope you are cuddling between your sheets and turning off the lights for a good night's sleep. Of course, if I heard correctly, there is a party tonight in your apartment complex. Earplugs for the party noise, right? You probably have your own secrets, although you were always a great sleeper. As a baby, when the phone would ring while you were napping, you would lift one hand and cover your ear, never waking up. Here's to a good night's slumber. Here's to a nice end to the semester tomorrow. Here's to four years of all the right habits.

See, it's that "I can" attitude.
Dad

1/11/12 Your Final Semester? Happy or Sad?

Dear Austen,

 Once again, the house seems empty without you. That feeling may never go away. Thanks for being home for such a long stint, as we really enjoyed this Christmas and New Year's season. We found a good tree, had a fun Christmas with the entire family, saw our share of movies, and ate our share of good dinners. Pretty good from my standpoint. Although I was disappointed to see the holiday season end with your return to your USC apartment, at least we got you moved in with all of your stuff. Right now I am looking at your index card with this semester's class schedule. What a difference from last semester. Last year's card was filled with classes with almost no empty spaces. This semester? You do not even have a class that meets three times a week. Just one of your classes meets twice a week. Hopefully, you will have time to practice your voice, piano, guitar, drumming, and songwriting. Hopefully you will enjoy your teaching-aide school experience. Maybe you can relax a little and enjoy free time with your friends, or perhaps with Skyler or us? We like your long weekends with no classes (zero) on Mondays. If you decide to come home on a holiday weekend, that's a four-day weekend. Another advantage for those parents whose kids attend a college in their local city.

 Congratulations on your prompt acceptance into USC's master's-level graduate program. I saw an article in today's paper that reported that the majority of Californians were supporting a new ballot initiative for increased funding for K–12 education. Your timing for a move into teaching may be excellent, as I would expect the schools to begin to receive some of the funding they have lost over these last four years. At the same time, I want to express my encouragement to not feel locked into any set path. As mentioned in earlier e-mails, you are likely to have four to six different careers over your lifetime. That is not just different jobs, but different careers. I think you will be an outstanding teacher, but it does not mean you cannot follow other passions. It does not mean you cannot take breaks. Look at me. Once I received my medical license and was certified to practice medicine, I took a year off to write. I recommend that type of break for everyone. It's a wonderful opportunity to experience a different part of life and learn more about yourself. So many parents want their kids to work on a linear path. I do not understand it. Life offers too many adventures to focus on a single career or a regular paycheck.

I know my weakness for wanting to write "if I were you" e-mails, so I will try to refrain. But I wanted to pass along one warning. I noticed in your paperwork that a letter for scholarships would be forthcoming. In medicine, they sometimes offer scholarships if you are willing to work in a certain area. For example, some states will pay for your medical education, once you have been accepted into a medical school, if you are willing to commit to working in one of their communities. If you ever receive that type of restricted scholarship offer, turn it down. When you finish the master's program, after all these years of education, you want to select where you live and where you work. That was one of the nice benefits about being a physician, and it will be one of the nice advantages of being a teacher. When it was time for me to work, I selected the community first and the job second. You will be in the same predicament. Don't get locked into a geographic location. You want to be able to decide where you raise your family. Keep that flexibility. It makes a huge difference in the quality of your life.

Which does not mean you have to stay in Southern California.

Dad

1/31/12 Another Scholarship? Thanks!

Dear Austen,

    I could not be a luckier or prouder father. Once again, you have given me a present: another scholarship. I doubt if you ever calculate the math, but that makes the total sum of your scholarship for college and graduate school sizeable. In personal terms, that means much less work for me and much less stress on me. For the future, it also means I have more freedom to pursue my next attempt at writing a book. My writing may still crash and burn, but you, more than anyone else, have given me the flexibility to pursue one of my dreams. So many heartfelt thanks. If you can do for your students what you have done for me, giving me a better chance to follow my dreams, you will be a fantastic teacher. Now I wish you could step back and appreciate all you have accomplished. I think you take your hard work, your success, and your achievement for granted. I know there are many things far more important than the above external rewards, but give yourself a much-deserved pat on the back. For now, I hope you can relax with all of your remaining classes and with your additional work as a teacher's aide. I will look forward to finding out if you have any free time between graduation and the start of graduate school, as we would love to celebrate with a family trip.

    With so many options already settled for next year, Mom and I enjoyed our lunch with you today at the CPK restaurant. We both felt you were hitting your stride. It's amazing when passion meets purpose. The result is usually something meaningful. We were very impressed with you and your personal growth, plus impressed with your level of music acumen. It sounds as if you have also hit your stride with your teaching through the USC's outreach program and your acceptance into the USC MAT graduate program, and it sounds as if you have hit your stride with your songwriting. You once told me it often takes two hundred songs for songwriters to find their sense of self, and it seems as if you are hitting that point. Each time we listen to one of your new songs, typically en route to some Los Angeles restaurant after picking you up at your apartment, we are blown away by the quality of the melody, the quality of the lyrics, and the quality of the instruments. So, congrats on all fronts. I wish more people had a chance to hear your songs, but that part is not my choice. I am just lucky that I have that opportunity. If your daughter is a history or business major, do you get a chance to see her creations? Not unless you read an essay or see a presentation. What matters is that you have selected your craft and taken control of its development, and you now have the ability to utilize it to sustain a career where you are helping others.

We think you have successfully hit all the key points.

Dad

2/13/12 Another Grammy Show?

Dear Austen,

As I was watching last night's Grammy show, I thought how that connection was another advantage to your four years at USC. That school has worked out great. We have loved having you close to home. The Thornton School of Music has provided you with an excellent education. You have been lucky with your extracurricular activities. To be a Grammy member and have the chance to participate in the show's preparation and then attend the Grammys with great seats—that is pretty cool. I have loved your observations of the quality of the musicians at the Grammy show. How many of them exude intensity during rehearsal, making certain all the sounds of the band hit just the right notes, and how many of them are casual during rehearsal, not producing as good a product. I can't hear the difference. The audience does not hear the difference. But a good musician can hear the difference. When it came down to your considering USC as your college, I did not even think of all of those additional, extracurricular factors. As a parent, I had to step aside and trust *your* instincts and vision. But I would have loved to have been educated on all of the USC advantages—and all of the NYU advantages. With Skyler and NYU, and then with you and USC, I took the tour, saw the campus, and listened to the staff presentations, but I did not really learn the true value of either school. In retrospect, it reminds me how we have to look beneath the surface. Many of the strengths for each college are hidden, not revealed until well into your education. With both of you, we got lucky. You and Skyler made great choices.

Maybe the hidden strengths are meant to be discovered later?
Dad

2/19/12 Plans for Graduation?

Dear Austen,

After reading the material on your graduation, I agreed with your sentiments. I do not see any logical reason to eat dinner with twelve hundred people I do not know. Therefore, I am not going to make reservations for the 2012 Baccalaureate Dinner on Thursday night. It would be more fun for the four of us to go out to dinner by ourselves at a nice restaurant. However, if something develops that changes your mind, please let me know. Your desires would trump my own thinking. Just remember that I suspect you would be receiving an award at that dinner, as they tend to announce awards for each academic program. But I know you well enough to appreciate that you couldn't care less. Plus, I know you would enjoy our family banter, especially over an expensive meal, far more than some announcement of your name and an award placard.

Here is my plan. I am going to make reservations for two hotel rooms for two nights at the Los Angeles Bonaventure Hotel for your graduation. Since I would suggest a restaurant far removed from school for our graduation celebration, I think the Bonaventure would be a fine starting point for driving to some distant restaurant. If you disagree, please let me know. But we will have two rooms for those two nights, so you will be spared the chaos of the graduation night celebrations at your apartment complex. Of course, if you decide you to want to go to a party, you have a green light. However, I realize your predicament. You are graduating on Friday and starting graduate school on Monday, and we need to move you into a new apartment over that weekend. You would think they would give you more time between finishing undergraduate school and starting graduate school, but life is not like that. Once you step onto the conveyor belt, it keeps you moving forward, usually faster and faster, without many exits.

Lastly, there is the main graduation ceremony and then the smaller, separate graduation for the Thornton School of Music. That will be fun to attend so you can say bye to all of your friends. Then you will be done. We can relax in the afternoon, celebrate on Friday night with another dinner, and go to work on Saturday morning moving your possessions to your new apartment. After four years of living with roommates, you are finally going to have your own single studio apartment. I realize it is not anything special and it will be off campus, somewhere in downtown Los Angeles, but it will be your own apartment with your own possessions. You can decorate your space as you would like, not having to worry about boundaries with a roommate. Of course, we will need to pick the furniture, have it delivered on Saturday, and then scramble to put everything together before Monday. After four years of hard work, you graduate and then jump into harder work without having a chance to exhale. That still does not seem right. But, in truth, it comes as no surprise.

Such is life in America.

Dad

3/09/12 Applause for Surviving another Long Day

Dear Austen,

    Congratulations on surviving yesterday's lengthy day. Maybe it will be one of those days that linger in the recesses of your mind, periodically intruding into your thoughts as you age? Let's see. You had to get up at 6:00 a.m. You were out the door of your apartment after 7:00 a.m. and scrambling to your local grade school. You taught three classes of jazz. You returned to college, scarfed down your salad, and studied from noon to 1:00 p.m. before hurrying back down to the practice room so you could be ready for your voice lesson at 2:00 p.m. Who can sing when they have been lecturing all morning? Although I know your lecturing is teaching, there are still moments where you have to raise your voice to maintain control of the students. After the singing lesson, you had just enough time to get to your midterm in music and TV at 4:00 p.m. Then you had a rushed dinner with another salad, another midterm, your film class at 7:00 p.m., followed by a full movie premier with the directors and actors, finally getting to your apartment around midnight. Just another day of college, yes? Another day of no pressure, right? Who could forget a day like that? At some point in a student's college life, the student should write down one of the busier days and pass along the list to the parent. Maybe then the parent would stop offering advice. Of course, nothing would stop me. For you, I am including the list as a reminder that college was not that easy. That the time in college was precious. Maybe we were not much help in any of your courses. But maybe we can at least help you remember some of the many challenges through these e-mails.

    It's too easy to forget, yes?
    Dad

3/19/12 Spring Break? Already Over?

Dear Austen,

 You did not go to Hawaii for spring break or do anything exciting, but you still provided us with much pleasure. For us, the days were productive. We were able to find you a neat apartment in downtown Los Angeles for graduate school. We were able to look at some furniture with future delivery dates right before the start of graduate school. Over the break, you were able to write your film essay, read ahead in several books, and better prepare for your recital and upcoming teaching classes. You are still going to feel overloaded as you head into these six weeks, but you would have been more overloaded if you had not been home for this past week, and if you had not been so productive with your work. As you head to your gospel choir tonight, give thanks to the Lord. Your spring break at home worked out for the best. Think of all of those good meals, starting with Japanese and ending with Mexican. We enjoyed each and every meal with you, plus you returned with bags of groceries for the next couple of weeks. Just sorry you are back at school, already working on another project. We thought this semester would be easy. Maybe life does not work that way. Maybe we should be honest and admit that life gets progressively more difficult. There is no way around that truth. And it gets faster and faster. Maybe that is why I am feeling such a need to prod your memories? But will you keep any of these e-mails? Mom is saying there is no chance!

 Tonight, as I was thinking about you, I was wondering if I had any advice left to offer. After four years of e-mails, what else can one father say? Oh well, you know me. As I already explained, it is the final 20 percent of effort that leads to 80 percent of success, so I will try to offer some fresh ideas in these final e-mails—my final 20 percent of effort. Did I tell you to take more breaks from your stress? Check. Have I ever offered an acupuncture treatment or a massage treatment to ease your nervous system? Check. How about a congratulations for your most recent paper handed back to you by the professor with "brilliant" written across the top? Check. But here is something new. Try lowering your standards, if possible. Could you, over these next six weeks, submit something with purposefully created mistakes? Do you know the theory that it is the imperfections—the cracks in the wall—that let in the light? What makes your mother so delightful? It's all of her special idiosyncrasies, all of her imperfections. Maybe you should switch gears and look at your grades. Maybe you could try to toss a B into the mix. I know the answer, you are not about to look at any grades, and you are not about to stop learning. Should I try to offer something different?

How about dreaming more of your future and living less in the present? That goes against my usual dictum. Think about it. Within eighteen months, you will be teaching. I am confident that you will find a good position. Find a school that fits your needs. Or find some school system with a chance for future advancement. Of course, you have to get through the next year of your condensed master's program. I know how hard you work, so if you need a short break, you are once again welcome to come home any weekend. We will do your high stack of laundry. We will take you to a nice dinner or movie. We will get out of your way. You will have time to work on your graduate projects. Come on, you only have to survive another year of school and then move into work. Move into your real twenties. Those years, I promise, will be great and exciting years. Maybe you will fall in love. Maybe that will not happen until your thirties. Life is about loving, not just work. Good times are coming. Believe in your future. Did that help at all? I am guessing, like with so many of my e-mails, the answer may be a polite no! I am guessing you hit the delete button. Do you realize how much that hurts?

Oh well, I will make one more attempt. I attended a lecture by Jack Canfield, the author of the *Chicken Soup* series of books. He was once a teacher, but he was frustrated by the difficulty in getting students motivated. So he wrote his first book on motivation and started speaking. Over the years, he developed a new career, writing and speaking, far removed from the classroom. I would view your upcoming classroom as the starting line, not necessarily the finish line, for your career. That holds true for almost all of your fellow seniors. They become too preoccupied with the first job and the security of that first job. Again, just remember how security is the lowest form of happiness. When you consider the various possibilities, think of where the first job will lead. Then be prepared to discover new options, new avenues, and new adventures. You are going to have many jobs. You are going to have many careers. As long as you keep learning, that should not be a problem. They are just steps on your journey. Enjoy that journey. And forget about the destinations and any so-called rewards at the end of the destination. The real rewards come in those special moments that occur in anyone's life. Seize those moments. Make them last as long as possible. My moment with Mom has lasted a lifetime, producing two wonderful women. Three beautiful women, counting Mom!

Should I keep trying for more points? No?

Dad

4/08/12 My Random Thoughts? Coming to an End?

Dear Austen,

It is Sunday night. You and Mom are asleep, and I am listening to your new group of five songs. Before I comment on the songs, I want to thank you for joining us for Easter weekend. It was fun on Friday night, seeing *The Hunger Games*. It was enjoyable on Saturday night, eating at the French restaurant in Laguna Beach. It was also relaxing today at the Easter brunch overlooking the ocean. For you, I hope it was a relaxing weekend to give you a break from your final weeks of stress. Remember, you are "Team Courter," supporting yourself with positive self-talk, a positive attitude, and a commitment to do your best without comparison to others and without thought to expectations. You have to fight against any negativity from others, any limitations from others. Do not let their "water" seep into your own ship. What's that famous Amos line? "All the water in the ocean cannot sink your ship unless you let it in." You deserve clear sailing! You deserve to enjoy the journey. For you, if that translates into learning as much as possible, then learn to your heart's content. You have my permission to skip the drug-crazed raves at USC. You have my permission to forgo the outings with Skyler to one dance club after another. What works for one person does not always work for the next, even when two people are close, loving sisters. Do what you want! What an unusual father—encouraging you to follow your dreams, not my fantasies, or someone else's suggestions. Hmm…didn't I say the same thing when you were a freshman?

By the way, I think you will be a great teacher. I think it matches your personality and offers you a chance for a wonderful life. You will have a chance to enjoy vacations and summer, and you will have time for yourself and your family. You will have the chance, and the time, to pursue other hobbies. I think your satisfaction from all of those features will exceed the satisfaction from any paycheck. On that note, I still think you are a brilliant songwriter who could sell her songs if you ever wanted to. You have grown progressively better and better with each single year. I loved your five new songs, and you did not even share that you had cowritten two of the songs, per teacher instruction, with another songwriter. I support that collaborative approach. Cowriting songs with another musician, helping another try to create his or her own career with some better songs? That sounds like fun. If your songs with the cowriter are as strong as your individual songs, I think that musician will make it. If not, it will not be for the lack of outstanding material. So, enjoy these final collaborations. Enjoy these final days of your senior year. Enjoy your final days of USC.

Sort of like enjoying my final e-mails, yes?

Dad

4/22/12 Ready for the Shock of Your Life?

Dear Austen,

    I do not have to repeat all my negative observations of my mother. Do I like her focus on material possessions? Do I respect her focus on wealth instead of character? Do I applaud her continued self-preoccupation and selfishness? Do I tolerate her racism and prejudice? Do I become nauseated when thinking of her lack of acceptance of your mom? Do I tolerate all of her criticisms of you and Skyler, regarding table manners and her view of appropriate etiquette? Do I forgive her poor treatment of my dad in the last days of his life? Do I ignore how she has avoided any chance to help any of us, even letting us buy her car? The list is endless. To each of these questions, the answer is no. I know everyone is supposed to love his or her mother—and I love my mother for giving birth to me and giving me this miracle of life—but do I respect my mother's values? The answer is more than obvious. But, against that backdrop, we asked my mother if she wanted to move into our house, especially knowing you would be at graduate school and out of the house for most of the year. We asked, and she accepted. She has reached the stage where she cannot prepare her own meals, she cannot take care of her house, and she should not be driving. She drove through another red light last week, barely missing a car accident. Without our help, her options would be limited. So, when she sells her house, she will move into our house.

    Why did I extend the offer? Please note that the offer came with Mom's full support, as she is always so kind. Do you remember my analogy of the orange juice? My orange juice is my orange juice. No one else's. Yes, my mother is the stimulus, often driving me to the breaking point. She is like the hammer pounding the orange. Nevertheless, I have to take ownership of my negative feelings toward my mother. I need to be able to push them aside and do what is right. For most of the past decade, I have been able to push aside those feelings and go to my parents' house every Saturday morning to help my dad and mom. With my dad, it was easy. There was nothing but admiration and love. For my mother, it is not so easy. For a couple of hours one day a week, I can handle it, as I just stop listening. Can I handle it for 24-7 with her intruding into our daily life? I am going to turn my downstairs office into her bedroom. I will move my computer and books up into Skyler's now-empty bedroom. My chart work will be done from Skyler's desk. How ironic is that? I pushed her to work hard into the night, and now I will be pushing myself to work hard into the night. I deserve that twist of fate. We will build cabinets in the garage for my mother's clothes, we will redesign the closets for additional space, and we will change the downstairs bathroom with steel rods by the toilet and shower for better stability. We will do everything we can to make her life better, not worse.

I am a great believer in positive thinking. What you believe and what you think about is usually what you get. Am I optimistic about the results of my mom living with us? I hate to admit it, but I, too, have my limitations, my character faults. No matter how hard I try, I am like Han Solo in *Star Wars*: "I have a bad feeling about this." Do I think she will be critical of our house, since it is not decorated to her usual level of elegance? Do I think she will criticize Mom's cooking, especially since we eat mostly vegetarian meals? Do I foresee more criticisms of you when you come home on the weekends with your casual attire? Do I picture future arguments where she lashes out at each of us? Do I imagine, as she grows older, her pushing or shoving Mom? Yes to all of the above. I have this feeling she is going to progress from "Nonny" to "the Nonster." The beast among us. I try to visualize a different series of events, but those visions dissipate with every attempt. So why am I bothering to make the effort? I consider it a life lesson. How can I preach the right habits to you and Skyler and not demonstrate any attempt on my own? I will preach the value of character. I will preach the importance of giving, not taking. I will preach the benefits of acceptance and tolerance. I will preach the rewards of treating people with respect. I will preach the benefits of forgiving. I will preach the peace that comes with increased connections with others and with God. Maybe "preach" is the wrong word. I will try to "demonstrate" the hidden wealth within those habits. If I fail? Remember, since she cannot climb stairs, you can retreat up to your room. Me? I will be right behind you, heading to Skyler's room.

One final point. Remember my other analogy of the bamboo tree and its growth in the sixth year. I am also a strong believer in the 80:20 rule. Around 80 percent of your success comes from your last 20 percent of effort. I am looking at this last effort—moving her into our house—as that 20 percent. In theory, it could be the turning point. Maybe the bamboo tree will sprout to sudden heights. Maybe my mother will change when she sees the level of happiness in our household. Maybe our relationship, and especially my mother's long-term relationship with Mom, will improve when she sees how kind, considerate, and loving Mom is all of the time. Nope? Then I will turn my belief in the other 80:20 rule. Around 80 percent of our happiness comes from just 20 percent of our activities. If my mother does not change, if she continues to be superficial and self-preoccupied, and if she continues to criticize all of us day after day, we will have to turn, as a family, toward those 20 percent activities, which give us 80 percent of our happiness. The four of us (you, Mom, and me, plus Skyler when she is home) will have to focus on those activities that give us the most joy. We can still go out to dinners up in Los Angeles. We can still take a family trip to Maui, leaving my mother with a caregiver. We can still focus on those key activities, and see if 80 percent of our happiness is enough for us. Let's view it as an adventure, not just an experiment. Let's hope it does not turn into a train wreck. Shocked? I hope you read this e-mail while sitting down, not standing up.

You never have to take us into your house. Ever!

Dad

5/01/12 What a Show! Congratulations!

Dear Austen,

I just want to express my admiration and appreciation of your final senior-year recital. I think it was impressive that you decided to sing only female composers. I think it was equally impressive that you researched so many different songs to come up with your wonderful selection, and I think it was impressive that you arranged everything by yourself: the site, the staging, the accompanist, the film technician, the program, and the food. The best part of the show? It was your singing. I had not heard your classical voice in months, except through the bedroom wall while you practiced. I had focused more on your pop voice and your original songs. With your classical voice, I thought you sounded as good as I have ever heard you. I agreed with your voice coach, who observed that it would be a loss if the world did not get to hear more of your beautiful voice. Still, I think you are making the right decision to become a teacher, because it is more aligned with your preferred lifestyle and more aligned with helping others.

I also want to thank you for your last weekend at home for your regular college career. It was a typical snapshot of your college weekend at home. I was not surprised how your body collapsed right after your spring recital, requiring plenty of hydration with green tea, plus resumed healthy eating and daily exercise. I was also not surprised by your weekend studying, even though you could have refrained from opening another book. Learning? It is just part of your nature, even on weekends at home. Now, can you remember these images? Regardless, I wish you luck over these final college days, and I wish you luck with your two back-to-back finals on Thursday. I am not wishing luck for any grade; I am wishing luck so that you are satisfied with how much you have learned. Personally, I think it's absurd for the college to schedule two finals around the dinner hour without giving you time to eat. Do they expect you to take the second final with an IV? Do they expect you to eat dinner at 10:00 p.m.? Maybe they are toughening you up right before you step into the real world. We will look forward to hearing from you when you have the chance, perhaps on your walk to your apartment after your final exam?

As a final snapshot, we snuck two cards into your suitcase right before we packed your car. In addition, Mom drove to the post office, right after you left, to mail you a final card, congratulating you on finishing your college career. Hopefully, that card will arrive tomorrow morning as you wake up to freedom. We have enjoyed sending cards all these years, sneaking them into your suitcase or backpack. How many cards have we sent over your USC career? A couple hundred? How many of them were covered with a picture of some dog? Another snapshot to remember, yes? Oh well, we will look forward to moving you into your new apartment. Now is the time to flip the page to your new life. With all of your hard work, you should feel pleased with your personal and professional growth. Don't underestimate how much you have changed, how much you have grown. Too many students never reach your level of understanding. And don't underrate your future happiness. We just want you to be happy doing something that adds meaning to your life and adds meaning to the lives of others. Somehow, you have gone against the grain. I think the personal rewards will be immense and lifelong. Far greater than anything financial.

Call us Team Courter.

Dad

5/13/12 Your Graduation? Congratulations!

Dear Austen,

 We want to congratulate you on your graduations on Friday, May 11. We enjoyed both commencement ceremonies. We are very proud of you and your growth in your craft. Thanks, too, for saving me so much unexpected money with the latest group of the merit-based scholarships for your master's program. If I added up all of your scholarships, it would be several hundred thousand—probably much more. You are awesome. You have grown from a young lady to a grown beautiful woman, and one who is going to be an outstanding musician and an awesome teacher. What a transformation over four years. What a great place USC has been to help you through that transformation. Again, we could not be any prouder of you. We are only sorry that you do not have time to celebrate this accomplishment. Our celebration will have to wait until after graduate school and the master's program. Right now, you are driving to your own solo apartment for the first time in your life, not to celebrate, but to get ready for another year of hard academic work. An old apartment building on Sixth Street, not far from where the homeless gather. Lock the door, close the bolt, attach the chain, and get yourself a good night's sleep. I know, I know. I sound ridiculous, as if I have not grown over the past four years. Maybe that is the hidden truth. The college student grows and transforms, but the parents, left behind in the burrows, remain unchanged. After all, here I am offering advice when I started these e-mails promising to do just the opposite. Parents, what can you do with them? I know! Make them your lifelong friends? Let us know how to apply for the position, as we are more than ready for the part.

 To remind you that I do show restraint, I would like to point out how I offered no advice to any member of your graduating class. If you remember, I listened to all of Skyler's NYU graduation speeches, and I was dying to have stepped to the microphone and offered my own suggestions for life. Really, I think so many of these speakers miss the mark. Are you curious what I would have said at your graduation? You probably can guess, but beware. It would have been different from my imaginary speech to Skyler's graduating class, as I have learned much over your junior and senior years. As stated before, the roles seem to reverse at times during the college experience. The parents become the students, and the students become the teachers. We have to help one another through this transition, hopefully reaching a point where we become better people and where we develop an even stronger family bond. Which is why we are officially applying for that lifelong role of friends. Even if you just need a pair of old codgers to just walk your dog or tend to some future kids, we are there for you, ready and willing. Mom and me.

Hoping, of course, the position is permanent, not temporary.
Dad

5/15/12 My Final Graduation Speech?

Dear Austen,

Now, what would I have said to your graduating classmates to prepare them for life? Would I have lectured on the importance of finding your gift, creating your passion, and developing your purpose? Would I have addressed the need to push aside society's focus on income, and would I have encouraged them to follow their interests and dreams, making life an adventure, not just a job? On the topic of money, would I have tried to clarify the difference between wealth and personal happiness? Would I have cited the tabloids and all the problems of the wealthy? How we spend more but have less? How we build larger houses but still have broken homes? How we take more pills but have less health? How we connect more today on the Internet but actually communicate less? How we preach tolerance but still show prejudice? How we pretend to stand for peace but repeatedly create conflict? Would I have asked your classmates to reevaluate all of those issues, coaching them toward a more rewarding life with giving, not taking? Nope. All of that material has been well covered.

Instead, I would have warned them how life can be like stepping onto a conveyor belt, how it can transport you forward on your career, constantly picking up speed with each year and every decade. I would have warned them how hard it may become to step off that conveyor belt. After all, most companies make money off your hard work, and most companies want you working harder and harder, right until you drop at the end of your career. I would have encouraged them to consider taking at least three or four six-month planned vacations or breaks during their careers. I would have encouraged them *not* to save those breaks for retirement or the end of their lives. I would have used myself as an example, sharing how I had taken three significant breaks in my career, each time giving up income. I would have highlighted the benefits of those breaks for learning more about myself and my life options, I would have encouraged them to use those breaks for reevaluating their current careers and future goals, and I would have suggested how those breaks can be used to unearth talents, clarify passions, and change life paths. I would have quoted Steve

Jobs, reminding them to pause from time to time, making certain they are following their hearts, not someone else's goals.

Of even greater importance, I would have encouraged them to use those breaks for expanding two other key components in their lives. The first component is personal development. Careers force you to focus on work skills, not life skills. I would have recommended setting aside time during these breaks for self-exploration. I would have told them the story of Wayne Dyer. How, when walking one night, he came across a man who was searching for his lost car keys under the light post close to his car. The man explained he had accidently dropped his car keys as he crossed the lawn to the curb. Wayne stopped and helped the man for fifteen minutes, searching through the grass and bushes under the light post. When they could not find the keys, Wayne finally asked the man, "Is there any chance you could have dropped the keys over there on the lawn where it's dark?" The man responded, "Yes, that's exactly where I dropped them." Confused, Wayne asked, "Then why are you looking over here?" The man did not hesitate with his answer, spoken while still searching around the lamppost, "I am looking over here because it's light. Over there it's dark." Wayne Dyer implored all of us to examine new areas, especially those "dark" areas, which we normally don't explore.

In that vein, I would have highlighted how few people read nonfiction books after graduation. While working, we are often too busy for outside reading. That is another reason for the repeated, long vacation breaks. Travel? Yes! Decompress? Yes! But read some nonfiction books? Why not give it a try? I would have offered the suggestion to read some of the authors who focus on personal growth or successful life habits. I would have recommended Benjamin Franklin, Henry David Thoreau, Russell Conwell, Dale Carnegie, Og Mandino, Norman Vincent Peale, Napoleon Hill, Earl Nightingale, Zig Ziglar, Steven Covey, Wayne Dyer, Anthony Robbins, Brian Tracy, Michael Broder, Deepak Chopra, Tom Peters, Denis Waitley, Jim Rohn, Marianne Williamson, Kerry Johnson, Don Miguel Ruiz, James Huber, Daniel Burros, Barbara De Angelis, Jay Abraham, Peter Lowe, Robert Allen, Paul Pearsall, and many others. Do you think any of those names would have been remembered by the graduating seniors? Probably not. But maybe the idea of personal development would have struck a chord with some of them. Maybe it would have inspired them to take those well-deserved and much-needed breaks from constant employment and put those breaks to good use.

For the second component, something else to focus on during those work breaks, I would have encouraged reevaluation of their commitment to their relationships, coupled with an attempt to improve those relationships. I would have emphasized how much of their happiness in life, much like their happiness in college, comes from their relationships, not just from their work. I would have applauded any break around the time of a marriage, around the time of the birth of a child, and whenever a person hits a period of staleness with either career or family. That is the best time to reevaluate and reenergize your relationships, your family ties, and your friendships. I would have also emphasized how the quality in a relationship does not occur without sufficient quantity, without sufficient time together. As examples, I would have used my time with your mother in Spain before we were married or the time of your birth when I took four months off from work to help care for you and Skyler. Those periods cemented a great relationship and a wonderful family. Lastly, regardless of these longer work breaks, I would have highlighted the advantage of annual long vacations with your family. Too many people get sucked into working week after week, paycheck after paycheck. I would have quoted more Steve Jobs, encouraging them to stay hungry and stay foolish, even as they grow older. Annual long vacations help keep those foolish, hungry impulses fresh and alive. Explore the world. Explore new cultures. But explore them with others. Go for those experiences. Don't stay on the conveyor belt just for the money. Experiences, relationships, and personal growth make up the triad that trumps everything else in life.

So, that would have been my message to your fellow graduates. That's my message on how to reach your highest level of happiness. So, how different am I after Skyler's college experience and your college experience? Would I have made those recommendations six years ago? Would I have made those recommendations without learning so much from the two of you? With your graduation on Friday and the start of your master's program on Monday, would you have agreed with most of my points? Will you be planning your own annual vacation breaks? Have you given any thought to periodic longer breaks? Skyler is already planning on a six-month break at her five-year mark of employment. That decision shows more than intelligence; that decision shows wisdom. Maybe the two of you can travel together sometime in the future. Renew and rejuvenate together. Or with your significant others. Oh well, you have heard my pitch for a better life. Do you like it? I hope so. However, like Skyler, I am sure you are delighted I remained silent on your graduation day. For my silence, do I get any reward? How about a series of shared vacations over the course of your life? Or better yet...

A lifelong friendship with you?

Dad

ACKNOWLEDGMENTS

I want to thank my two daughters, Skyler and Austen, for giving me permission to publish this private correspondence from each of their college careers. I suspect that many daughters would scatter at the mention of such a request, but my daughters stood their ground, gave the request due consideration, and supported my own dream of leaving a footprint. For me, this reflects the strength of their character and the closeness of our friendship. The two of them represent my best contribution to the world. I appreciate them as much as I appreciate life. I offer my love and thanks.

I want to thank my wife, Priscilla. When you meet over a dead body, your relationship is bound to be special. For me, she has been my companion for life, my partner in romance, and a constant supporter of all of my crazy, idiosyncratic pursuits, including the writing of these e-mails. My only question for her is overused but true: How did I get so lucky to have her fall in love with me? Somehow, against the odds, I rolled a pair of aces and got very lucky. In fact, we've gone through life calling each other by the same nickname: Ace.

I want to thank CreateSpace for publishing this book. This is my second book with this company, and they have been a delight with both books. Their team has been outstanding. I want to especially thank the designers, the editors, and the marketing team. My perspective remains unchanged. When you enter a physician's office, your care is not determined by the quality of the doctor; it is determined, more than you realize, by the quality of the staff. The same holds true for any book. The real credit should go to the entire team at CreateSpace and its own special family.

ABOUT THE AUTHOR

William Courter, MD, earned degrees from Williams College, New York Medical College, and the University of Southern California. A board-certified physician in psychiatry and neurology, he has served as the associate medical director of the Orange County Health Care Agency in Orange County, California, and as a national consultant for difficult medical, psychiatric, and substance abuse cases across the United States.

Courter has been a keynote speaker for multiple organizations on health, career paths, relationships, and personal development. He is the founder of the Boomer Health Institute and the author of *The Boomer Survivor Kit: An Indispensable Guide for Yourself * Your Relationships * Your Life*. He has created two websites, www.boomerhealthinstitute.com and http://www.drbillcourter.com/, and produced a series of YouTube videos.

Courter currently lives in Coto de Caza, California, with his wife of over thirty years. His two daughters also live and work in Southern California.